PLANNING THE FUTURE STRATEGY
OF YOUR BUSINESS

PLANNING THE FUTURE STRATEGY
OF YOUR BUSINESS

Edited by

EDWARD C. BURSK
Editor of the Harvard Business Review *and*
Professor of Business Administration
Harvard Graduate School of Business Administration

DAN H. FENN, Jr.
Assistant Editor of the Harvard Business Review

McGRAW-HILL BOOK COMPANY, INC.
New York Toronto London **1956**

PREFACE

THIS BOOK, the seventh in an annual series, is based on the proceedings of the Twenty-Fifth National Business Conference, sponsored by the Harvard Business School Association, June 11, 1955, which was attended by some 1,800 businessmen—alumni and friends of the School—from all over the country and abroad.

The theme of the Conference, "Planning the Future Strategy of Your Business," in the words of the General Conference Chairman, Mark W. Cresap, Jr., Executive Vice President, Westinghouse Electric Corporation, "acknowledges the intensity of competition and emphasizes the need for strategic business planning to exploit fully the new facilities and resources of business resulting from the vast expansion program of the past decade."

The morning and evening sessions, consisting of speeches that consider the over-all theme in the light of particular company practices and experience, constitute the bulk of the material in Part I.

The afternoon sessions were conducted purposely on a very informal basis, in an attempt to let the subject develop in line with the group's interest. Introductory talks or case presentations were designed to stimulate discussion among the businessmen present, and the resulting interplay of ideas forms the basis for the chapters in Parts II, III, and IV, as well as for the question-and-answer sections of two of the chapters in Part I.

This material has been screened and reorganized into suitable form for reading. We stayed as close as we could to the actual words of the participants, for the sake of first-hand flavor and veracity. However, in many cases the very quality of dynamic, spontaneous discussion would have caused lack of clarity and continuity in cold print, so the "editing" has been done with a generous hand.

We should say generous hands, not hand, for the Editors have been assisted immeasurably by the HARVARD BUSINESS REVIEW Editorial Staff, including particularly Miss Louise B. Morse, Miss Virginia B. Fales, Mrs. Kathleen G. Linnell, Miss Jean E. Hardy, and Miss Elizabeth H. Knox.

Edward C. Bursk
Dan H. Fenn, Jr.

CONTENTS

Part Three **NEW VIEWPOINTS AFFECTING STRATEGY**

Part Four **PLANNING FOR YOUR OWN FUTURE**

Part One

BASIC PLANNING

INTRODUCTION OF THE THEME:

Planning the Future Strategy of Your Business

Donald K. David

I AM PLEASED TO WELCOME readers to this book, which is based on the Twenty-fifth National Business Conference at the Harvard Business School.

Those who attended the conference and, I believe, those who will be reading this volume are joined by the same professional concern for competent and responsible management that has drawn businessmen to the Harvard meetings for a quarter century.

This newest volume in a series based on the conferences over the past seven years deals with a theme appropriate in its timeliness and comprehensiveness. In recent conferences and their published counterparts we have concentrated upon the problems of administration once strategic decisions have been taken. Here we will look

Note: Mr. David at the time of the conference was Dean of the Harvard University Graduate School of Business Administration, a position which he held from 1942 to his retirement in 1955.

at the strategic decision itself and the elements of effective planning.

Strategy I take to be the marshaling and disposition of the material and human resources of a business to achieve, under the spur of competition and the uncertainty of the unknown, certain specific and socially acceptable goals. Thus strategy precedes action.

Without conscious appraisal and reappraisal, basic strategy is easily neglected. In the hurly-burly of war and of shortages of materials and productive capacity, for example, conscious strategy is superseded by opportunism or emergency. Mediocre planning is permitted for some time by the momentum of a rapidly expanding economy. But as economic forces settle into a new equilibrium, the sting of competition reminds delinquent planners that strategy can become obsolete. Then tactics become desperate, and improvising wastes the resources for future planning. The dangers of drifting are more easily seen in retrospect than beforehand. But a well-considered course can be set only in advance and then only when goals are set and their attainment scheduled.

Ten years now of uneasy peace have seen enormous expansion in our economy. They have revealed, under test of transition from war, the vitality of our economic system. We hope that the changing of tactics apparently undertaken by Soviet Russia will mean long-term strengthening of the prospects of peace. If so, our individual firms must take an even harder look at the problems of using expanded capacity fully, steadily, and intelligently. Our individual companies must achieve survival and growth under more and more challenging conditions. Those weak or slow or without imagination will fall behind as competition continues to grow keener. If firms fail the test of competence in large numbers, they imperil not only themselves but our economy as well, for in business as in private life we are free but interdependent.

With the new urgency for reconsidering basic strategy so abundantly clear, it becomes all the more important to realize the scope of strategy and the range of considerations strategic thinking must encompass. In this connection, it should not be surprising if I emphasize the idea which in different ways I have expressed many times before: that the strategist must plan *responsibly,* with the goals of the American society as clear in his mind as the need for his company's success in competition.

The strategic planning which we are considering here is not shrewd maneuver or corporate conniving, destructive of competition. It cannot be laid down at the expense of our economy as a whole. Not to elude the need for achieving superiority fairly, but to outrun competition and pace the performance for all—that is its purpose.

We think today of linking the goals of the company with the goals of the community. We proceed on the premise that the conduct of business is consistent with the American idea of individual freedom and individual responsibility for maintaining the condition of freedom. So we plan, as well as act, with our responsibilities in mind—to employees, owners, community, competitors, and, yes, to ourselves as men with professional objectives and satisfactions.

We should plan also to give meaning to our individual and total economic achievement. Our basic strategy should encompass awareness of the nonmaterial ends being served. The pressures under which strategy is forged lead us too often away from the positiveness of purpose which is at the heart of our business activity. We know that in total we have made a free society which advances the public good further than any other system of social organization has ever done. We know that our strength as a society begins with (though it does not end with) our material strength, which has upheld the cause of freedom for years and made possible all our lesser cultural and humane accomplishments. We know also that in turn our material strength resides in the thousands of nuclei of initiative, independence, and energy which are our business organizations. Every creative achievement rising out of practical affairs makes a solid contribution to our society. This contribution we should not only recognize but plan for, put into words, and include for appraisal in our reviews of progress.

If we can make progress in isolating and stating the relevance of individual strategic decisions and basic planning to the strength and achievement of our whole system, we shall make it possible for a skeptical world to reappraise what the American achievement has been. We will also clarify our own purposes, and see them less earth-bound than we may have thought them. We may as men in business adjust to values as individuals which will permit full exercise of the professional tasks of management. If this happens, our American achievement will become even more notable. Communism can be defeated not only by force but by the will of the peoples of the world who still have a choice to make.

The thinking that we shall be doing—as this subject is discussed in the chapters that follow—is important, not only to each reader and participant individually, but to all of us as men with a professional interest in the real and potential achievements of American business.

PLANNING THE BASIC STRATEGY OF A LARGE BUSINESS

Ernest R. Breech

MR. CHARLES H. PERCY of Bell & Howell, whose discussion of strategy planning in a medium-size business also appears in this book, provided a springboard for the observations I shall make here when he testified recently in behalf of the Administration's foreign trade program before the House Ways and Means Committee. He remarked then that American industries are competing not with cheap foreign labor but with the efficiency of the automotive industry.

Those words of Mr. Percy are kind and flattering. We in the automobile industry would like to accept the compliment. If he is right, we can all pose as efficiency experts (though I remember that Charles F. Kettering once defined an efficiency expert as a mechanic away from home).

But it is the significance, rather than the compliment, that I want to bring out. I do feel that the competitive situation in our industry

Note: Mr. Breech is Chairman of the Board, Ford Motor Company.

has put a premium on industrial efficiency and that our experience, especially at Ford Motor Company, may be relevant to many other businesses in meeting their future markets.

We at Ford have been preparing for almost a decade to hold our own in what we foresaw would be a rich but hotly competitive market. We believe that we have a new kind of market today, that we are dealing with a more prosperous and more selective consumer, and that we must plan our business accordingly. We are acutely aware also of many external, social, and political forces which condition the environment of business and will affect our planning.

We are confronted on all sides by difficult, almost imponderable questions. What will be the effect upon our business in five or ten years of the fast developing new technologies—of automation, electronics, atomic energy? What about defense planning? What about the great and swelling demand of American working people for greater employment stability? And so on.

I cannot hope even to begin exploring all these questions in a few brief moments. I can, however, try to give you my impression of what it takes to make a go of a modern industrial concern in today's and tomorrow's competitive market. I will draw for that purpose upon our own experience with the reorganization of Ford Motor Company. Our whole story, basically, is one of preparation for a tough buyers' market. Moreover, I believe our company to be an almost classic example of the introduction of modern management methods and the results thereof.

Our strategy for the future was laid out ten years ago. It has stood up well under the test of time, and we are still broadly adhering to it.

When a new management team under Henry Ford II undertook the reorganization of Ford Motor Company, it found itself short of everything but determination. It faced the postwar market with run-down plants, obsolete products, almost nonexistent financial control, an inadequate engineering staff, and just sufficient cash to meet its daily operating requirements.

As we looked forward into the future, we saw that we would not be able to last when the competitive market returned unless we remade ourselves completely into a strong, modern, and going concern.

What guided us then still guides us today. What we went after was precisely what it will take for any firm to be competitive in the rich but hard-fought market of today and tomorrow. And what it takes, above all, is competent management, flexible and big enough to respond swiftly to changing market conditions; research and engineering adequate to meet the enormous strain of modern product competition; plants and machinery efficient enough to compete with the best of the industry; and a financial control system which provides sound forecasting, keeps operations efficient, and is geared to produce peak profits.

Let me point to just a few high lights of our experience and try to extract from them some general applications.

DECENTRALIZATION AT FORD

One of our first steps back in 1946 was to set up a modern organization featuring a program of decentralization—breaking up our business into many smaller profit centers, each run like an independent business and held accountable for its profit performance. Along with this process naturally went the delegation of responsibilities to managers and the authority necessary to carry out those responsibilities.

In order to make that system work—and this was vital—we set up an incentive system based on supplemental compensation, and made it clear that rewards would be commensurate with performance.

We also set up an orthodox line and staff organization with an administration committee and various operating subcommittees to deal, for example, with product planning, merchandising, industrial relations, purchasing, scheduling, manufacturing, foreign operations, and public relations. Each group develops basic programs and recommends them to the executive committee.

I wish I might say that once the organization is set along these lines, it remains put. It does not. So far as we are concerned, no book on organization has ever been written that can be applied dogmatically to any given company. A theoretically sound and logical organizational setup can and often does founder on the hidden shoals of human nature.

While the modern executive may seek guidance from the textbook, he remembers always that he is dealing with individuals and not with theoretical abstractions. Organizations are nothing more or less than groups of people with a common purpose. They must be rearranged from time to time so that the abilities of the management personnel at hand may be used to the greatest effect.

Management organization, like medicine, probably will always be as much an art as a science.

The corporation is like a living organism. All of you have watched with much fascination, I am sure, the changes and evolutions that have taken place in your own business organizations over a period of years. There seem to be recurrent cycles in which management power and influence flow in toward the center and then out to the extremities. Strange, hard-to-diagnose illnesses occur in various parts of the organism; unsightly bulges appear anywhere that fat is permitted to accumulate. (Maybe that is why they call that common affliction a "corporation"!)

If the organism is permitted to sit still too long, it begins to develop hardening of the arteries, shortness of breath, and atrophy of the imagination. The executive must be constantly and critically sensitive to the health of the corporate organization, and he must be experimental, intuitive, and imaginative in dealing with it.

PRODUCT ENGINEERING

After we had set up our basic organization, we turned our attention to our engineering and product planning establishment. Unless you have the right product at the right time to meet consumer demands, you will not have much of a business.

In my opinion, the main goal of product engineering in any consumer goods company is obsolescence. Our job at Ford Motor Company is to render obsolete every car on the road—not merely by superficial changes but chiefly by dramatic and fundamental engineering and styling improvements.

Does that policy pay off? Look at today's automobile sales. Had the automobile industry been content to ride along with its 1949 or 1952 models, I venture to say that this would be much closer to a 4-million-car year than to the 6½ million-plus retail sales we presently anticipate.

The big reason for today's booming car sales is that the new models are far ahead of their predecessors in mechanical excellence, performance, and styling.

To do such a job in a company with diversified products requires a very substantial research and engineering setup. We must be able to work out simultaneously the design of many different current and future models, to push out ahead of competition in basic scientific research. We must have an organization large and flexible enough to meet crash emergency demands for special engineering projects.

To give you an example, in 1946 we had a total of only 2,300 engineering employees, including draftsmen, clerks, and sweepers; and their activity was budgeted at $14 million annually. Compare that with today, when our engineering personnel total 9,500, and the annual engineering budget is close to $95 million.

Over the same period, we have made available to our research and engineering men some $88 million for new facilities. In addition to building new research, styling, and testing facilities, we have invested heavily in a superbly staffed scientific laboratory which is working years ahead on the development of new and better means of automotive transportation.

The development of product planning procedures—like organizational planning—depends much upon individual personalities and the type of products to be designed. Our own procedures have come about through a gradual evolution. Maybe I should call it "trial and error."

In our industry, we work at least three years ahead on new models. Normally, we should have final management approval of basic new-model styling and design characteristics more than two years before the actual production year. Right now we are placing our bets on what we think the public will want to buy in 1957 and in 1958.

Rapid obsolescence is of course an expensive proposition. Tools, dies, fixtures—whole production lines or systems—might have to be scrapped in order to take advantage of some desirable improvement. It calls for a top-flight engineering and research organization, adequate and up-to-date facilities, plus careful planning and coordination with other components of the company.

FACILITIES PLANNING

Next is the vital problem of proper facilities planning. In order to maintain and improve our competitive position, we must of course have adequate and modern plant and equipment.

In our business, long-range facilities planning, to put it simply, means analyzing the market for our products over a certain period of years, determining what percentage of the market we think we can get, determining the type of products that will be characteristic of those years, and translating those findings into plant requirements. In other words, we ask what facilities we will need to produce standard volume.

Broadly speaking, we define standard volume as the average annual output of cars, trucks, and other products which we expect to maintain over a long period—five years or more.

Since standard volume is the basis not only of all our facilities planning but also for all prices and budgets, it becomes a critical determination. If we overestimate our standard volume and wind up with excess plant capacity, we of course pay the penalty of lessened profits. If we estimate on the low side, we incur the added costs and inefficiencies of overtime work to meet peak markets.

There is some theoretical dispute as to whether it is wiser to estimate conservatively or to build the capacity to handle peak loads. We at Ford prefer the former course. The profit on added volume in excess of standard volume more than offsets the overtime premiums during peak operations. Moreover, in any industry with a high seasonal factor, such as the automobile business, the use of overtime to secure peak volume is a valuable means of promoting more stable employment and better incomes for our working people.

While long-range planning is a matter of recurring study, short-range facilities planning—one or two years ahead—must receive constant attention. Each component of each new-model automobile requires facilities planning from metal stampings to automatic transmissions and engines.

Control of this effort is a vast job. All plans submitted for new products or models must be accompanied by rather detailed analyses of the facilities required. Obviously product planning and facilities planning must go hand in hand.

The complex job of both short-range and long-range planning, the rearrangement of existing facilities, and the engineering and integrating of new facilities require a vast and competent technical organization. Ford Motor Company employs currently more than 5,300 manufacturing engineers, as we call them, including our plant, facilities, design, and methods engineers.

Our cost control system operates as a spur upon every plant manager and foreman to analyze his operations continuously to determine whether more modern methods and machinery will do the job more efficiently.

Our current appropriations for modernizing and improving our machinery and methods run into many millions of dollars annually. We frequently find it to our advantage to replace two- or three-year-old machinery with newer and more costly machines. We keep a close watch over such modernization; every appropriation for this purpose must show clearly the anticipated cost savings and the expected return on investment. Later, actual performance is checked against these estimates.

FINANCIAL CONTROL

The success of the entire business depends ultimately on sound financial planning and reporting. A financial control system must have a clear objective—a yardstick against which to measure performance. In our case, as I have mentioned, all financial forecasts are made on the basis of standard volume rate of operations. At the beginning of each year every manager of a profit center must submit a profit plan for that year based upon standard volume.

These profit forecasts are reviewed individually with each manager and his principal assistants by the top officers of the company. All expense budgets of organizations that are not profit centers, such as those covering administrative and commercial expenses, engineering, and so on, are submitted annually and reviewed thoroughly in the same manner. In the monthly financial reviews all managers are present when the results of their operations for that month and the year to date are presented to the entire administration committee, all such reports being compared with the previously submitted financial forecasts, or profit plans.

In addition to the actual monthly and year-to-date profit statements, each month all operations furnish a forecast covering the next four months of the year, based upon the expected performance at anticipated volume.

Although most companies of any size are strong, some of them outstandingly so, on cost control, many of the same companies may be startlingly casual about pricing, or revenue, control. It has been our experience that large dividends of added sales and profits can accrue from a careful and systematic attention to revenue control. Pricing procedures for all our products are based on anticipated costs and revenues at standard volume, without regard to temporary fluctuations in the market. However, revenue control involves much more than setting sales prices—it involves the whole area of pricing philosophy, the determination of desirable product mix, and the selection of make-or-buy products on the basis of obtaining maximum profitability.

Under the profit center system, revenue control of intracompany sales between various divisions of the same firm gives invaluable guidance in make-or-buy decisions, provides a check on supplier prices, and is a useful test of performance. Moreover, requiring our own producing divisions to sell competitively to the end-product divisions (car, truck, and tractor divisions) has contributed enormously to the improved profit position of Ford Motor Company.

What I have said here suggests that the whole financial control system must be so designed as to highlight profitability. In our business we do that through a combination of the profit center system and incentive in the form of a supplemental compensation plan in which more than 3,800 members of management participate according to their own performance.

In the course of reorganizing Ford Motor Company, by 1948 we had set up a modern cost control system and a supplemental compensation plan. Having done so, we were disappointed to find that nothing in particular happened. We had built, or so we thought, a log fire under the company. But we had not, up to that point, applied the torch of internal competition.

In the fall of 1948 we called together several hundred of our top management men. We analyzed and compared the profit performance (or performance against standards) of each key operation, and showed how performance was reflected in the supplemental compensation fund. It was quite a show, and each man went out of that meeting determined to put his own house in order. Each man in turn set up similar meetings of his own supervisors, and the process continued on down the line. These meetings were held (as they still are) at regular intervals. The results were almost unbelievable.

Our direct labor costs were reduced from an off-standard of 65% in July of 1948 to only 6% off-standard in 1951, and manufacturing overhead improved 48 percentage points during the same period. We never could have achieved that performance without a real incentive system and internal competition that reached deep into our management structure.

LABOR AGREEMENTS

Because of the special current interest in the guaranteed annual wage, I suppose I should touch on what has occurred at Ford in the labor relations field.

Our company has concluded what we believe to be a sound and far-reaching agreement with the UAW–CIO. However, it is still too early to assess its effects. Moreover, the package as a whole is rather complicated, with implications which cannot be explained as quickly and easily as, say, a straight wage increase of equally generous size. So, rathei than go into detail about the contents of the package as negotiated, let me say something about the management planning that underlies it.

We have long been completely sympathetic toward the desire of our employees to lessen the risks of unemployment resulting from seasonal factors in the auto industry. We have sought consistently to stabilize our production and employment to minimize layoffs due to model changes by better planning, and to use overtime pay, wherever possible, to meet production peaks rather than hire temporary workers. We have made much progress in this direction.

We began some time ago to work on the details of a proposed plan of private supplementation of unemployment compensation which would give substantial added security to our workers in ways consistent with sound private-enterprise principles. We believed that such a plan should not shackle management's freedom to manage. It should be a definite determinable cost item with a definitely limited liability. It should not offer unemployment benefits so great as to remove the incentive to work.

Our present plan meets every one of those requirements. We believe it is a good plan—good for the workers, good for the company, good for the whole country. I am sure that anyone who has had a chance to study the plan in detail will agree that it solves a knotty problem which concerns not only American industry but the general public as well.

CONCLUSION

Obviously, business planning for the future involves the all-important functions of merchandising and distribution. Are we riding the crest of a boom that may taper off a few months or years from now, or is this the new norm of American economic activity? How big is our market, and how big is it likely to grow?

I think our expansion program indicates how we at Ford look at the situation. We see a constantly expanding market for cars and trucks over the long pull; and, frankly, we intend to take an increasing share of that market for our own products.

We believe it is our business, and that of other large companies, to *make* trends, not to follow them. A confident aggressive spirit, backed up by intelligent planning and hard-hitting management, can be contagious. I am sure most of you noted the recent upturn in steel production to meet the sustained sales performance of the automotive industry. It has served as a powerful stimulus to over-all economic activity.

The market of the future promises to be unlike anything we have known before. We see no ceilings to that market except the ones imposed by our own shortness of vision.

That market, needless to say, will be hotly competitive.

In planning the strategy of the larger business—particularly in the consumer goods industries—clearly we will not be competitive in the year 1965 with the products or tools or methods of 1955.

Staying competitive will mean a bold, venturesome outlook on investment in new products, new plants and equipment. It will mean seeking constantly to make obsolete existing products and being ever ready to adapt our businesses to the needs of the atomic age.

Business management must be stronger than formerly in such areas as scientific research, product and manufacturing engineering, financial forecasting and control. It must have real flexibility and strength-in-depth of organization so that it can respond hard and fast to changing competitive situations. It must be imaginative. It follows, then, that management must provide enough incentive to attract and hold really capable men at all levels—and in the last analysis, all else depends on this.

With a well-staffed management team in which an aggressive risk-taking spirit is backed up by cool-headed, analytical planning, there will be no problem too tough to be solved.

PLANNING THE BASIC STRATEGY OF A MEDIUM-SIZE BUSINESS

Charles H. Percy and William E. Roberts

INTRODUCTION

THERE'S A JINGLE that might have been written especially for the corporate president, the executive vice president, and the division head: "The world is so full of a number of things, I'm sure we should all be as happy as kings." Sometimes our world—and our days—are all too full.

For example, do the following sound familiar?

> *The morning mail.* Included are requests from the Chamber of Commerce for a speech on foreign trade, from a public service radio program planner for a talk on aid to education, from a service club for a talk on "The Social Responsibilities of the Industrialist." A share owner writes for information on dividend policy. A security

Note: Mr. Percy is President and Mr. Roberts is Executive Vice President of Bell & Howell Company. The various sections of this chapter are by Mr. Percy and Mr. Roberts alternately, with Mr. Percy leading off.

18

analyst has a query about anticipated earnings. A group of teachers wants to tour the plant and exchange ideas with company executives.

The telephone. It rings steadily. A distributor in Holland calls about a new trade fair. An irate customer can't get service in Mule Shoe, Texas. A key dealer calls frantically about some fair-trade violation.

More mail. A distributor from Thailand announces an impending visit. A key dealer suggests cooperative advertising . . . "but keep up your full schedule of national advertising."

Your meetings. A civic lunch for Project B (the host had come to luncheon for Project A). Back to the plant for a budget board meeting. Review a new product release. Turn down gracefully (impossible!) a request to introduce a friend to the director of purchases; discuss two new appointments in the manufacturing division and a major capital equipment acquisition. Write a column (due yesterday) for the employee newspaper.

End of the day. Into the brief case goes the balance of the day's mail (or yesterday's) along with the reading matter marked "must." Before turning off the office lights, take a look at the sign on the desk, which reads, "MY JOB IS TO BUILD OUR COMPANY'S FUTURE!"

Such activities, the norm for many business managers, were standard procedure in our company for far too long. But eventually came the realization that the man should run the job rather than the job the man. Through a gradual and cautious program of trial and error, we began to evolve a more intelligent mode of operation. Few chief executives would quarrel with the concept that their principal responsibility lies in planning the future of their businesses. Most would ruefully admit that the responsibilities of their office all too often combine to prevent their fulfilling this principal responsibility.

The technique for diverting time from immediately urgent to the ultimately important is a subject in itself.

The strategy can be summarized in three words: (1) *planning,* (2) *coordination,* (3) *execution.*

We have at Bell & Howell's what we call "participation" management; and, in order to properly tell the story of how our program is developed, our entire officer and division manager group should contribute to this discussion. However, since this would not be practical, Mr. Roberts and I will describe our 60-month program of long-range planning, our system of participation management, and the extent of our top management's responsibility in the execution and communication of company programs.

PLANNING FOR PROFIT*

The foundation of "profit planning" is the company's 60-month program. In setting our goals we take a retrospective look at where we have been, an objective look at where we are, and a hopeful look at where we want to go. We then chart a course which we believe will get us there. We keep an eye on economic forecasts, but I must admit that we do not let them influence our thinking too much. If the economic outlook is good, we are encouraged to go ahead with our plans. If it is foreboding, we try to determine how to buck the trend.

An important step is to analyze carefully our relative position in each field in which we compete. After a careful comparison of our past and present financial ratios—earnings to sales, return on investment, and inventory turnover—we establish goals to improve our position during each of the succeeding five years.

With the goals set, the detailed preparation of a 60-month program begins. We analyze our existing product line and review our new product development and research program. A sales forecast is made by months for the next 15-month period and on an annual basis for the following four years. Increases in hourly labor rates and salaries are projected, as is the lowering of unit costs through the anticipated effectiveness of cost-reduction programs. For expansion and capital equipment, future needs are analyzed, schedules are made, and financing is planned.

The 60-month program is a living document which never becomes static. At no time has it ever been bound together between two covers

* By Mr. Percy.

as an "approved program" for the company. Most of the time it is in the form of rough layout sheets which are under constant revision.

The object of the program is not only the program but also the thinking and planning that go into it. We are never satisfied with it, and I hope we never will be. Working constantly on a 60-month program makes the preparation of our current year's profit and loss forecast a great deal easier, more accurate, and more satisfactory than it might otherwise be.

The merchandising division establishes a detailed sales forecast by months for all products and models, and submits it to manufacturing, financial, and administrative management for critical analysis. This same procedure is repeated frequently throughout the year. Desired inventory levels are established and manufacturing schedules drawn up. Cost of sales and divisional expense levels are established by the budget board in consultation with division managers. Programs and expenses are continually revised to maintain the current year's profit objective. The forecast profit and loss statement and the anticipated balance sheet position projected one year ahead are submitted to the board of directors at its December meeting.

At this point Mr. Roberts will relate what our batting average has been for our current year's forecast, as well as for our five-year projections, and what action is taken when deviations from our planned program occur.

ACTUAL VERSUS FORECAST PROGRAM*

Flexibility is a must in a 60-month program. Looking ahead five years from a constantly moving current date makes planning for the immediate 12-month period easier. Both our long-range and short-range programs are constantly modified to meet new competitive products, the unforeseeable results of some of our own engineering and research efforts, the consolidation of newly acquired businesses, and other factors incalculable in advance.

Actually, our five-year planning is not directly measurable in terms

* By Mr. Roberts.

of "batting averages." But in keeping us aimed in the right direction it has helped to achieve a good batting average in our short-term, 12-month planning.

Over the past four years we have varied only slightly from our planned sales, expense, and profit budgets. Variation in expenses against budget, for example, ranged from 4.4% in 1952 to 1% in 1954. The variation from the preyear profit budget to actual was only 3% in 1954.

When deviations occur, as they frequently do during the year, we apply no magic formula for corrective action. Deviations are rapidly detected through weekly meetings of our sales analysis board. Then pertinent division heads and executives are gathered to determine what action is necessary. The answer may be overtime, the addition of double or triple shifts, duplicate tooling, new capital equipment, or around-the-clock engineering effort; it may be a price change or the appointment of a special task force to nurse the situation back to normal.

We try to make our near-term budgets for profits, sales, and manufactured products realistic and attainable. They are rarely missed although it sometimes requires ingenious and unusual effort to keep the program in balance.

Should some problem arise that cannot be remedied in time, we review earnings goals in the light of changed circumstances, and we immediately initiate steps to bring expense budgets into line.

Time will not permit a detailed review of our capital equipment planning. However, in brief, each division head develops and submits by November 1 a detailed list of his anticipated capital expenditures for the following year. The requested budgets are broken down in several ways. They are divided according to whether they are replacement, supplementary, or cost-reduction equipment. Each of these categories is, in turn, divided into two groups—"mandatory" and "desirable." The data are assembled by the controller, reviewed and balanced by the budget board, and then submitted to the president and the board of directors for approval.

Once approved, it becomes the total company dollar capital equipment budget for the ensuing year. However, each individual expenditure against the budget must be fully justified by the division head and approved by the controller before actual purchase. Cost-reduction equipment must presently meet a rigid rule of paying for itself within 18 months. The measuring stick is almost always: What is the rate of return on investment?

COORDINATION OF MANAGEMENT EFFORT*

At Bell & Howell we believe firmly that our business should be the expression of the ideas and objectives of our entire management group and, as far as humanly possible, of our employee group. We have experimented with many ways to encourage the free expression of opinion throughout the company, and have developed a pattern for coordinating our management effort and keeping us all running on the same track. The best way, we have found, is to have the top management group help lay the track by participating in the development of the 60-month and current year forecasts.

But occasionally it helps to get far enough away from the program to take an objective look at it. To do this our officers and division managers literally move to the Fin 'n Feather Club in nearby Elgin, Illinois, once each quarter. Here we spend several days working together without the interruption of telephones or the pressure of supervisory responsibilities. The setting is beautiful, the atmosphere informal. Sports clothes are the order of the day, and, despite the customary skeet shoot, we have never lost an executive! In addition to crystallizing our thinking about our future program, this meeting helps to ease tensions that may have built up between purchasing and manufacturing, manufacturing and engineering, or engineering and sales.

For some time afterward the atmosphere is completely relaxed back in the organization—and then, suddenly, we know we have to go back to Fin 'n Feather again.

Round-robin reports by division managers at our monthly staff

* By Mr. Percy.

luncheon keep each of us informed on all major developments within the company. Recent accomplishments can be reviewed and near-term forecasts analyzed.

We lean heavily on various management boards to coordinate the functional phases of our program. They are not committees. We feel about committees a little like the description by the chancellor of one of our large universities:

> The first time he saw a camel, he got out of the jeep, stood right next to this ugly looking thing with its drooling jowls, baggy skin, and great humps, and he thought, "Good Lord, that looks like it was put together by a committee."

Although the responsibility of these boards is entirely advisory, they are effective in achieving a more closely knit operation and in tapping the specialized knowledge of top management people.

The heart of our management program is the research board. All ideas for new products are first submitted to this board, which helps to guide new product ideas to fruition. The members of the board include the president, executive vice president, and treasurer, the engineering, manufacturing, and merchandising vice presidents, the head of our product planning activity, and the assistant vice president in charge of production engineering and tooling. Thus, all major operating divisions are able to contribute their viewpoints and participate in discussions and decisions on new product development.

Market research and merchandising department ideas on product features, appearance, and price are usually obtained before the first line is made on a sheet of drafting paper.

Sales, engineering, manufacturing, and financing problems get a thorough going-over before—not after—new product development work is begun.

RESPONSIBILITIES OF SPECIAL BOARDS°

Our sales analysis board, which includes top merchandising, manufacturing, purchasing, and market research people and the executive

* By Mr. Roberts.

vice president, meets once a month. At these meetings individual product projections for the next 15-month period are studied month by month and compared with planned manufacturing and projected inventory schedules. The sales, manufacturing, and inventory programs are reviewed, and confirmed or modified in the light of changed conditions; weak areas are detected and corrective action planned. All statistical data are presented graphically.

Supplementing the sales analysis board, a smaller group meets each Monday and briefly reviews sales and manufacturing progress toward budget goals. Negative trends are thus detected in time to bend them back to meet or exceed budget.

The manufacturing board is composed of manufacturing, planning, tooling, production engineering, quality control, and methods engineering personnel. Acting as a two-way information channel and a sounding board for unusual problems or new manufacturing ideas or techniques, it coordinates the functions of the manufacturing division.

The budget board, which includes the president, executive vice president, treasurer, controller, and vice president of manufacturing, controls the purse strings of the company. It develops all budgets, in cooperation with the division heads, and recommends them for approval. Annual divisional expense budgets, manufacturing schedules, capital equipment budgets, inventory objectives, and the cash forecast are its responsibilities. It must operate within the current earnings target, with the 60-month goals constantly in sight.

Our boards have become a device for overcoming the specialization that tends to divorce the outlook of operating experts in engineering from that of experts on sales or manufacturing. But they don't take major planning chores out of the operating people's hands; they don't take away from the division head the responsibility which is his for meeting company objectives; they don't become substitutes for the regular line and staff organization. The boards are merely superimposed on the operating organization as a device to make possible wider interdivisional participation by top executives.

EXECUTION OF PROGRAM*

We would agree, I am sure, that the basic purpose of a free society is to develop the individual to the greatest possible extent. Should we not also conclude, then, that a company's chance for success is greatest when it encourages such growth and development on the part of each individual within the organization? We believe so, and therefore our objective is to try to create the proper working climate and sufficient incentive for every person to work as conscientiously and intelligently as if he were working for himself. This is the goal we keep constantly before us.

Once our target has been established, our job is to shoot for it—and to shoot with an expectancy of success. We are entirely dependent upon the people of our organization, to whom we delegate all necessary authority and responsibility. Decisions are made at the lowest possible level. We try, as much as possible, to manage through the rule of exception; that is, once a plan has been established and the authority delegated for its execution, no further authority is required from any higher source unless an exception must be made because of changing circumstances. This removes 90% of the routine work from the manager's desk.

But top management would be remiss if it assumed that its job was now done. For in addition to the never-ending job of future planning, the president and the executive vice president must go to work for the operating divisions of the company to help implement plans and programs already made. This job has many facets, but I will mention only two: the communications program and the continuing task of evaluating divisional and individual performance.

We have proved again and again Thomas J. Watson's words: "None of us is ever enthusiastic about anything until we understand it. Knowledge creates enthusiasm, and it is enthusiasm which inspires us to work and move forward."

When the organization, from top to bottom, understands the overall aims, objectives, problems, hopes, and aspirations of the company,

* By Mr. Percy.

then it can do a better job of carrying out the company program.

It is often said that "big business" has every advantage. Size does offer advantages, but it has inherent disadvantages. If the small or medium-size business seized every opportunity its size offers, it would soon find itself becoming bigger at a faster than normal rate. One key advantage of smaller size, of course, is the ability to meet face-to-face with every member of the organization and his family.

It was just six years ago when I spoke at the first Bell & Howell "family night." Since that time family night has become an annual affair for our Chicago plants as well as for our film plant in Rochester, New York. We hold an annual meeting for our shareholders; and family night is based on the theory that people who have invested their lives in a business are just as interested in its operation as those who have invested their money. Attendance figures prove the point.

At each meeting we discuss our outlook for the future, whether it be good or bad. We discuss questions and problems about our general company program and those which we feel are on people's minds. Meetings are not dull and drab, for a proper balance of showmanship and visual aids holds the attention of both the masculine and the feminine members of the family.

We talk about profits. And in this connection let me relate a little piece of experience:

> I remember back in 1938, when I was a novice in our apprentice training program, I was working on an assembly line putting together an 8 mm. camera. Another worker turned to me and said, "Chuck, the customer pays $100 for this camera and, according to my figuring, it costs the company about $15 to make. Pretty sweet for someone."
>
> I know that a top executive realizes this is not true, but at that time I was 18 and I believed it. When I was transferred to the accounting department as part of my training program, my suspicion was confirmed, because the organization was so set up that the fellow who handled direct labor wasn't allowed to talk to the fellow who had control of material costs, and the controller was the only one who ever put costs together.

But as I went through the department, I jotted down the costs **on** this camera, and I was amazed to find that only an 8% profit margin was realized. And I vowed then, if ever I had the chance, I would talk about profits to the people of our company.

So we talk about profits—and we never speak defensively. Year after year we prove that it is good for our employees as well as good for the company to earn a reasonable profit. In many different ways we ask the question whether an employee would like to work for a company that did not earn good profits. "Would you feel a sense of security?" "Would you have confidence in the company management?" "Would you feel that you had opportunity for the future?" We are proud of making a good profit. In fact, we are ashamed when we don't.

I believe that it is management's increasing willingness to talk about profits, to explain their purpose and function in a free-enterprise system—that is responsible for the public's growing understanding of business. We believe we have developed a sincere desire on the part of most of our employees to help the company build its future by helping it to become more profitable. We know that this desire has become an *intense* one since we have introduced a liberal profit-sharing plan!

The next section will cover a few phases of our informational program and the methods used to evaluate divisional and individual performance.

INFORMATIONAL PROGRAM *

We use many channels of communication:

¶[Our monthly executive meetings are attended by approximately 300 executives and shop foremen, who see and hear a carefully prepared presentation of important company problems or programs. The meetings afford an excellent opportunity to inform the executive group of pending changes or actions before word is passed along to the employee group and to the public.

* By Mr. Roberts.

⟪Our company publication, *The Finder,* is another effective means of communication. Published twice monthly, it includes an "As I See It" column by Mr. Percy, which has proved to be tremendously effective.

⟪Frequent letters to the homes of all employees have also helped to keep open and maintain our information channels. Any really important news about the company is first given to our executives; then it is usually followed by a letter to our employees before it is released to the public.

⟪We have a liberal and effective suggestion system and we maintain an "open-door" policy. All of our top executives encourage anyone with a serious problem to bring it directly to them if he can't get it solved by his superior or the personnel division.

⟪A key information channel was employed in the last quarter of 1954 to explain our profit-sharing plan. We felt it so important for every single employee to understand the plan that we prepared detailed instruction material and developed a training program. First our entire executive staff was trained in using and presenting the material. Each executive then gave a detailed explanation to a small group of department heads and foremen. These supervisors, in turn, told the story in meetings with their employees. This was supplemented by *Finder* articles, bulletins, and letters to employees' homes. The plan was not a simple one to grasp. It needed and it got careful and complete explanation. All questions were answered fully. As a result it was enthusiastically received, and 91% of our employees signed up to make voluntary contributions to the plan.

⟪This technique has been used successfully for the introduction of other important programs, and we will continue to use it in the future. We feel it is extremely important to bring the foreman into our communications program.

PERFORMANCE EVALUATION

Divisional performance and personal performance are evaluated in several ways:

1. Each division head submits a weekly report briefly outlining important accomplishments and problems. Such reports are primarily

informational, but when trouble spots show up, they lead to corrective action.

2. Six-month and year objectives are established for each division in cooperation with the division heads. At the half-year and full-year points, accomplishments toward established goals are tallied, and the results are weighed in considering bonus amounts and salary increases.

3. At six-month intervals, every individual in the company is merit rated by his superior, after he has rated himself. The two ratings are then compared and discussed. Such merit ratings are made for everyone, from the president on down. The program has acted as a constant personnel audit by each department and division head and a gauge of progress for each employee. It has contributed substantially toward having the right man in the right job.

An important "by-product" is the fact that it opens a broad avenue of communication *from* the employee *to* management. Supervisors say it brings them closer to their people and their people closer to them and the company.

SUMMARY *

In a few words, the strategy we have outlined can be summarized. First, we attempt to establish reasonable yet challenging goals through planning in which our top management group participates. We try to coordinate our efforts so that we all shoot for the same goals. We delegate authority to the fullest extent possible. Enthusiasm for our programs is stimulated by the dissemination of information so that participation is achieved at every possible level. Performance toward established goals is constantly evaluated, and achievement is fully rewarded.

From beginning to end, our strategy depends on faith in people —faith in the members of our organization. The job of management selection, training, transferring, weeding, evaluating, and promoting is one that can be shared with other members of top management. But it is never one that can be completely delegated. It is for this rea-

* By Mr. Percy.

son that, while our operating divisions at Bell & Howell report directly to the executive vice president, the industrial relations and personnel divisions report to the president. It is in this area of management evaluation that Mr. Roberts and I have our longest, most searching, and most unhurried discussions. No joy can ever equal ours when events and performance prove that our confidence was not misplaced. No disappointment is greater than that which comes from the failure of someone to measure up to our expectations or his own actual abilities.

Bell & Howell's growth has been part of the growth of a dynamic industry in a rising economy. But that is not the whole story. Our increase in sales from $13 million six years ago to over $40 million last year has exceeded the average for our own industry and for business as a whole. It was due in large part, we believe, to the thoughtful planning and concerted effort of a number of our officers, division managers, and other members of our organization with whom it has been Mr. Roberts' and my privilege to work. Their enthusiastic approach to their work, their ability to analyze a problem, and their initiative in solving it will be responsible for whatever measure of success we achieve in the future.

We are constantly attempting to do a better job of organizing and delegating our work. We seek to develop executives with the human touch. We place in positions of key responsibility men who like and respect the people with whom they work and who can inspire others with enthusiasm. We look constantly for men who can stimulate the imagination of others and help them develop their own capacities to the fullest.

However, it is well for us to remember one thing. We could not continue to improve unless we had areas in need of improvement. In this we are indeed rich. We have many unanswered questions, many unsolved problems. I'm sure we always will.

But in the midst of past and present problems, we can never forget that the primary obligation of management is to take the long view. We must evaluate the past, work in the present, and think in the future.

QUESTIONS AND ANSWERS*

From the floor: I am interested—and somewhat puzzled—by one aspect of Bell & Howell's "participation" management.

My organization has about 500 people in it, and is pretty small in comparison with some of the large companies. We have a lot of talented young men, however, who are charged with ideas and raring to go, and we are anxious to hear their suggestions. And I couldn't help thinking, as Mr. Percy reported on the way his company operated, how bogged down we get when we try to get all these people into the act, how even our little organizational problems seem to get choked in committee sessions. Yet I understood from his presentation that Bell & Howell had around 300 people getting together every month. How is it possible, as a practical matter, for a company to drag everyone into the act? And how can it control a management committee?

Mr. Percy: I became very enthusiastic about management participation—we had never had anything like it in the company before—but I must confess that at one point I made the unpardonable mistake of letting it go too far, and it was hard to pull it back on the track again. You just cannot let this type of thing get out of hand.

After we started having everyone at the meetings, these conferences had to be held after working hours. This made arrangements much more difficult, of course. When we found that meetings were unnecessarily long and that reasons for calling them were often invalid, we instituted a training program on conference leadership. We had agendas made out ahead of time, including the stated purpose of the meeting, the starting time, and the closing time. If the chairman conducted the meeting improperly, the committee members quickly criticized him for it and thus brought him back on the track. We no longer try to consider everything in these con-

---

* In a subsequent meeting, Mr. Percy answered questions pertaining to his formal presentation; this chapter section is drawn, more or less verbatim, from the discussion that took place at this meeting. George P. Baker, James J. Hill Professor of Transportation, Harvard Business School, acted as moderator.

ferences. For instance, no one in the company is wise enough to judge how money taken in through sales should be prorated and expended; this is now a problem for the budget board.

I think we are no longer plagued by too much "meetingitis," as we called it, although we did have trouble for a while controlling our kind of participation management. We used to have dinner meetings once a month from 5:15 to 8:00, but we found we could save several thousand dollars a year by eliminating the dinners, and we now meet for only an hour and a quarter, from 5:00 to 6:15. This gives us plenty of time to present our monthly reports and to inform our executive staff and foremen about important company plans.

The smaller quarterly meetings of our top executives are another matter. They do need to be physically removed from the plant and free from all interference. These meetings, incidentally, provide a wonderful chance for our secondary line of management to run their divisions by themselves for a day or two every quarter. We think it is valuable experience for them to be completely on their own without any of the top management staff about.

From the floor: Mr. Percy has stated that his long-range, five-year planning makes his short-range, one-year and two-year planning a lot easier. How is this true?

Mr. Percy: By becoming familiar with what our cash position is likely to be several years in *advance* of any coming year—barring unforeseeable happenings such as the acquisition of a new business or our competition coming out with a revolutionary new line of product—we find it much easier to estimate our position for any particular year. By the time 1955 came around, we had been planning and working on it for three or more years. Most of my personal time now is going into 1957 and later years—1957, incidentally, will be our fiftieth anniversary, and we have been thinking about it and working on it for many years. We think it will be a fine opportunity for a special drive in several directions. Detailed planning for 1957 should be much easier with all this general, long-range planning in back of us.

From the floor: In Mr. Percy's discussion of profit planning, he has mentioned that he looks at the present objectively and the future hopefully. What is the point of this distinction between "objective" and "hopeful"?

Mr. Percy: "Hopeful" is one word that almost everyone associated with our company uses extensively. Businessmen have to be optimists; we would get nowhere if we looked with pessimism to the future. We have to figure ways for our company to keep going regardless of the way the economic indicators point and in spite of what our competitors may do. Our theory used to be that when the indicators drop down, then we buttoned down. Now we try to accelerate our new products ahead faster than originally scheduled and intensify our sales efforts. In other words, we, like other managements, will try to buck any adverse trend—that is our nature. When I said that we look to the future hopefully, I meant we all believe that if any year doesn't turn out the way we thought, at least the approach we took made it better than it might have been.

From the floor: I think if any company can instill the spirit of optimism that Mr. Percy describes into its whole organization, the company will grow and prosper. Even the smallest organization can get some place if it is inspired this way; and if a company isn't optimistic, it might as well toss in the towel and quit. My business is located in New England, and I am afraid that a great part of the mills in our district have failed and closed up largely because of a lack of enthusiasm and get-up-and-go.

From the floor: In the planning of profit, how far can a small company go when it has departmental control of expenses and a number of departments contributing to the products?

Mr. Percy: I think our company's experience with budgetary control is very encouraging. We started when our sales figure was $13 million. Then we had only one man in the budget department and our budgets were handwritten in pencil. I think we operated more or less out of our hip-pockets until we got into the field of budgetary control and understood what it could mean as a management tool.

Now if we don't get our budget out to our operating department heads by the fifteenth day following the close of the month, the budget control department is criticized by the department heads— the figures have become that vital. Our budget people bang out the budgets on IBM machines. All department heads get a detailed accounting breakdown of the year to date and the past month, compared to the budgets for these same periods that they had agreed to at the beginning of the year. Our system started out on a very modest basis, but we now have seven people in the department, which is headed up by a former industrial engineer who leaned in the direction of accounting and financial controls. As the company grows and we add divisions, we immediately place them all under budgetary control. This is one of the few "musts" in our expansion policy.

From the floor: Is there any real, reliable standard of profit for a firm that has no competitive price to deal with? In other words, in a mixed product operation, in order to get a real profit motive, haven't you got to use outside market prices rather than any incentive you can create inside your company?

Mr. Percy: I think that question is pertinent because it applies to a great many areas of business where prices are regulated, as in the case of railroads and utilities. Utility prices are set by regulation, not by the market as in the case of highly competitive items such as raw materials. I think that is the point of the question. Incidentally, I recall a visitor from England asking one time how we went about making our prices, and one of our vice presidents replied that we just made an effort to meet our overhead!

Now, in pricing and profit making you are dealing with an equation where there are a number of variable costs which at best you can only partially determine. The further the items you have to buy are removed from the finished product, the more leeway you have in your pricing policy. For instance, basic steel moves within a very narrow price range, while cameras move within a wide range. Profit possibilities depend on this range factor. The more engineering labor and skill you put into your product, the more you take your article out of the narrow price bracket that it would otherwise be in.

Today many companies have found that they just could not make a living by manufacturing a standard product. Therefore they have tried to put something into their product that would remove it at least somewhat from the arena of competition. There is no doubt that many engineering improvements—in design, in improved packaging, in color, and so on—have been made with the idea of achieving freedom in pricing operations. Pricing for profit is the central problem of business, and I don't know of any formula; but I do know that there are certain assumptions made which are not always correct— namely, that the price cannot be changed and that the nature of the article cannot be altered. There is more latitude in the game of price and profit than that.

From the floor: This is all true, but my point was that to be realistic in creating a profit incentive inside your company you need a valid economic yardstick. This yardstick is your ability to sell the product, and this depends on the competition of the market.

From the floor: Mr. Percy has referred rather indirectly to the acquiring of other firms as part of a business's growth process. What should be the criteria in purchasing smaller outfits? What should a company look for in a firm it may want to buy?

Mr. Percy: This is a very interesting question, since everyone is preoccupied with the present merger trend.

In the past six years Bell & Howell has studied over a hundred purchase opportunities, many of which might have been excellent moves. Then last year we took action for the first time, and bought two companies—a venture that has proved very interesting but at the same time has posed something of a problem.

Now, our real customers in the photography business are young couples, who are especially interested in taking movies, primarily of their children. This is fine, since everyone is having babies. But then when people get older, they become more interested in taking still pictures and travel shots. Germany and Japan have pretty well blanketed the camera market, and so our company has concentrated on colored slides and slide projectors. One of the firms we bought is the world's biggest slide projector manufacturer.

Our problem was to convince the two new companies that our sales and production policies were right, and that they should go along with our strategy plans. In one case we have had outstanding success in winning over the firm's personnel to our way of doing business (perhaps because they became part of the parent organization); in the other case, we have had a great deal of selling to do. We believe in persuasion, not regulation, and we want the managers to accept our program willingly before they start operating under it. The second company's executives have taken their time in "buying" some of our ideas, and therefore installing some of our procedures has been rather a slow process. But when they do adopt a procedure, it is usually from conviction that it is good for their division—and we anticipate that it will "stick" longer.

THE ESSENTIAL COMPONENTS
OF BUSINESS PLANNING

Meyer Kestnbaum

FORMAL BUSINESS PLANNING, in the sense in which we use the term today, is a relatively modern development. To be sure, every aspect of business activity requires some degree of planning as does every other purposeful activity in life. However, we have come to recognize only recently the degree to which planning can be used as a tool of management.

Those of us who remember Wallace B. Donham's salty observations will recall one of his favorite maxims, "The first rule of business is to do the best that can be done in the circumstances." He had in mind the need for practical judgment. But the emphasis on circumstances is significant. Mr. Donham certainly did not intend to convey the idea that circumstances control our destinies. On the contrary, he meant that it is the function of business management to deal with circumstances. The whole concept of planning rests on the assumption that

Note: Mr. Kestnbaum is President of Hart Schaffner & Marx.

it is possible to anticipate circumstances, to devise methods for dealing with them, and in some measure to control them.

It is probably fair to say that the management of every well-conducted enterprise makes it a point to reappraise its position from time to time, to re-examine its objectives, and to review its plans for the future. In a small enterprise, for example, these plans may be expressed in certain decisions and attitudes without ever being reduced to written form. On the other hand, the improvement budget of a large railroad is a voluminous document prepared in meticulous detail.

It is in the nature of planning to determine which factors are significant:

> The department store will be concerned not only with the everyday problems of merchandising, but also with the growth of shopping centers and the effects of decentralization. In an industrial community, merchants will be influenced by the prospects of their local manufacturers; in rural communities, they will pay particular attention to the agricultural outlook.
>
> Thus, the circumstances of individual companies even when they are engaged in the same type of business may differ sufficiently to affect the way in which they plan. One may be preoccupied with the need for facilities which require additional capital; the other may be greatly troubled by its pattern of distribution.
>
> The availability of labor, the quality and temper of the labor supply, and wage differentials also are critical factors in a great many business decisions.

Business planning is particularly sensitive to the factor of change. Even during periods of general prosperity the textile industry, the coal industry, and some sections of the railroad industry have encountered difficulties.

We have seen, for example, substantial changes take place in the relative importance of some of our basic raw materials. The competition between natural and synthetic fibers has already had far-reaching effects on both producers and distributors of textiles. The chemical revolution that has taken place in recent years has had a violent impact on many industries, and now we are becoming aware of the impressive possibilities of new developments in electronics. With the development of atomic energy for industrial use the next few decades will probably produce changes equally if not more profound. It is the responsibility of those who plan to endeavor to take these changes into account.

HISTORY AND DEVELOPMENT

Millions of business decisions are made every day; and while most of them are of a routine nature, they all flow from some kind of planned activity. But it may help identify the essential components of planning to review some of the factors that have stimulated American industry to organize its activities more carefully.

There is little evidence of formal planning in the early history of our business system. The development of retailing is a case in point. Many of our great department stores and mercantile organizations grew up during the latter part of the last century. They were founded by men who had little formal education or training. Many of the founders came from other countries. These men learned retailing on a small scale; some of them started as peddlers, but they had enough imagination to see the opportunities that existed in growing communities in a rapidly expanding country. It may be noted in passing that their efforts stimulated that expansion.

These early merchants kept very little in the way of records; they had no operating budgets, no formal buying budgets, none of the carefully detailed systems of merchandising controls with which we are familiar. The overhead of the modern department store would have startled them. But it would be naive to assume that they were less sensitive to the hazards of merchandising than are their successors, or that they were less alert to merchandising needs and opportunities. They knew how to select merchandise and how to sell it. The need for elaborate planning techniques simply had not yet developed.

Much of the detailed control and planning that is characteristic of large-scale retailing had its impetus in the drastic drop in commodity prices that took place in 1919 following the boom stimulated by World War I. Retailers generally were caught with heavy inventories, and many sustained staggering losses. The result was that, to prevent a recurrence of these losses, elaborate systems were established for the control of inventories. Under these new programs merchandise management was organized as a separate function, and the basic responsibility for the management of inventories and for merchandise planning was transferred from the buyer to the merchandise manager.

In the case of the smaller specialty stores it was the depression of the 1930's that stimulated more detailed plans and procedures. On this point I can offer some personal testimony. No longer than 30 years ago it was the exceptional merchant in the men's wear field who attempted anything resembling merchandise planning. Merchants generally were more interested in selling than in watching their stocks. They paid little attention to turnover; very often the only effective restraints on inventories were those imposed by limited capital. Gross profit margins varied widely according to the over-all cost of doing business. Stocks were frequently unbalanced; price lines were haphazard. I wrote many letters in those days urging retailers to work out seasonal buying plans and operating budgets and to improve their gross profit margins.

The world has changed in 30 years. Retailers now write me to demand higher markups.

Planning in our manufacturing industry reveals a pattern of development parallel to but somewhat different from that which took place in retailing. The early manufacturing companies were founded by men who were ingenious and inventive, and who knew how to turn out a product. They dealt with many problems, and certainly much planning was necessary, but such planning as they undertook was usually directed to the advancement of specific objectives. For they were spared many of the vexing problems that now confront us. It was not difficult to find markets in an expanding country. Wage rates were low, and the labor problem as we know it had not yet developed. Large-scale immigration assured an ample labor supply; the factory owner could usually count on finding people waiting for jobs at his gate. Taxes were low, risk capital was available for promising enterprises, and the era of extensive government intervention in business had not yet dawned.

These company founders were pioneers and builders. We may be sure that for the most part they placed greater reliance on practical judgment than on theory or research, but also that they were quick to appreciate the value of engineering ability and the possibilities of technology. It was their constant striving for better methods that first exhibited the American genius for production. As these enterprises became larger and more complicated, as more people participated in management decisions, as various staff functions were developed, the simple need for coordination of all these activities forced management to work out specific procedures designed to achieve specific goals.

Planning for production does have the great advantage of dealing with empirical factors—the development of facilities, the scheduling of materials, and the careful analysis of processes and costs. It recognizes opportunities for research directed to the solution of specific problems. The growing influence of the Taylor System with its emphasis on highly detailed production planning accustomed manufacturing industries to the planning process. So by the turn of the century efficiency had become widely accepted as the guiding principle for production. Today we associate productivity with our way of life.

This emphasis on productivity exerts constant pressure on other aspects of business management. The economies of full production are so dramatic as to put a great premium on the ability to sell and distribute merchandise. Our economy places a great value on selling ability and promotion techniques. To support mass production we have found it profitable to develop such devices as installment selling and to extend consumer credit to limits never dreamed possible.

NEED FOR BALANCE

It would be too loose a generalization to suggest that retail planning is essentially cautious, whereas the planning which has emanated from our manufacturing industries tends to be expansive. Retailers have frequently been more alert to the possibilities of products than have the manufacturers themselves. Nevertheless, it must be acknowledged that production rather than distribution has been the driving force in our economy.

The development of over-all plans that strike a proper balance between the need for production and the opportunities for distribution is one of the most challenging demands made on top management. It is at this level that some of the most difficult management decisions must be made. What pricing policies, what merchandising policies, what advertising and promotion techniques are needed or can be devised? What type of organization can be assembled to carry them out? What merchandising risks are justified? A serious miscalculation on any of these points can be costly.

But because we are more sensitive at the moment to the problems of selling than to the problems of production, a few comments about selling plans are in order. We have more information about markets, more accurate income statistics, and perhaps a better understanding of the psychology of the consumer than we have ever had before. This is an area in which much excellent research has been done, and obviously the existence of mass advertising media provides us with powerful tools. But the fact remains that some companies have been much more competent than others in appraising their market opportunities and in building their plans accordingly. I can think of no better example than that currently afforded by the automotive industry:

> It was generally predicted that with the end of the Korean boom the high rate of automobile production would decline. The opinion was also widely held that the industry would have to reduce its prices in order to sustain even a normal volume of production. It is safe to assume that any one of the larger companies could have produced an economy car. Instead the leading companies adopted an entirely different approach, and we have witnessed one of the most revealing developments in the history of merchandising.

> It took great courage to plan for the increased production that has been achieved, and considerable merchandising genius to recog-

nize that public imagination could be captured by cars that were larger, more powerful, and more attractive than those that were already owned by the consumer. The fact that the automobile industry elected to expand and trade up at a critical moment has strengthened general confidence in the market for all products.

Occasionally the estimate of the market is too conservative. One case that comes to mind is the decision of a number of the domestic airlines to stay out of European air travel:

> Most of the airlines came to the conclusion that a handful of airplanes could carry all of the passengers that were likely to travel between the United States and Europe and that the opportunities in this field were limited. Other than Pan American, which was already committed to intercontinental travel, only one of the domestic airlines, TWA, elected to enter this field. It is possible, of course, that in terms of their own situation, the other airlines may have decided wisely, for the business is highly competitive and many of the European airlines are subsidized by their governments.
>
> The example is cited only to illustrate the fact that able experts greatly underestimated the size of the market. On the basis of all current statistics their conclusions seemed sound, but statistics do not always enable us to predict the future. It took imagination to foresee the tremendous increase in airplane travel that has developed during the last ten years.

We are constantly searching for simple principles that will help us appraise the potentialities of the market. Here is what has been advanced by more than one retailer as the underlying principle of merchandising: *supplying what people want, when they want it, at a price that they are willing to pay*.

This sounds persuasive, but unhappily it is not capable of wide practical application. People do not always know what they want until they see it, and we observe every day that they have been made to want things that they had not dreamed of wanting until these things were presented by someone with enterprise and imagination.

The same qualifications apply to predetermined ideas with respect to price. Where there is little to distinguish one product from another, the consumer naturally seeks to buy most advantageously. Yet the consumer has evidenced time and time again his willingness to pay a higher price for goods that have distinctive style or quality or some other feature that makes them more desirable.

It is generally assumed that market analysis can proceed with considerable accuracy in fields such as retail merchandising where we are dealing with reasonably stable markets. In the aggregate this assumption tends to be true, but uncritical reliance on records and statistics can lead to bad planning. The pressure to match last year's sales is difficult to resist, and in an effort to do so many mistakes are made. An unusual selling event that made good sense last year may not be reasonable or possible at the present time.

Furthermore, last year's sales record tells us what we did but not what we might have done. The figures do not reveal the opportunities that were lost or the sales that might have been achieved with more adequate stocks. There can be no doubt that retailers have missed opportunities to sell better grades of merchandise simply because they have made no provision for them. The sales records tend to be inconclusive on this point for the simple reason that sales performance is determined very largely by what is offered for sale.

To plan without the benefit of previous experience is foolhardy. To regard past performance as conclusive is unwise, for experience is a great teacher but not necessarily a reliable guide to the future. In the hands of unimaginative persons, procedures designed to reduce the hazards of merchandising can limit that spontaneous quality of retailing which is one of its principal assets.

All this illustrates the pervasive effect on business planning of estimates of the market. More could be adduced. It would be interesting, for instance, to review some of the postwar planning that was done during the early 1940's. Much of this was either academic or naive. It was widely predicted that the end of the war would precipitate large-scale unemployment. Many companies felt that the way to offset a decline in their own production was to invade another field. A surprising number of companies, for example, made plans to engage in the manufacture of appliances—some with unfortunate consequences.

On the other hand, the well-planned research and development carried on during the war period was productive of amazing results. A number of important new industries came into being, and others have been able to adapt to civilian use many items developed for military purposes. Such research has now become a major factor in business planning.

NEED FOR TRAINED PLANNERS

The long-term implication of increasing recognition of the importance of trained personnel is no less important. That the separation of ownership from management in business would enlarge the need for trained executives was recognized many years ago. We have since come to realize that trained people are needed at all administrative levels. They are not likely to be supplied in sufficient quantities by our educational system. Furthermore there is some question as to how much of this responsibility should be imposed on our schools and colleges. Differences of opinion exist as to the relative merits of vocational and general education. The issue is too complicated to be discussed here, but I would express the view that the long-term trend in the colleges is toward greater emphasis on general education, and that the training function is one which must be undertaken very largely by industry.

The dramatic announcement recently made by General Electric of the establishment of a business administration college, operated entirely by the General Electric Company, illustrates the degree to which our largest industries have come to recognize the importance of the development of executives. Ralph Cordiner is quoted as saying, "Not customers, not products, not money, but managers may be the limit on General Electric's growth." If this is true of General Electric, it is likely to be true of all of our great industrial organizations.

Although there have been notable advances during the last few years in the techniques of personnel training, I believe that we are still in the early stages of this development. Every personnel audit that is made reveals the fact that our needs are great. Every business is interested in finding superior people, but there are not enough superior people to go around. Fortunately many people of average ability can be trained to carry more responsibility—and I would predict with some confidence that training programs for the upgrading of second and third line personnel will become a major activity of business during the next decade. Not every company is in a position to do what General Electric proposes, but other companies will develop their own plans, and in some cases it may be possible to work out on a cooperative basis training programs for the benefit of an entire industry or area.

The problems of markets and of personnel have been emphasized thus far because they are common to all business. But the areas of business planning are too varied to be neatly catalogued, and the planning process itself is too complex to be neatly defined. Nevertheless, some general observations can be made.

THE PLANNING PROCESS

A distinction needs to be drawn between specific plans and the planning process itself. At the end of a certain period a detailed plan is presumed to have served its purpose. (The function of planning, on the other hand, is one which is never completed.) Further, plans are formulated as guides to action; they involve means and ends. They are prompted very largely by necessity. Some of the most successful procedures developed by American business have been born of adversity.

Greater emphasis on formal planning has been stimulated by a substantial improvement in special techniques. We have much better facilities than ever before for analyzing markets, for testing consumer reactions, for determining the most effective use of advertising and promotion. An extraordinary amount of work has been done in the field of personnel management. We are paying greater attention to public relations, and recent events suggest that a number of our companies are beginning to pay a little more attention to stockholder relations.

It would be foolish to suggest that a *plan* will convert a mediocre executive into a good one, but there can be no doubt that the habit of planning, if carefully cultivated, can contribute to the quality of a business management as a whole. For one thing, a carefully drawn plan helps prevent oversights and mistakes. This is particularly true of an integrated operating plan that is based on careful estimates of sales, expenses, and capital requirements, and with supporting schedules dealing with organization, materials, and processes carefully worked out. If the principal executives in an organization have participated in the preparation of the plan and the allocation of their separate responsibilities, if the basic assumptions are reasonably sound, one may conclude that the plan will prove an effective device for the coordination of a whole series of complicated activities for the allocation of responsibilities and for the appraisal of results.

The process of appraising results is not an easy one. There is a presumption in favor of good performance when the sales quota is met or the operating budget adhered to, but this is by no means conclusive. We have all seen a bridge player bid four, make his contract, and feel a degree of satisfaction, although someone looking over the player's shoulder can testify to the fact that there were six tricks in his hand.

In the matter of meticulous planning we have something to learn from the military. In developing the principles of logistics military planning has applied some of the techniques of science to the movement of men and materials. And in considering the capabilities of an enemy, military planning puts great emphasis on provision for all possible contingencies.

Plans can go wrong for many reasons. Some of the underlying assumptions upon which the plan rests may prove to be unsound. The basic strategy may be badly conceived. Many plans fail because people overestimate their capacity or underestimate the difficulties which are to be met. A plan also can fail if it is not properly executed, if its timing is bad, or if it has not been properly explained and sold to the persons who are expected to carry it out. Many good programs have been doomed to failure from the outset because of an inadequate provision of means. All too often something entirely unexpected intervenes to render the plan ineffective.

We must have constantly in mind the fact that planning is a function of the human spirit, that it reflects human strengths and human weaknesses. Very few plans are completely objective. And the qualities of those who plan vary. The sales manager's approach usually differs from that of the treasurer. Businessmen are conditioned by their experience. Plans made in good times tend to be optimistic; when business is off, all plans take on a conservative cast.

The effect of these psychological factors is evident in sharp changes in inventory policy, one of the most troublesome factors in business planning. On the whole, inventory policy tends to aggravate cyclical changes. The day may come when more rational policies with respect to all future commitments will contribute to greater stability.

FUTURE RESPONSIBILITIES

If the developments of the last few decades are indicative of future trends, we may expect that the conduct of business will become increasingly complicated, not only because of the developments within business itself, but also because business has developed closer ties to the community. Businessmen cannot be insensitive to the broad economic and social changes that are taking place in our country. The ability to deal with these changes will test the quality of business leadership during the coming decades.

It is obvious, for example, that government has assumed larger responsibilities for the maintenance of a high rate of business activity. To an increasing degree the climate in which the business system operates will be affected by government policies. No business can afford to ignore the practical implications of national commitments to high employment and to the maintenance of economic stability. There was a time when Americans were willing to accept the uncertainties caused by fluctuations in the business cycle. Times have changed. They now press for economic security. We find it difficult to withstand the political pressures caused by even moderate unemployment.

We may expect, therefore, that of necessity *business management will gradually assume a larger share of responsibility for the stability of the economy*. What better evidence could be offered to support this proposition than the 1955 bargaining negotiations in Detroit? It has not yet been seriously proposed that business has a legal obligation to adjust its pricing and inventory policies to national economic policy, but the weight of public pressure even in these areas has begun to make itself felt. Witness the furor caused not long ago by the increase in the price of coffee.

We have a right to be optimistic about an economy that is supported by a highly productive industrial system. So long as we have a free economy, however, the conduct of business will be fraught with risks and business planning will be difficult. Certainly these can never be reduced to an exact science.

Business must always deal with factors that are unpredictable. It must recognize the element of chance. Many of our most important scientific discoveries were made by chance, but it must be remembered that "chance favors the prepared mind."

Plans for large affairs call for boldness and imagination. Plutarch tells us of one of the ancient Greeks who was asked whether he could play a musical instrument and who replied, "It is true I never learned to tune a harp or play upon a lute, but I know how to raise a small and inconsiderable city to quality and greatness." It may be that we ask too much or make unreasonable demands on those who lead our nation and our economy when we hold them to such a standard; but when we consider that the quality of the planning which we undertake at this critical time will determine our survival and our growth, we find it difficult to be satisfied with less.

Business planning at its best represents a happy combination of art and technique:

> Insofar as planning is based on knowledge and experience, it calls for analytical ability, for no body of experience, no sets of facts or statistics should be accepted uncritically.
> Insofar as planning requires the development of methods and procedures, it calls for skill and ingenuity.

Insofar as planning addresses itself to problems, it demands resourcefulness.

Insofar as it deals with people (and all plans are carried out by people), it requires an understanding of the forces which motivate human action.

Since all planning is based on some estimate of the future, it puts a premium on the qualities of imagination and foresight.

Finally, and above all, planning always calls for the exercise of judgment.

It would appear that the ideal planner needs all of the moral and intellectual virtues, plus an astonishing collection of skills.

As we improve our range of knowledge and apply this knowledge to practical problems through technology, as we improve through education and specialization the services available to business, we gradually substitute information for opinion, judgment for intuition. In many respects the development of business management has been similar to the development of flying. Most of us remember the early pilot whose most important asset was a kind of intuition which enabled him to fly "by the seat of his pants." He had few instruments, fragmentary weather reports, a plane of limited range and capabilities, but he also had unbounded faith in man's ability to fly.

The airplane industry has developed a whole series of devices which have taken much of the guesswork out of flying. The modern businessman, too, has at his command an extensive set of guides and controls that were not available a generation ago. But technique is no substitute for art. The expansion of our knowledge has by no means simplified the problems of management. On the contrary, we have enlarged the area in which planning takes place, and we have imposed on business leadership very much larger responsibilities. The complexity of our society and its dynamic quality call for the type of planning that is born of wisdom and that is inspired by what has been so aptly called "the vision of excellence." There has never been a time in history when planning for business was as difficult or as complicated as it is today. There has never been a time when its opportunities were as great.

QUESTIONS AND ANSWERS*

From the floor: All businessmen seem to be preoccupied with the growing social responsibility of industry. How will this way of thinking affect industrial personnel policy? In other words, how can companies train their potential managers to recognize industry's new and great role?

Mr. Kestnbaum: This attitude develops in two ways. Some awareness of social responsibility trickles down from the top management, and some of it comes from the pressure of public opinion. Management's learning process has been difficult in some cases; I think the development of labor relationships since 1932 is a lesson in accommodation through hard experience. Companies had to develop theories and practices for dealing with labor problems as they came up against them face-to-face. Industry accepted the necessity for collective bargaining arrangements only after it had felt the repercussions of strikes and angry and widespread criticism of its policies.

Public pressure on industry today is great. The merits of a strike are tried in the public press, and the positions of both management and labor become the subject of general debate and discussion. The United Automobile Workers realized that the country was intensely interested in their fight for the GAW, and their maneuvering was on that basis.

Then, of course, a realization of business's responsibilities can be acquired in a man's formal learning process. The professional education offered at Harvard Business School and other schools of business administration is very valuable for this reason. I remarked about the importance of general education programs in our colleges; one of the functions of general education is to give future businessmen an understanding of how our economy operates and just what its responsibilities are. For the purpose of training managers, a general-

* In a subsequent meeting, Mr. Kestnbaum answered questions pertaining to his formal presentation; this chapter section is drawn, more or less verbatim, from the discussion that took place at this meeting. George P. Baker, James J. Hill Professor of Transportation, Harvard Business School, acted as moderator.

ized liberal education is more to be desired than much more vocational training.

Professor Baker: I wonder how much Mr. Kestnbaum thinks a company should vary its policy away from the maximum-profit motive in the interests of general social responsibility.

Mr. Kestnbaum: If it is ever going to be a question of a company adjusting its prices according to what people may want to pay, we will all go out of business. Any firm that starts to lose money because it has altruistically lowered its prices so more people can afford to buy its products will disappear very quickly. The best rule for businessmen to follow, if they want to meet their social responsibilities, is: "Run a good business."

This is not to say that the profit motive should be pursued blindly. A good business is not merely a business which makes a lot of money for its stockholders. For instance, we can all remember when it was common practice for an industrial plant to call in workers every morning and let them stand around, hopefully waiting for work. If there was a job, they were given something to do; if there wasn't a job, they had to go home. This layoff practice has disappeared, and no good business will ever be run in such fashion again. This is a case where trade unionism and general public pressure combined to influence business policies.

However, I will say again that the best contribution any of us can make to society is to run a good business—and when I say good, I mean good. We must have the highest standards and the best designs. Our products must be what our advertising departments say they are—they must be honest. Our economic system is only as strong as the total of all our businesses; and if many of us turn out shoddy products, we can injure America's economy.

Good businesses are run in a responsible manner. Today when people go into a store, they know what they will have to pay for their purchases because retail merchants follow a fixed and uniform price policy. Today the American public can rely on the manufacturer's guarantee of his product. Incidentally, 60 years ago our firm became the first apparel company to advertise nationally a guarantee of satis-

faction or the customer's money back. People predicted that we
would be bankrupt as a result of this move, but we found it to be a
very intelligent policy.

In other words, my answer to the question is that we, as business
people, can fulfill our obligations to society in the everyday process
of running our businesses. In the long run, the interests of business
and the nation in general are identical, not opposed. A healthy and
growing economy is what we are all striving for. Businessmen should
be proud of the contribution they are making toward this goal, not
apologetic because they are making money.

From the floor: Mr. Kestnbaum has mentioned the importance to
sales managers of understanding the attitude of the consumer without relying wholly on market analysis statistics. Now, can you plan
your production in a general fashion merely on the basis of consumer attitude? Can you appraise your market opportunities ahead
of time through this type of informal estimate?

Mr. Kestnbaum: Yes, I think businessmen can gauge the market
informally by observing general trends. Some of these trends can be
very clear. For example, men in our industry can easily observe that
people are wearing more sport coats and slacks and fewer business
suits. This particular trend is growing at a rather steady rate. Then
there is a definite shift toward the wearing of summer suits—30 years
ago men did not wear especially light clothing in the summertime,
but today they do. Of course, there are some things that cannot be
predicted. I must say that in the type of business represented by my
company every season is more or less of an adventure.

By observing consumer tendencies, we do find that we can plan
six months ahead for such things as variations in style and fabric.
We distribute our clothing through retailers, and this is where we
sometimes run into difficulty in proving our market estimates correct. We use advertising and salesmanship to induce the consumer
to buy what we think he wants, but sometimes retailers do not agree
with our analyses; they do not sell our products as we should like to
have them sold and as we feel they can be sold. This is why so many
organizations have set up their own distribution machinery. In my

opinion, automobile manufacturers could not sell nearly as many cars as they are selling today if car sales were channeled through department stores.

Perhaps this story about two young Harvard Business School graduates is pertinent to the discussion of business planning:

It seems that after leaving the Business School these two boys decided they would engage in the retail business. Their fathers had lots of money, and they had no difficulty in securing enough funds to start a very attractive men's store. Having benefited from their courses in management training, they had markup charts, budgets, markdown controls, and a planning division. They had research activities and marketing analyses. They had the works.

After three years, in the course of which they lost most of their original capital, their fathers got tired of supporting this venture. The men's store was chalked up as a failure, and the two Business School graduates went out and got paying jobs. Their property was sold to a merchant who owned the small haberdashery next door to the big store. This man, surprisingly enough, began to do very well. In fact, after two years he had paid off the purchase price, and after four years he had bought the entire building. Shortly after that, he was recognized as being a highly successful businessman by the head of a manufacturing company who was interested in learning more about merchandising.

The father of one of the young Business School men went to call on the merchant and said, "I am just curious about your success. With all the education my son and his friend had, and with all their capital and other advantages, they were definitely unsuccessful. You have had, I understand, only a limited education, and you had limited capital. What is your secret?"

The merchant replied, "Maybe those boys didn't know how to figure. With me, it is very simple. I buy something for $3.00, I sell it for $5.00, and I am satisfied to make 2%."

Techniques are important in business, but they are no substitute for the kind of judgment and imagination that is essential to good planning.

THE NATURE OF CONSERVATISM

Joseph W. Alsop, Jr.

I YIELDED TO THE TEMPTATION—I succumbed to the honor—of the invitation to contribute to this discussion, because I have something rather serious to say that I think should be said to businessmen. For, as Dean David pointed out, businessmen do not plan the future strategy of their businesses in a vacuum. And they can have—and should have—influence on the shape of the world in which they operate—not only for their own good as businessmen but for the good of the communities which surround them and support them.

My friend, Professor Arthur Schlesinger, Jr., has an interesting article on "The New Conservatism: Politics of Nostalgia" in *The Reporter* of June 16, 1955. It begins with a loud audible sniff. "No intellectual phenomenon has been more surprising in recent years," writes Schlesinger, "than the revival in the United States of conservatism as a respectable political faith." Professor Schlesinger goes on to demonstrate to his own satisfaction that conservatism may

Note: Mr. Alsop is the author of numerous books and articles and coauthor of the syndicated newspaper column, "Matter of Fact."

be a possible faith in countries like England, where it can draw its leadership from the members of an ancient landed class imbued with the aristocratic spirit of *noblesse oblige*. But, says Schlesinger, conservatism is not a possible faith in America because, here in America, the leaders of any imaginable conservative party must be businessmen. And to prove his point he quotes the elder Henry Cabot Lodge to the following effect:

> "The businessman dealing with a large political question is really a painful sight. It does seem to me that businessmen, with few exceptions, are worse when they come to deal with politics than men of any other class."

POLITICS AND TRADITION

I radically disagree both with Professor Schlesinger and with old Senator Lodge. I think conservatism is a possible political faith. It is my faith. And I do not think businessmen are disqualified as conservative leaders. Yet I must say that after three years or so of the first conservative, business-minded, business-led administration this country has had in more than two decades I write this as a depressed and worried conservative. The history of our century teaches, after all, that there are two things which are automatically fatal to a conservative party in a Western democracy. One is a Dreyfus case and the other is a Munich. And I fear we have been having both on the installment plan during these three years.

I shall attempt to document this somewhat controversial assertion as I go along. I believe that the errors—if they have been errors—of the Eisenhower Administration have flowed from a misunderstanding of the nature of conservatism. I think the errors are not fatal yet. But I am sure they will ultimately be fatal unless leaders of the conservative interest themselves insist upon corrective action. So it is to the nature of conservatism that I wish to address myself. That nature can be shortly summed up. *The true conservative is one who is obstinate about moral questions and flexible about practical questions.*

Being obstinate, digging your heels in, and proclaiming that "they shall not pass" is always a very dangerous thing to do in politics. Yet true conservatives will fight like tigers, they will go down in the battle if need be, in order to conserve the great tradition—I know no other word—that gives its moral tone and flavor to their society. This is the *style* of all true conservatives—to be reverent of their society's great tradition; to be touchy when it is called in question; and to be always seeking to strengthen and revivify it.

Without this style, conservatism loses its excuse for being. It then becomes no more than a political attitude of the have's designed to protect what they have from the inevitable depredations of the have-not's. And any political movement that altogether lacks a sense of higher mission, that exclusively considers crass material interests, will ultimately come to grief among the stern, remorseless laws of history. That is why every successful leading group in history has always had an ideal which was morally convincing to the group and morally impressive to other people in their time, although of course some of these ideals may now seem morally horrifying to us.

Now, the great tradition in America is two things at once: it is humane, and it is libertarian. I will not attempt to discuss here the persistent materialist attack upon the humane aspect of the American tradition. The increasing shallowness of American culture, the constant weakening of every link with the intellectual past, the pragmatic debauch of American education, the transformation of our people into a mute mob of listeners to singing commercials—all these things seem very alarming to me.

I am a New Englander with a strong inherited respect for capital. I cannot help being alarmed when our intellectual capital appears to grow less and less as our material wealth increases. I regard this moreover as a moral problem, for the choice between things of the mind and orchid-colored plumbing is essentially a moral choice. But this problem is a whole topic in itself not directly linked to politics and therefore beyond the narrow limits of any special competence that I may have.

As a Washington newspaperman, however, I feel fully competent to speak about the persistent and terrifying attack on the second aspect of America's great tradition—the libertarian aspect. It is this attack that I have in mind when I speak of a Dreyfus case on the installment plan. People seem to forget nowadays that individual liberty *is* what America *is* all about. Or maybe I should say that individual liberty *was* what America *was* all about. For I am not so sure that we can use the present tense any longer, when Thomas Jefferson seems to be widely suspected of subversion because he included the Fifth Amendment in that great Bill of Rights that was designed as the sacred shield of the individual against the capricious power of the tyrant state.

The first leader of the current grand assault on the American liberties has, of course, lost his former importance. The Senator from Wisconsin has suffered a political setback from which he will not easily recover. He has been defeated by the Eisenhower Administration. But meanwhile, unhappily, the Administration has also perhaps unconsciously been borrowing the Senator's famous methods and putting them in a pseudorespectable dress.

As a result we have seen in these two past years a long series of shocking injustices perpetrated upon individuals—upon a great man and high officer of Harvard University, Dr. J. Robert Oppenheimer; upon a loyal, intelligent, and devoted public servant, John Paton Davies, Jr.; upon many little men like the unfortunate Abraham Chasanow, who was casually held disloyal on the basis of anti-Semitic poison pen letters and spent his life savings to extort an apology from a reluctant government. These cases make me ashamed of my country, and that is an emotion I do not enjoy.

Yet I do not sound this warning to you because of these injustices to individuals. You know of them already. I sound a warning, rather, because of the system behind these cases about which I am sure the great majority of you know very little.

THE "SECURITY" SYSTEM

This system has been erected quietly behind the persuasive curtain of the word "security." But by this system a great many of those liberties which our forefathers fought to establish forever are already being effectively denied to citizens of this republic. Nameless, faceless accusers are now permitted and encouraged to destroy careers and reputations without check upon their motives or their truth. Hired informers and paid witnesses are now the petted servants of our machinery of justice. Every ancient protection of the citizen's privacy has been torn away with eager hands. Without regard to law or custom, everything concerning him is now to be inquired into, right down to the respectability of his garbage pail.

That is no joke, either, for it is now common for our federal flat-feet to ask a man's neighbors whether his trash and garbage appear to include an excessive allowance of bottles; and on one occasion that I know of, this charming question was asked a distinguished foreign resident of Washington about a neighbor who happened to be one of the highest officials in the State Department!

In truth no check is placed upon the swollen investigative police working in darkness, with their dossiers bulging with poison pen letters. These men, for good or ill, have a free range through the lives of our citizens; and, if they choose to point the finger of suspicion, the career of the man pointed at is all but automatically ruined.

With each passing day the purview of this system is incontinently extended, so that already, besides our unfortunate diplomats and bureaucrats and government scientists, those who are exposed include such groups as school teachers, workers in defense industries, and even inhabitants of federally financed housing projects. And who can tell whether a slight change in the high command in Washington may not bring leaders of business and captains of industry into the system, so that you too will be wondering whether your garbage pails are suitably presentable, and trying to imagine what sort of poison pen letters your enemies may write under appropriate encouragement, and puzzling about how any man can prove that dangerous thoughts do not lurk in the most secret recesses of his mind.

If I sound bitter, if I sound indignant, it is because I *am* bitter and indignant. Thoughtlessly, with good intentions under the guise of insuring the national security, we have created a monstrous machine which is already a disgrace and can become in other hands a mortal danger to the America we know.

Maybe the old rights and liberties are shopworn nowadays. Maybe it is foolish to think that an American citizen has a right to face his accusers and be tried by peers under the rule of law. Maybe the wise men's warnings against hired informers, that go back to the acid words of the Roman Tacitus, and against the police who operate in darkness, that go back to the time of the Spartan Krypteia, have lost their former validity. If these things are so, the founders of this republic labored with a false end in view. But being an intensely, indeed passionately, conservative man, I do not think these things are so. And therefore, as the first safeguard of a healthy American conservatism, I would urge the root and branch reform of this so-called security system that succeeds only in breeding insecurity and injustice.

I wish I could stop here, saying that American conservatism can insure its future by this simple act of moral courage—by doing no more than to correct abuses which more and more sensible men are beginning to see as abuses. But, alas, in these complex and testing times being a true conservative is not a simple business. There are not only the moral problems that demand the kind of obstinate defense of our great tradition which any sturdy-minded man can compass. There are also the great practical problems which make even more taxing demands on those Americans who would solve them successfully.

THE REAL ISSUES

I do not pretend to offer you solutions of all these practical problems. I venture only to suggest that the terms of their solutions will become easier to discover if we go back to the A B C's and try to be very clear in our own minds about what conservatism really is.

What then are these A B C's? There is a grain of permanent truth concealed in the rhyme that "Every child that is born alive is either a little liberal or else a little conservative." From the dawn of history every society has been crudely divisible into two groups. On the one hand, there are those who are, on balance, satisfied with their lot in society and with what the society does for them; and the satisfied are naturally hostile to change. On the other hand, there are those who are, on balance, dissatisfied with their lot in society and think the society should do better for them; and the dissatisfied are ever inclined to welcome change.

The interaction, the pulling and hauling between the satisfied and the dissatisfied, between those who are hostile to change and those who welcome it, is the dominant motif of every society's inner history. If the society is both healthy and free, the interaction will be continuous but peaceable; the pulling and hauling will be vigorous but not violent.

But within these two great groupings of the satisfied and the dissatisfied there is a further subdivision of the utmost importance. As there are those among the dissatisfied who would make a violent revolution to achieve their ends, so there are those among the satisfied who would go to any lengths to resist change of any kind. And this extremist attitude among the satisfied is unconservative, because it fails to take into account the first and highest law of history. This is the law that change comes in the end to all things, all men, and all societies. In societies, above all, change is the great theme. Socially speaking, there is no being; there is only becoming.

There have been ruling groups in the past, of course, and on the other side of the Iron Curtain there are ruling groups today, that have been successful for a while in arresting the process of change. By means of force they have frozen their societies into the rigid mold that happens to suit them. But inevitable change too long resisted is like irresistible flood water too long dammed up. When the change comes at last, it is not gradual and partial and controlled. It sweeps all before it, uprooting everything, altering every feature of the once familiar landscape, destroying the good with the bad in order to create the merely new. In a certain measure, something like that happened—I am inclined to think—here in America in 1932. Few can doubt that if Mr. Hoover had dealt a bit more flexibly with the new forces let loose in our society, Mr. Roosevelt would not have found it so easy to carry his New Deal to such lengths of change.

An appreciation of the problem of change is especially important for conservatives in a free society. In unfree societies, as on the other side of the Curtain, the masters of the society can prolong the social catalepsy for great periods of time—perhaps for centuries. They can give Lord Keynes's answer to the man who urged him to think about the long run before proposing radical economic remedies. They can say, "Well, after all, in the long run *we* shan't be here." But in a free society, urgent practical problems demand prompt and practical solutions that win the consent of the large majority. If such solutions are not forthcoming, a Mr. Hoover is rapidly and tumultuously replaced by a Mr. Roosevelt.

For these reasons, the great rules of true conservatism in a free society are (1) to give ground gracefully when ground must be given; (2) to do what really needs to be done with as few regrets as possible; and (3) above all, to do it yourself instead of waiting for the other side to profit by your inaction, and do it much worse later on.

As I have tried to suggest already, these rules of expediency do not apply to the moral base of the society. If *that* is jeopardized, everything is jeopardized; so *that* must always be fought for at all costs. But economic problems, defense problems, resources problems, and foreign policy problems belong in the practical rather than the moral category. Our taxes may be raised or lowered; our forces may be increased or decreased; our alliances may be altogether reversed; I even dare to say that our industries may be nationalized or not nationalized without affecting our society's moral base which is individual freedom.

The measures themselves may be pernicious and foolish, as I think the nationalization of industry is pernicious and foolish. But as any unprejudiced man can see in England today, even so radical a step as nationalization has only changed the society's shape without direly altering its spirit.

In brief, then, true conservatism approaches practical problems with no ideological preconception. The fact can be easily demonstrated from both history and the situations now confronting us. At the beginning of the last century the economics of Jeremy Bentham were in the highest degree radical. They constituted a violent attack upon the mercantilism that was then the prevailing economic philosophy of the satisfied; and a violent attack, too, upon the privileged position of the great landed interests that then dominated the English society. Ogden Mills must have been thinking of these points when he once denounced me for calling him a brilliant conservative. He declared that he was one of the few true liberals because he was a true-blue Benthamite. But I think very few other people would now regard Benthamite economics as anything but intensely conservative. Or take as a minor modern instance an American problem that is clearly going to demand a solution in the next 20 years:

> All over this country the pressure on water resources is daily increasing. The demands of the urban centers and of industry are rising. At the same time the water table is steadily dropping. Any practical solution will certainly require federal planning and federal intervention on a considerable scale. So, are we to remain true to free-enterprise principles and so end by dying of thirst; or are we to give a little on principle and so solve the problem in the only practical way available?

THE REAL AIMS

The aim of true conservatism, in short, is always to conserve, as the word implies. But the method is to recognize when change is unavoidable and to conserve what truly may be conserved while sacrificing those things that must be sacrificed to save the rest. And true conservatism is inordinately difficult nowadays precisely because it is not easy to separate what can be conserved from what must be sacrificed.

You may think it very odd of me to trace the disaster of the Munich settlement to neglect of these conservative principles that I have been trying to outline. Yet I venture to say that this was the real cause of Munich. Overpowering military strength gave Adolf Hitler his long free run. His strength was overpowering because the Chancellor of the Exchequer, Lord Simon, used to tell the British chiefs of staff, "You must not forget, gentlemen, that Britain's economic strength is Britain's first line of defense." Lord Simon was in effect expressing the prevalent view of the British business community, that a rise in the tax rates to pay for the defense effort that Hitler's challenge necessitated was a greater risk to Britain than the risk of ignoring Hitler's challenge.

When Neville Chamberlain got off that famous airplane brandishing that famous umbrella and promising "Peace in our Time," he was the most popular prime minister Britain had ever had. But when the final accounts were balanced, the old British economy lay in ruins, British industry was largely socialized, and the businessmen that Chamberlain spoke for had been all but banished from politics. For they have no voice whatever in the revived Tory party of Eden, Churchill, and Salisbury. And all this happened essentially because the wrong choice was made—because the leaders of Britain in the 1930's would not sacrifice the tax rate in order to conserve Britain's position in the established world balance of power.

As I have hinted already, I greatly fear that the same dangers now hang over American conservatism. In Europe, the outlook may have brightened for the moment; but on the Free World's most vulnerable flank in Asia the deterioration has been rapid and fearful, from the moment when we so eagerly granted the Chinese Communists the Korean truce which narrowly saved them from utter war exhaustion. About Asia we have talked very big, but we have acted very small; and it is hard to know now where the Free World's retreat in Asia can be stopped. Behind this retreat, moreover, there is the effective disarmament, not concealed from the enemy by huckstering talk about a "new look" in defense, that has left us with less real strength in the Pacific than we have ever had since Pearl Harbor. And behind this disarmament, in turn, there is the same order of priorities that prevailed in Britain: tax problems come first, the budget second, and defense third.

This may be pleasing for the moment to all of us who greatly dislike paying taxes, as every normal citizen does. But there are times, alas, when it is better to pay through the nose than to take the ultimate consequences of not paying. In the short run, it is an unconservative act to increase the corporate and personal income levies. But in the long run it is even more unconservative to lose your country and the world.

THE RESPONSIBILITIES

In truth, the choices nowadays grow more and more disagreeable as the penalties of wrong choices grow more and more horrendous. Yet despite my reputation, I am no pessimist. I do not think the errors that I believe have been committed are irrevocable errors. I think, too, that a majority of American conservatives are beginning to suspect that they are errors; and therefore I hope they will be corrected within the permitted time.

We are witnessing, after all, a most fascinating act in the American political drama. In the first century and a half of our history the American business class built this country. To free enterprise and vigorous business initiative we owe the vast wealth and enormous power that make America the envy of the world. But in all this period, despite very great political influence, the American business class never directly ruled the country. Businessmen paid the bills. Politicians friendly to business did the work. And beyond the relatively simple act of writing checks for the usual intermediaries between business and politics, businessmen had very little knowledge of the workings of our political system. They did not need that kind of knowledge in the simpler American past.

But the past—and I regret it—is dead and gone. The dates marked upon the tombstone are 1932, 1941, and 1946—when the Soviets first showed their true postwar intentions in Azerbaijan. Nothing, alas, can revive the past. And in the grimmer, uglier, more dangerous world we live in today, the businessmen who are the natural leaders of the conservative interest in this country cannot leave politics to second-raters. They must now learn to perform the tasks of politics as well as the task of economic creation. I think the signs say they *are* learning.

There is no reason on earth except the political inexperience of most businessmen why former Senator Lodge should be right. There is every reason why the American business class should now bend all its energies to proving him wrong. And if businessmen grasp the dimensions of our modern problems, and reflect a little upon the nature of conservatism, it is my belief that after this dark interval American conservatism may yet go down in history as the preserver of human opportunity and the savior of freedom in the world.

Part Two

MANAGEMENT STRATEGY AT WORK

GETTING THE ORGANIZATION TO WORK EFFECTIVELY AS A TEAM

Edmund P. Learned

IN THIS CHAPTER I want to discuss the management skills required to fix responsibility while ensuring contributions to the solution of problems from all qualified personnel regardless of organizational element.

In order to simplify the development of this area, I am assuming agreement on certain basic facts. In view of the observations made in Part I of this book, there can be little question of the wisdom of both long-range and short-range planning, and the importance of objectives and strategy in charting the course of a business. Every one of the authors has emphasized the importance of management teamwork in concrete ways, thereby making a remarkable contribution to the theme of this section of the book.

Businessmen can afford to ask certain questions fairly often.

Note: Mr. Learned is Professor of Business Administration, Harvard Business School.

1. What are the basic elements of our industry?

2. What functions do we perform as well as, or better than, any of our competitors?

3. What about our products—can we improve on them in such a way as to put ourselves out in front and enable us to make a greater contribution to the economy?

4. What new opportunities or products might our organization develop in order to make a contribution to profits, to general economic well-being, and to the growth possibilities for our employees?

Looking back at Part I, you will notice that in virtually every chapter the importance of profits is emphasized; the planning of business is considered as if it had an impact on our economic well-being; and the role of men in achieving these results is ranked high. Really the only new term that I am adding in the above series of four statements is *growth*.

Two other facts of business life that are practically always with us are basic to this discussion: First, business problems, programs, policies, or procedures tend to cut across any conceivable formal organizational lines; this is one reason we need management teamwork. Secondly, businessmen like to fix responsibility, grant commensurate authority, and hold executives and supervisors accountable for results even though they redelegate a part of their authority and responsibility to subordinates.

Here, again, I am adding nothing original. Practically every author in Part I emphasizes the importance of profit controls, profit centers, and the development of men of managerial capacity who can measure up to the responsibilities assigned.

One of the most difficult conundrums of organization teamwork, then, is how to fix responsibility this way and yet ensure cross-departmental cooperation at the same time. This teamwork is increasingly important because of the complex nature of internal and external problems of management. Organizations in general have become larger, and the growth of scientific knowledge and the proliferation of specialists have not made the job of a responsible leader any simpler. There is a greater need than ever for management leaders who will be able to reconcile the divergent activities, attitudes, and needs of the various functional and technical specialists.

The authors of the earlier chapters have implied that there is no real way to chart an organization and make sure it will stick. But that very fact makes it all the more necessary to continually examine the facts as they are, the people you have, and the objectives of the firm. Then we must adjust the organization, the people, and the combinations of men and events to achieve the desired results.

Consequently many of us accept the utility of well thought-out lines of organization. In other words, in a complex world you just have to think through the ways in which one activity can be related to another. Thus, we also accept the value of job descriptions as a part of the process of developing organizational understanding; and we realize the importance of standards for the evaluation of people who have received the delegated responsibility.

The fact remains that people are our main block to effective teamwork. Each individual brings all his personal aspirations, backgrounds, and values to the work place, and he seeks to achieve personal growth and development on the job. To put it another way, individuals try to achieve and develop their personalities in connection with their work. Every businessman of experience knows that he has a problem of reconciling the individual personality with the opportunities and requirements of the company situation.

Different sizes of firms and different executives deal with this basic phenomenon in a variety of ways. But, as a general rule, it seems to me that management can contribute to effective teamwork by realizing that it is dealing constantly with both a conception of teamwork and with the day-to-day perceptions of problems by members of the organization.

CONCEPT OF TEAMWORK

Generalizing out of the experience of watching a number of companies at work, I suggest that a sound concept of good teamwork consists of these four elements:

1. Problem solution as the basic focus of organization effort.
2. Achievement of a general management type of solution.
3. A task force or group to contribute to the problem-solution process.
4. Finally, and most important, a man with the primary responsibility to lead a group to the definition or solution of a problem.

Let us test the validity of this concept by seeing how it works in actual experience.

In the case of the smallest firm, most of the effort and coordination is carried by the owner. In the case of a partnership, it may be divided in some fashion among the partners, according to interest and aptitudes. But in the medium-size and large-scale organization, whether company or government agency, the job is more complex. Here is where the concept of teamwork finds its greatest need and opportunity (although the same principles apply less formally in smaller companies).

According to this concept, the president or some responsible executive assigns a problem or the definition of a problem to some specific individual who might be described as the captain of a task force team. He is the man who is charged with getting a result—he and nobody else; there never is any doubt. Who the particular person is may vary from time to time; but he is likely to be an individual from whatever department on the organization chart has the greatest interest in the problem under consideration. In other words, the person who gets the assignment is the man who has the greatest (but not the exclusive) interest in it.

The captain will be responsible and accountable first for getting the problem defined and then, if possible, solved. He will take the initiative in utilizing any personnel to be found inside the company, regardless of the department in which they work. If he needs to go outside for help, he will seek it. He will lead this informal task force group in the attempt to come up with the kind of an answer that the president or the executive who assigned it would like to develop himself if only he had the needed time.

I think most top executives, if they look back, will recall that when they were lower in the organization and were "catching" this kind of problem from above, they brought a lot of enthusiasm and interest to its solution. If they think they could develop the same kind of solution now if only they had the time, then they are very fortunate that they do not have the time. As a matter of fact, not only have they lost touch with the facts, but when they pass a problem down the line, they ensure its getting better attention than if they did it themselves—better in the sense of the quality that represents a well-rounded answer, a general management solution.

TASK FORCE LEADERSHIP

The principal leaders of this so-called task force, and all the departmental participants, should rise above selfish personal or departmental interests. They should be able to perceive the company-wide implications of the matters under discussion even while expressing the view of their departments. But how do you get people to do that? Maybe they *should,* but will they?

At this point, let me make it clear what is meant by a task force. It does sound something like a small-scale military force; and as such it might be composed of people used to taking orders. There is a real similarity in that both the military task force and the kind of team I am talking about have a single definite objective. But otherwise my kind of team is more like a football team, with a strong quarterback —a group of men of equal range but different skills; and when you get a picture of drawing ideas from everybody, it becomes quite a democratic, unmilitary-like concept.

Of course, the team doesn't always function smoothly. You have the problem of the ball-grabber—the aggressive person who gets an idea and wants to run with it to the exclusion of the rest of the team. And, at the other extreme, since you are dealing with a cross-section of the organization, you have the problem of diversity of opinions. Clear communications up and down, agendas for meetings, and so on, are ways to take care of such problems.

This concept of teamwork is designed to reach down into the organization and across departmental lines; it is not the simple working together of the executives at the top—not that that is always easy, either.

It is more a method of approach than any prescribed procedure. Here, for example, is one simple form:

> The boss says to me, "I wish you would look into this matter," and I say, "Yes, sir," in the best Navy style. And when I say, "Yes, sir," I mean I will look at it, I will get an answer, I will get it fast, and it will be a good one. I do not have to call a meeting of anybody, but I can think of Henry Smith, I can think of Joe Doaks, I can think of Bill Green, in different departments. So I get on the telephone or I go see them face-to-face, and they give me something I have not thought of, a new idea. In the search for a solution of this problem, I become, in effect, a changed man.
>
> When I am through, I have consulted everybody that is in this "conceptual task force" in my mind. The people involved do not necessarily even know they are members of a task force; yet the ultimate solution arrived at will work out better because most of the men that have to make it work helped lay the track. That is why I have used the word "conceptual" with "task force," and why I used the words "face-to-face," or "over the telephone."
>
> In other words, I had a concept of a problem, of its breadth and its depth. I had a concept that I could get some help and I reached out for the help. I listened to what others had to say; they changed my mind because they thought of something that came within their knowledge and skill and experience that wasn't in *my* knowledge and skill and experience. I saw that it made sense, and I incorporated it in my solution.

Maybe this isn't a team, but it does constitute a team effort. As far as I am concerned, it does not make too much difference whether or not the members really meet, because if I have consulted the right people, I have brought in the areas of their interest and given them a chance to describe their viewpoints. Also, if I found I had to disagree with something they said, I probably went back and talked further with them about it. In other words, I have greased the wheels as well as laid the rails. It is the results that count; and if I have gone through this process, I may not have a formal team in the sense of a group that has met together, but I do have group effort in a broader sense.

This kind of a flow of ideas is conditioned by how you use it. If the task force captain behaves as if the solution came exclusively from him, he will not continue to get answers very long. Hence the kind of men who can get results tend to be magnanimous in giving credit to others.

Here is one way to look at it: Teamwork isn't something that happens; it is a state of mind of the man who is responsible for handling a problem. It is an attitude of accepting the fact that he doesn't know all the answers, and can't do the job by himself.

The leader of the group must have an especially broad view of the problem itself and of the types of people who can contribute to the answers. Only then can he reach out for the appropriate interdepartmental assistance and collaboration.

This leader must be able to resolve differences. They inevitably exist in any human organization, and he has to work them out in a timely and friendly fashion. Furthermore, he ought to be able to state any that remain for the benefit of a superior who may be involved in the subsequent review. He must be expeditious in coming to grips with a problem and should not let a minority view prevent action or recommendation, though he ought to respect minority views and in the interests of fair play and cooperation should state such views courteously and reasonably when presenting the majority solution.

Unfortunately, minority views are not often treated with respect, and few executives state them with emphasis especially when they are being reviewed by higher echelons. This is an important matter. If you treat the minority with respect, if you understand its position, if you give it proper emphasis when presenting the problem to other people, you will often find the minority going along with the majority. Moreover, not only the leader but also the various members of the group should be able to listen understandingly and respectfully to the positions of others, evaluate them, and modify any of their preconceptions accordingly. Such men will be able to contribute effectively to management teamwork. They are bound to become real leaders in the companies for which they work.

A few other features of the task force concept may be mentioned. Any department head involved must delegate some real responsibility and authority to his department's representative on the force. If the department has a preliminary view on the issue, or even settled convictions, its representative should know them. Nevertheless, he should be permitted to respond to the facts presented by all members of the group. Management will never get the quality of answers it wants if the intelligent representative of one department is not allowed to respond to the evolving facts and discussions of the entire working group.

It is understandable that on major problems higher echelons of management are likely to review the efforts of the informal task force. In order to facilitate this process, the subordinates ought to keep their chiefs informed about the trends of the discussion. A superior who has a preconception of an answer may be shocked by a final recommendation which conflicts with his view, but may not be upset at all if he has been briefed on some of the major factual findings and principal differences developed while the group was discussing the problem.

Another practical suggestion is that all the work of the group does not have to be done in an assembled meeting. A great deal of time is wasted by committees who feel everything has to be done by all members. There are some things that have to be done together; then the group can disperse and work individually, or in small sections, to reassemble as necessary. One of the great arts of administration is to know when to farm a job out and when to conduct it through a discussion in the presence of the whole group.

I do not mean to imply that "teamwork" is the *only* device to accomplish your business objectives, nor do I say that all problems can best be handled this way. Some companies have found that profit centers with some internal friction are effective—Mr. Breech suggested this in his chapter. If you conceive of an organization as being sound when it is organized around its process flow of activity, you are simply recommending that your organization be built around the work to be done. If you are organizing it that way and you have the parts figured out correctly, much of what we are talking about will not be necessary.

However, the fact remains that some problems will still have to be solved. Isn't there a distinction between the routine of day-to-day operations and trying to define a problem, establish a policy, or build a procedure which you don't do very often in the stream of events? Just because there is more operation than planning in business in terms of the total activities of all the people that are involved, it does not follow that, having organized your activities and formulated your objectives, you won't need to formulate a new procedure or determine a new policy. So there is always recurring need for teamwork in the sense that I have been using it.

Sometimes it is as simple as suggested by this experience of the manager of a large hotel:

> Operations were unprofitable by his standards, so he decided to go clear to the bottom, to the people who were doing the day-to-day work, and to do so himself rather than through any formal organization. He said to the people something like this: "You have been working here a long time. You must know something about what is right, and you must have some ideas of what is wrong. What are your suggestions?"
>
> And he began to get some answers, perfectly obvious answers. Implicit in his questioning was a belief that people at the work level have some ideas about what goes on and what could be done better. He had shown them considerable respect simply by asking them a question; he had implied a compliment. Just by listening to what they had to say, he got a real dividend. They had good recommendations for him.

Most situations, unfortunately, are more complex. The thing to remember is that the type of problem you face constitutes one of the conditions which help to determine whether a task force concept, or any other teamwork practice, will work out successfully. But there are other conditions, as well, which must be examined.

IMPORTANT CONDITIONS

One condition is the attitude of top management. Many people have raised the question of the junior executive who wants to develop a teamwork project, but cannot because his superiors do not approach the business in that fashion. He can, of course, make suggestions, but unless the boss has given him a clear idea of how far he can go and what the framework of the policy is, he is going to tread on somebody's toes even though he may have the best interests of the company at heart. The example of the hotel manager was significant in that he was the top man and as such decided to take the step that was designed to stimulate teamwork and organizational cooperation. Granted, then, that the junior executive can make suggestions, and run some risks of getting slapped down, still the best impetus for teamwork comes from the very top.

Another condition is the creation of a right atmosphere in meetings for a good exchange of information. People cannot listen effectively when they have something to say; they just have to get it out of their system. Maybe this is one explanation for the length of so many meetings. As soon as you have got everybody heard once, then you can begin to get people to listen. It requires real personal training to develop a good habit of listening to what other people have to say.

This human phenomenon of not listening when you have something on your mind to say is one reason why a chairman of a committee or the leader of a task force group has to go through the process either in meetings or in face-to-face contacts of listening effectively to the people who have something to say and of protecting their right to say it. When he has demonstrated this capacity, he has a better opportunity of inducing them to hear and perceive what other people are saying. Much time can be saved for large groups if a part of this process takes place outside of group meetings.

In this same connection, the impact of one difficult person on a group process is worth touching on briefly. How can you make an effective teamworker of an executive who feels he must always prove he is right? A person who holds such an attitude has a disability for fully effective teamwork. It is often hard for fellow executives or even superiors to make such persons perceive their own habit pattern and its implications. Where it exists in extreme form, some effort to widen a man's perception of his own behavior justifies much of the time that is spent upon it. There is no known panacea, however, for inducing men to change themselves. Each case has to be considered on its own merit, and any person trying to influence another person might as well assume at the beginning that he will have a certain percentage of failures.

In fact, one of the biggest tasks any administrative leader has in an organization is to induce everyone in it to learn to accept everyone else as he is and to maximize strong points of personalities and to overlook as many of the weak points as possible. But we never can get away from the fact that people are human. They do have emotional reactions. The administrative leaders, who have emotional reactions also, must develop the ability to submerge their own feelings and take as objective a view of the situation as possible, doing whatever they can to help other people establish better personal relationships.

This is no easy assignment. Few men ever achieve perfection in this regard. If that is your goal, you are certain to be disappointed in yourself and be frustrated. Someone has said that a 6% return on a financial investment is a good one; why should we expect to do better with people, a commodity far more changeable and complex? Of course, measurements are hard to make in this area, but from my observation of companies that have really adopted the attitude and concept discussed here the return has been far beyond anything like 6%.

Then there is the simple problem of time. How can line management find the hours in the day to participate thoughtfully and effectively in a specialized, problem-solving task force? Time may be gained in a variety of ways.

One way is by delegating the task force assignment to a subordinate. This gives him experience, contributes to growth, and keeps the superior available for more important duties.

Another way of handling it is for the executive to delegate some of his other tasks to subordinates and take on the task force assignment himself. It is necessary to evaluate which of these alternatives is the appropriate one in each specific situation.

There is a third possibility: rethinking out one's work. An executive may eliminate some activities as really unnecessary, albeit they are interesting to him.

Breaking down the barrier of a kind of instinctive segmentation is another important condition of teamwork. When an executive assigns a problem to a subordinate and the latter's report reveals a lack of consultation with other interested parties, a few well-planted questions such as "Have you talked with the purchasing agent?" or "Have you talked with John Smith in the personnel department for his view of this problem?" will serve to point out the deficiency. The behavioristic refusal by such a superior to accept a partial analysis will go a long way in inducing the subordinate to reach out for help. This procedure is bound to have an impact if consistently followed. If it does not, you may be faced with finding a man better equipped to handle the particular job.

How about the problem of leadership? As I have indicated, this is a most important consideration. But leaders can be found, and to believe otherwise seems to belie much fruitful experience. Much hinges on the definition of the leader. If you assume that he knows all the answers and should know more about the problem than the people he consults, the whole task force concept falls of its own weight. This assumption seems to me, however, to be an error. A great deal depends on an individual's faith in himself and faith in other people. How much does he really believe in the capability of other men to make a contribution to a solution? Many men rise very high in business on the abilities of others, and they do it without making other people feel that it is at their expense.

The task force leaders of medium and large-scale businesses who have been successful have had the capacity to bring to the problem the personal skills that are available in an organization. These are the men who believe that the opinion of a group obtained either in a discussion or on an individual, face-to-face basis will give a better view of the problem than the limited view of the leader or the limited view of any member. These men have faith in themselves and their ability to distinguish these specialized contributions and to integrate them into a meaningful whole. They believe in the give-and-take process, and have confidence that it will produce a well-rounded, well thought-out answer. They are willing to state differences of opinion, to respect differences of opinion, and, when necessary, to present these to higher echelons for review and final evaluation or approval.

These attitudes, if prevalent in an organization from the top down, will make for the most effective operation of the teamwork concept. This condition is the really indispensable one.

CONCLUSION

Informal groups have found this task force concept effective, and individuals who work on a person-to-person basis, either face-to-face or over the telephone, can use this same concept. Basically, it involves a set of attitudes and a set of assumptions about other people. It is not necessarily a continuing formal organization. When the problem is solved, or the problem is defined, the task force is dissolved. The next problem comes along, and we put together a new task force with the necessary leadership and the necessary resources to get a solution. In other words, this is not a technique of formal organization but rather, as I have been trying to emphasize, a concept and a set of attitudes toward problem solution.

Finally, the art of leadership in problem solution involves not only the concept of the breadth and depth of a problem but the perceptions both of the leader and of all the members of the group. I have developed a list of questions, which I append here both to illustrate what I mean by perceptions and also to stimulate readers to do some further thinking on the question of teamwork. Thinking through on your own is always much more valuable than being told by someone else.

THE ORGANIZATION YOU WORK IN

1. In what ways, if any, do (*a*) form of organization, (*b*) method of operation, or (*c*) attitude of individuals *contribute* to or create *obstacles* to achieving effective management teamwork?
2. What effect does delegation of responsibility or decentralization have on teamwork?
3. What staff functions contribute the most or the least to teamwork? Why?
4. What impact, if any, does the control function have on management teamwork?
5. What departments or types of people seem to have the least perception of how to become effective members of a team?

YOURSELF AND THOSE YOU WORK WITH

1. Are you suspicious of other men? Why?
2. Do you believe that subordinates and men from other departments have creative capacity and good ideas to contribute to your company?
3. Are you willing to let people make mistakes as a part of the cost of growing?
4. Can you distinguish those activities or decisions which you must handle and those which you can delegate?
5. Do you let people say what they think, or do you conduct yourself so they say what they think you want to hear?
6. Once you have delegated a responsibility, can you stay out of the details and let the person with delegated responsibility do a job, develop his capacity, learn from experience, and be judged by results?
7. How have you helped others widen both their conceptions and their perceptions?

CAPITAL INVESTMENT CONTROL

Ross G. Walker and Russell B. Read

INTRODUCTION

SOME OF US who have studied company budgeting policies for a number of years have found over and over again that there is no hard core of settled practice governing decisions on capital expenditures. Only a short time ago I heard one production manager say most emphatically—and he spoke from a good many years of experience—that processing capital expenditure proposals through to financing was one of the few areas of management in which he had never been completely happy with the results. "Handling capital expenditures has lagged far behind the procession," he said.

Note: Mr. Walker, who makes the introductory observations, is Professor of Business Administration, Harvard Business School; Mr. Read, Planning Director, Westinghouse Electric Corporation, discusses the problems of capital investment control in terms of his company's practice. John B. Matthews, Jr., Assistant Professor of Business Administration, Harvard Business School, served with Mr. Walker as comoderator of the session on which this chapter is based.

The uncertain foundations of policy characterizing this particular management job are unfortunate for two reasons:

> 1. They are bad for management because of their bearing upon the quality of decisions made on new plant purchases.
>
> 2. They are bad for national planners who want to improve the control of capital expenditures as a step toward greater economic stability for the nation as a whole. Of course, to what degree individual management practice in handling capital expenditures should yield to over-all regularization of national economic affairs is by no means a settled question.

With the variability of capital budgeting policies as great as it is today, it is good for us to be reminded now and then of the need to learn whether they must necessarily remain that way, or whether the uncertainties of practice are but a manifestation of our general ignorance of the subject.

That individual managements should make their own decisions to fit their personal views of prospects we must grant wholeheartedly. But we cannot help wondering if improved approaches to the timing of capital expenditures within the framework of individual initiative would not after all mean a solider foundation for national planners to build on, and still keep the individual management job where it belongs.

We have asked a representative of one of our front rank companies, which for years has been pushing toward more systematic procedures for controlling new investments, to describe the present status of its practices. But we should bear in mind throughout the discussion that what this company is now doing is not necessarily a perfect model for all to follow. It is only a step in the company's search for such a model. That this great organization will ever be entirely satisfied with its attainments in this search is probably only folly to expect or even to hope for—the complexities of today's capital expenditures problem are too many and varied to be strait-jacketed across the board in terms of any single permanent framework of company policy.

In the following section Mr. Read of Westinghouse discusses the two steps of (1) determining projects eligible for financing, and (2) deciding upon the mode and extent of this financing for particular budgeting intervals.

IMPORTANCE OF CAPITAL
INVESTMENT CONTROL *

There is no single area of management decision which surpasses in importance that of capital investment. There is probably more soul-searching, and possibly more crystal-ball technique, in this area of decision than in any other. Capital investment decisions have two prime characteristics which explain in part the reason for the importance accorded to them by every management. I mention them not to prove that planning and control of these investments is important —this fact we accept—but rather because a statement of these characteristics may be helpful in establishing a setting for this discussion. Here they are:

> 1. Capital investment decisions are fundamental to the future prosperity and stability of the enterprise. Capital investments carry with them advantages or handicaps which will be "locked in" for years to come—often beyond the span of any one management. They involve more uncertainty and require a longer and better forecasting judgment than probably any other aspect of business management.
>
> Because of the strategic nature of capital outlays, they reflect in large measure the quality of the planning, the foresight, the attitude, and the ability of the operating managers who propose them. They afford therefore a key point in the control of business; if capital investments are wisely planned, there is reasonable assurance that other facets of the business are also being wisely planned. Expenditures for plant and equipment, supported by the necessary product research and development, are the *key* to growth and prosperity of the business.

* By Mr. Read.

2. Capital expenditure decisions normally involve a high degree of selectivity. In an aggressive company, there will usually be more projects proposed than can be safely digested at any one time. Consequently, management is generally faced with the problem of selecting the best from among the many proposals which will appear over a given period.

SCOPE

Capital investment control is a subject of such breadth that I shall not attempt to cover it in its entirety—and could not if I tried. But it occurs to me that it may be possible to launch a discussion of this subject around the two basic characteristics just cited.

The first—the fundamental, strategic nature of these investments—suggests that *basic* capital investment control rests in the soundness of the over-all planning of the business and the integration therewith of capital expenditure planning.

The second—the problem of selectivity—indicates the need for a systematic means of organizing, classifying, evaluating, and, finally, authorizing capital expenditure projects.

In commenting on these two points I will try to sift out and express what appear to be the essentials in a sound approach to each. Without attempting to describe mechanics in detail, I will draw upon practices in my own company as a means of illustrating certain points. I do not imply that mechanics are not important. They are, particularly in a multiplant, decentralized organization, where a failure to make the ground rules clear may bog down the whole effort.

At the outset, it might be well to define "capital investment." Usually this is synonymous with the term "facilities expenditure," which in turn might be defined as "any expenditure to acquire or construct land, buildings, or equipment which is, under accepted accounting practices, capitalized in the accounts." In Westinghouse, we broaden this definition to include any nonrecurring expense directly associated with facilities projects such as rearrangement; and, in the case of new activities, it includes training programs, moving of employees, and overhead costs up to the time shipments begin. Likewise any major alteration or rearrangement in connection with buildings and equipment is included; ordinary maintenance of course is not included.

BASIC PREREQUISITE

One of the main problems in developing a good facilities program is the tendency to view it as an end in itself rather than as an integrated part of an over-all business planning program. If the objectives for the product line can be clearly expressed, the need for facilities can be identified. And if the needs can be identified, the search for capital projects will be stimulated and focused. This suggests that the basic prerequisite in capital expenditure planning is the developing and maintaining of a set of well-conceived long-term sales and profit objectives for each product line.

In our case broad objectives are formulated in the spring of the year. At this time, they get quite a going over as to whether they are acceptable objectives. The facilities program, which comes along about four or five months afterward, is begun when agreement is reached regarding the broad objectives the divisions and the company are shooting for.

Every year each of the 33 operating divisions, for each of the approximately 85 different product lines, takes a new fix on the future. It takes a new look at what it thinks its market will be five years ahead, the share of this market it feels it can capture, the sales volume that will result, the over-all assets required to support this volume, and the profit return objective it is shooting for.

These sales and profit objectives are the beginning in the planning process—the targets for performance. But the mere setting of concrete goals forces an analysis of the market, of product scope, of marketing plans and strategy; and translating these goals into specific plans requires an examination by the division manager and his key people of every aspect of the operation of every product line.

Thinking in terms of facilities only, the fifth-year product-line sales objectives, when compared with present capacity, can serve to in-dicate rather concretely the extent to which capacity has to be increased to meet the goals. And with this capacity gap expressed, the facilities needed to close it can be identified.

If the production volume required to meet the goal is substantially greater than the present volume, it may not only signal the need for increased capacity but it may indicate the approach of a volume level which will support new, lower cost manufacturing processes, and consequently a different type of equipment than presently used.

This long-term look may thus tend to prevent piecemeal facilities replacement and expansion by pointing the way to opportunities for complete process changes and improved plant layouts. Certainly the present trend toward automation makes this forward planning even more important.

The comparison of present performance with the long-term ob-jectives should also inspire a cold appraisal of the product from the standpoint of its present and future competitiveness—its ability to capture the share of market set as an objective. This, in turn, may direct research and development effort toward necessary product im-provements, innovations, and new products. These will, in most cases, require capital expenditure before they can be put into pro-duction.

The comparison between present profit performance and that set as an objective will also help in defining the amount of product *cost reduction* which is necessary to meet the objective—particularly if this analysis considers the pressures which are likely to exist for lower prices. This, in turn, may point up the need for product re-design or process improvement for cost reduction, both of which will probably result in facilities requirements without which the savings from the redesign or reprocess could not be realized.

I do not infer that an analysis of technical advancement in ma-chine tools, depreciation status, maintenance costs, down-time, and the like, may not be helpful. They are supplementary aids in un-covering potential profitable capital projects. But an analysis of the volume increase required to meet a specific volume goal and the cost decrease required to meet a specific cost goal may do more than anything to force to light the capital investment opportunities in new, enlarged, or different facilities. In other words, *the real vehicle to profit is the product, not the plant.* Thus, facilities planning is only one part of the over-all profit-planning job. It is likely to be more effective if viewed against the over-all product-line plans for expansion, product improvement, and cost reduction.

The manner in which profit performance is measured in the company is also significant in capital investment planning and control. Where return on investment is the basic measure of profitability of a product line or operating unit, there is likely to be a greater awareness of the importance of working the assets as hard as possible. This provides a sort of built-in control which is not in evidence where the sole measure of profits is percentage of profit to sales.

PROPOSED CAPITAL INVESTMENTS

So much for the stimulation and focus which can be given broadly to capital equipment planning by integrating it with the over-all profit-planning job. Let us assume that the capital asset requirements of a given operating unit of the company have been broadly identified and the unit is now ready to build up a proposed program. We turn to the problem of organizing, classifying, and evaluating the proposed expenditures. Again, for illustration, I shall draw upon Westinghouse practice.

Each operating division's facilities program, developed once each year, is expressed in two ways: (1) by a five-year projection of capital investment necessary to support its fifth-year volume and profit objectives, with the major expansion projects (those of $1 million or over) listed separately; and (2) by a detailed program for the next one-year period, with a list of all projects, large and small, which the division proposes to initiate.

At Westinghouse we have found that two simple but fundamental rules aid greatly in formulating and subsequently evaluating the program:

1. The facilities expenditures are dealt with on a *project* basis, identified where possible with a specific product line and aimed at a given purpose. For instance, if production capacity for a certain product line is limited by two bottleneck situations requiring two additional pieces of equipment, even though they are in widely separated locations in the plant, the two items of equipment would be combined into one project. Included also, would be any rearrangement expense and associated equipment such as conveyers. This project approach emphasizes the purpose of the expenditure rather than the equipment itself, and helps to permit a well-rounded evaluation of the complete project.

2. Every project must be classified *according to purpose.* Our classification system, which is not unique, contains four classes.

Expansion projects are those intended to provide greater capacity for existing products or for manufacture of new products. Their justification lies in the expected additional sales, profits, and return on investment.

Product improvement projects are those in support of product redesign, quality improvement, or broadening of the line primarily for the purpose of improved salability. These are justified by an appraisal of the competitive status of the line with respect to the needed improvement.

Cost reduction projects are those intended to reduce cost or expenses by replacement of equipment, by different equipment due to redesign of product or reprocess, by manufacturing in lieu of buying, and so on. Their justification lies in the return which the projected cost savings represents on the investment.

Necessity projects are those which are essential to continued operations but not falling within any of the other three classes—projects required by law, or for reasons of safety, health, or employee relations, and so on. Generally, they do not lend themselves to an economic evaluation.

True, some projects of a broad nature may contain some elements of each of these four purposes, but they will usually represent one primary or controlling purpose.

Classifying the projects in this way, or in some similar way, has at least two beneficial results: (*a*) it points at once to the type of information needed to evaluate each project and subsequently to justify its position as a candidate for inclusion in the capital budget, and (b) it permits the division manager and finally the corporate management to quickly see whether the program appears to be reasonably balanced among the four categories.

After the division has prepared its proposed program, it rates each project in three degrees of preference:

> For expansion projects and cost reduction projects this preference rating is determined by relating the projected earnings or savings to the amount of the investment. A project promising a return on investment of 20% to 30% is rated C, 30% to 40% is B, over 40% is A.

> Both product improvement and necessity projects are rated on the basis of their importance in comparison with rated cost reduction projects. For instance, a necessity project of such importance and urgency as to take priority over an A-rated cost reduction project— e.g., an expenditure to correct a serious fire hazard which could jeopardize the earning power of the whole plant—would be rated A. The rating of these projects indicates their degree of postponability, using as a point of reference the ratings which have been given to projects which can be rated in terms of earnings.

The programs then come into headquarters and are screened thoroughly by our group general managers, who represent another level in our organizational strata. They may disagree with the division manager's rating or they may not understand it. In this case someone from the division will come in and explain questions that develop.

The program will finally be taken to the company's top management planning committee which in turn may take exception to some of these ratings. While the division is not represented at these meetings, its general manager has a right—in fact, is encouraged—to question a low priority assigned a project by the planning committee, which may mean its being lopped off the capital expenditures budget.

We do not have any formal way of trying to spell out different degrees of risk. Consideration to risk is given indirectly in the evaluation of the economic life of the project. In considering the possibility of obsolescence of equipment or of plans that are being projected, we have to make an estimate of what the economic life of that equipment is going to be, which in turn means an estimate must be made as to how long the product is going to be good. The machine may last 20 years, but the product may be obsolete in 4 or 5 years, so indirectly the risk factor does enter into the economic life of the particular facilities involved.

We have not found it advisable to set different acceptable rates of return for our various divisions. We do have different objectives —long-term objectives—for different divisions, but we have not tried to set a different minimum for various categories of risk or various kinds of operations. We consider 20% before taxes as the minimum acceptable rate of return across the board—though some divisions are inclined to set their own minimum return higher if they are operating in excess of 20%, and others which are not doing that well might be happy if they could obtain a 15% return.

SETTING UP THE CAPITAL BUDGET

In our approach to capital expenditure budgeting, the programs proposed by each operating division, organized by project, classified as to purpose, and rated as to preference represent, when summarized for the company, what might be called the *demand* for funds.

About the time this demand figure is developed each year, the top management of the company, aided by the treasurer's long-term projections of cash receipts and disbursements, arrives at a capital investment figure which it is willing to commit in the next year. This might be called the *supply* of funds.

This figure is fixed in consideration of many factors including projected cash generation in net earnings and depreciation charges, dividend requirements, and debt retirement plans. However, at this stage in the capital budgeting process it is our practice to assume that the supply of funds will be limited only insofar as it can be generated internally.

The fun comes when the irresistible force, represented by the demand, meets the immovable object, represented by the supply. These figures must be brought into balance.

The division programs, both individually and collectively, are examined as to the distribution of proposed expenditures among the four classifications of purpose in order that the general direction in which the proposed expenditures are being channeled may be appraised. For example, a program heavily weighted with necessity projects could indicate lack of attention to cost reduction or expansion requirements. Or one aimed largely at expansion might imply failure to have recognized the product improvement and cost reduction opportunities.

Projects in each program are screened and reviewed in detail. This is where the preference ratings which have been applied to each project come into use: the projects are arranged in order of their assigned rating. This means, in effect, that the projects are arranged in order of their ability to produce return on investment. The cut-off point is automatically determined when the list reaches the total of the available supply of funds. It may be determined sooner if the return falls below the minimum which is acceptable, regardless of available funds. Or, on the other hand, if there are projects below the cut-off point which exceed the minimum acceptable return, it will be necessary to re-examine the supply of funds and the assumptions which underlie it.

If we are successful in the balancing of demand and supply, the resulting list of projects represents the capital budget for the next year. These projects are called "protected" projects.

I might add that not quite all of the available supply of funds is earmarked for these projects. There is set aside a relatively small figure, about 5%, as a reserve to accommodate unforeseen but necessary projects which may—and, of course, always do—develop during the year. This reserve is useful in two ways: (1) It can be tapped for projects that just could not be foreseen—otherwise, unless the capital budget is to be exceeded, the projects would have to be deferred until next year. (2) The knowledge that there is this flexibility in the program avoids a tendency on the part of divisions to load their programs with projects which have only a small likelihood of materializing during the forthcoming year.

CARRYING OUT THE PROGRAM

The setting up of the capital budget—with its "protected" list of projects and reserve—does not constitute authorization to initiate a project. It serves to advise the operating divisions that they may proceed with detailed development of the project, architectural work, site investigation, equipment specifications, and so on, in reasonable assurance that the project will be authorized. Each project, when ready for initiation, must be authorized individually through approval of a specific appropriation request, which completely itemizes the project and presents the supporting information necessary for its evaluation.

However, in the case of projects which have been "protected" in the capital budget, there is considerable delegation of authority for approval of the appropriation: individual projects up to $50,000 go to the division manager; projects ranging from $50,000 to $100,000 are referred to headquarters management; those over $100,000 go to the board of directors. This procedure greatly reduces the time required for review and approval by top management, but top management still retains control of the major projects and a large proportion of the total funds. This year, for instance, about 500 projects, representing in dollars 15% of the total program, will be finally approved by the division managers, while about 150 projects, representing 85%, will require headquarters or board approval.

Once funds for a project have been appropriated, it is what we call an "open" appropriation. The necessary investment is recognized for purposes of estimating expenditures in the future, but it is not included in the new list of projects for the next year's program. In other words, from the standpoint of control, each year's plan is a new plan. But after funds have been appropriated, it is simply a fiscal plan.

There are numerous other procedures governing reports of capital appropriations, progress, expenditures, closings, revisions, audit, results, and so on, which are important for an orderly functioning of the system but are not necessarily pertinent to this discussion.

One point might be mentioned regarding follow-up in profit performance of a particular investment. This varies according to the importance of the project. But when you are using return on investment as a basic concept of running the business, the operating division manager will think twice before he will overstate the possibilities for a project, because the results will inevitably come back and boot him.

One of the ultimate tests of the effectiveness of a program of controls such as Westinghouse is following is the extent this program taps, through the people in the divisional and product-group levels, the maximum potential of capital expenditure opportunities. In our case, there is never much question that we get more ideas than we can physically handle. However, it is better to have the selection problem than the problem of scaring up the opportunities.

And this leads to a major problem: ideas are originated and developed through certain stages where they become firm and are strongly supported by the various people in the division, but they may not be related to total company policy and objectives. Accordingly there is a problem of how to control to get the best ideas and the right timing to fit into the total scheme.

Here the solution rests primarily in the soundness of the product-line planning which has preceded the facilities planning by several months. This product-line planning really sets the general direction for the allocation of funds.

As a method of summarizing this discussion of capital investment control, I refer you to the following exhibits:

> Exhibit I, the first form, is used by each of our operating divisions in expressing their long-term objectives—currently those for 1960— for each of their product lines. (There is a form which precedes this one—not shown here—which serves as a work sheet for projecting the 1960 sales volume.) The assets necessary to support the volume objective and the costs which will have to be attained to meet the profit objective are projected on this form. We consider the setting of these long-term objectives the basic prerequisite to profit plan-

ning, with which capital investment planning must be integrated.

Notice that on the right-hand side of the form, the fixed asset projection is further amplified—although at this point in the planning process it is still a very "broad brush" projection. The translation of this projection into specific capital asset requirements is a subsequent step—the translation remains fairly general for the five-year period, but it becomes very specific for the first year of the five-year period.

The other three forms, *Exhibits II, III,* and *IV,* are used in evaluating and organizing proposed projects as a part of the annual capital budgeting process. They pertain to the problem of selectivity —always present in capital investment control. *Exhibit II* is an analysis form for cost reduction projects, and is used in determining the return on investment which the cost saving expected from the project will represent. It has been helpful in evaluating the worth of these projects and has provided a uniform means of making such evaluations.

Exhibit III is merely a project list, an example of a form which each organizational unit uses in presenting candidate projects for inclusion in next year's capital budget. A separate list would be made for each of the four classes.

Exhibit IV is used by each division in summarizing its proposed annual program, analyzing the program by class, by preference, by size of project, and providing for a five-year forecast of capital asset requirements.

Further breakdown of information on the form shows an analysis —by preference, cost range, and so on, of the program developed for the immediate year, and the amounts of facilities expenditures which the division foresees as being necessary for the second, third, fourth, and fifth years of the planning period. Thus we get an approximate picture of the requirements over a five-year period needed to support the long-term objectives which have been reviewed and crystallized earlier in the year.

When these forms are submitted to company headquarters, the information is summarized to get the over-all company demand for capital asset funds, and the capital budgeting process—the balancing of demand and supply—proceeds as described earlier.

Exhibit I. Form Used to Express Long-term Objectives

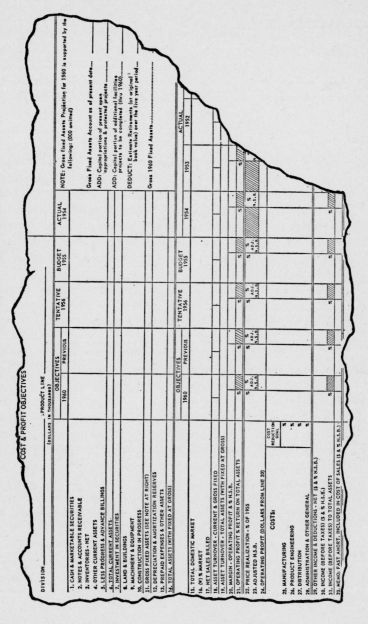

Exhibit II. Form Used to Analyze Cost Reduction Projects

COST & EXPENSE REDUCTION ANALYSIS
WESTINGHOUSE FORM 29136 A   ITEM _____ OF _____   DIVISION _____

SUBJECT OF ANALYSIS   DEPT.

                                                            SECTION | GROUP NO. | COST CENTER

DESCRIPTION OF PRESENT FACILITY

                                                            AGE | BOOK VALUE
                                                                | $
DESCRIPTION OF PROPOSED FACILITY

REASON FOR ANALYSIS

FACILITY VALUES

	I	II	III
	PRESENT FACILITIES	RENOVATION OF PRESENT FACILITIES	NEW FACILITIES
NET OUTLAY:			
A. Installed Capital Cost (a)			
B. Associated Expense (b)			
C. Less; Present Salvage Value of Present Machine		x x x x	
D. Net Outlay (Algebraic Sum of lines A, B & C)			
BASE FOR AMORTIZING CAPITAL COST:			
E. Salvage Value of Present Machine - One year hence			
F. Economic Life		(c)	(d)
G. Installed Capital Cost (same as line A)		+	+
H. Present Salvage Value of Present Machine (same as line C)		+	−
I. Estimated Salvage Value at end of Economic Life		−	−
J. Base for Amortizing Capital Cost (Alg. sum of lines G, H, I)			

SAVINGS CALCULATIONS & COMPARISONS - ANNUAL BASIS

EXPENSE COMPARISON:			
1. Amortization of capital cost	(e)	(f)	(f)
2. Amortization of associated expense (line B + useful life (g))			
3. Cost of maintenance			
4. Insurance and taxes			
5. Total (lines 1 thru 4)			
SAVINGS OVER PRESENT FACILITY:			
6. Line 5 comparison (h)			
7. Savings-direct labor			
8. Savings-direct labor-preceding or subsequent operations			
9. Savings-direct labor-premiums			
10. Savings-indirect labor			
11. Savings-defective work			
12. Savings-other than above			
13. Expected yearly savings (Algebraic sum of lines 6 thru 12)			
DETERMINATION OF RETURN ON INVESTMENT:			
14. Outlay (same as line D)			
15. Percent Return on Net Outlay (line 13 ÷ 14)			

PREPARED BY | DATE | APPROVED BY | DATE | COST OR EXP. REDUCT. DOCKET NO.

(a) Estimated capital cost of renovation or new facility, including freight, foundation, and installation.
(b) Associated costs not capitalized, such as rearrangement or auxilary tooling required as a result of this project.
(c) Estimated extension in economic life as result of renovation.
(d) Estimated economic life in consideration of expected technological improvements or product obsolescence.
(e) Present Salvage value (line C) minus Estimated Salvage Value One Year Hence (line E).
(f) Line J divided by economic life (line F).
(g) Useful life of Associated Expense is normally same as Economic life of facility but may differ under certain circumstances.
(h) Line 5 in Column I less line 5 in column II or Column III - may be either a positive or negative figure.

Exhibit III. Form Used to Present Proposed Projects

ANNUAL FACILITIES PROGRAM - PROJECT LIST

SHEET ___ OF ___

19___

CLASS NO. & NAME

DIVISION

(THOUSANDS OF DOLLARS - 000 OMITTED)

PROJECT NO.	URG-ENCY	PROJECT LINE OR DEPARTMENT	PROJECT TITLE (INDICATE BY ASTERISK PROJECTS FURTHER DESCRIBED IN SUPPLEMENTARY INFORMATION)	EST. FACILITIES EXPENDITURE		JUSTIFICATION				ESTIMATED TIMING OF EXPENDITURE		
				CAPITAL EXPENSE	TOTAL	CLASS 3 CLASS 1 EXPANSION		RETURN ON INVEST.	1ST YEAR	2ND YEAR	3RD YR. OR AFTER	
						OPER. COST SAVING	ADDITIONAL SALES	OPER. PROFIT				

TOTALS FOR CLASS (ENTER ONLY ON FINAL PAGE FOR EACH CLASS)

SIGNATURE OF DIVISION MANAGER   DATE

101

Exhibit IV. Form Used to Summarize Proposed Annual Program

FIVE YEAR MAJOR EXPANSION PROJECTS &
SUMMARY OF ALL FIVE YEAR FACILITIES REQUIREMENTS

(DOLLARS IN THOUSANDS)

FIVE YEAR MAJOR EXPANSION PROJECTS

PRODUCT LINE	PROJECT TITLE	YEAR OF INITIATION	ESTIMATED EXPENDITURES			ESTIMATED TIMING OF EXPENDITURES				
			CAPITAL	EXPENSE	TOTAL	1st	2nd	3rd	4th	5th	AFTER FIFTH

TOTAL - Major Expansion Projects

ANNUAL BUDGETED FACILITIES PROGRAMS

PROGRAM FOR FIRST YEAR (FROM FORM 2905)	SUMMARY BY URGENCY			SUMMARY BY COST RANGE				SUMMARY BY CAPITAL & EXPENSE			SUMMARY BY TIMING OF EXPENDITURE					
	URGENCY A	URGENCY B	URGENCY C	UNDER $25,000	$25,000 to $49,999	$50,000 to $99,999	$100,000 & over	CAPITAL	EXPENSE	TOTAL	1st	2nd	3rd	4th	5th	AFTER FIFTH
1 - EXPANSION - LESSER															
2 - PROD. IMPROVEMENT															
3 - COST REDUCTION															
4 - NECESSITY PROJECTS															
TOTAL - 1st Year															

2nd Year - Estimated Annual Budgeted Facilities Program

3rd Year - Estimated Annual Budgeted Facilities Program

4th Year - Estimated Annual Budgeted Facilities Program

5th Year - Estimated Annual Budgeted Facilities Program

TOTAL - All Company - Financed Projects for next Five Years

Remaining Expenditures on Company - Appropriations open at Dec. 31 this year

TOTAL - All Company Financed Facilities Expenditures

MEMO - Class 5 - Government Financed Projects - Next year

MEMO - Estimated Next Year's Depreciation & Amortization charges

MEMO - Estimated Next Year's Retirements on other Dispositions (at original book value)

MEMO - "Capital Portion of Additional Facilities Projects to be completed this 5 year period"

Includes rapid Amortization of ‘15

DIVISION

SIGNED   DATE

DEVELOPING MANAGERS

Myles L. Mace

I WOULD LIKE TO SUGGEST that there are four main ways of contributing to the growth and development of men for general management positions. One approach is off-the-job: attendance at advanced management programs. The other three approaches are on-the-job: (*a*) job rotation, (*b*) job progression, and (*c*) coaching.

ADVANCED MANAGEMENT PROGRAMS

There are at least three ways in which a course like the Advanced Management Program at the Harvard Business School can help men realize their potentials to fill the responsibility of general management positions. (I shall make my observations primarily in terms of the Harvard A.M.P. course, since I know it best.)

One result is a broadening of functional specialists. Today, with the increasing complexities of American business, and the need for hav-

Note: Mr. Mace is Professor of Business Administration, Harvard Business School.

ing the best possible business ability brought to bear on these specialized problems, we have two interesting results. One is that men are being confined to very narrow functional areas in an attempt to get the best possible professional specializing on the solution of those narrowly functional problems. The second result is to overcome the disadvantages of the fact that these same men are progressing up through the organization within relatively narrow channels.

A man may easily spend 20 years in his organization within a function of a function. For example, he may spend 20 years within the cost accounting group of the comptroller's office, or he may spend 15 or 20 years within the sales promotion activity of the marketing department. Then, when the man is needed for broader responsibilities, he just does not have the job experience and working knowledge to qualify him and equip him for fulfilling those larger jobs.

Now I think that while specialization is very good from the point of view of getting the most highly skilled person possible and having his abilities brought to bear on the solution of particular problems, such specialization, from the point of view of qualifications for broader management opportunities, cannot fail to be a real limitation and a real handicap.

It would be misleading and more than a little bit naive to suggest that men, by being at the Harvard program, or any other program for 12 weeks, can derive the equivalent of 10 or 15 or 25 years of experience in other functions. If a man has spent his time solely in production, or finance, or accounting, or public relations, it would be silly to assume that by some "quick pill" method he could in 12 weeks gain the equivalent of experience in other types of work. I do believe, however, that by considering various functions with a group of veteran performers from different areas of other businesses a man can gain an awareness of the operational bases of other departments. There is also another kind of broadening that takes place in a program like Harvard's. It is inevitable and almost unavoidable that men learn from each other, and thereby grow in breadth, adding to their qualifications as candidates for broader management positions when they return to their companies.

From an advanced management program participants may achieve a greater understanding of the human problems of administration. Administration—that is, getting things done through people on a cooperative basis—requires an awareness of some of the key concepts about people, why individuals behave as they do, and why groups behave as they do. Men in an advanced management program, with demonstrated abilities as administrators, are already aware of the difficulties of obtaining genuine understanding between people, but the study of case problems gives these individuals the opportunity of group exploration of the "whys" of personal behavior.

"Why do people behave the way they do? Why don't they behave the *right* way—that is, the way *I* do?" These are the questions they ask, and they begin very quickly to get some insight as to why they themselves think as they do, and why the businessmen to the right and to the left of them, or in back and in front of them, are taking different positions from what they might take on the same case problem. There are great possibilities for each participant to get a new understanding of human behavior, including his own. And as Professor Charles I. Gragg of the Harvard A.M.P. course says, "It is important to remember that administration is the art of handling yourself, not someone else."

The third value of an advanced management program, I think, is the opportunity for each man to personally examine his individual business philosophy. Away from the demands of a day-to-day job, he is able to think through the real importance of business, particularly his own, to the society and economy in which we operate. This may sound academic, and sort of misty and intangible, but this philosophic doctrine has been reported by a number of the men who have attended our A.M.P. course as being one of the greatest values they have derived from it. They are stimulated by being together with a group of other business pros who are equally interested in trying to do, as my ten-year-old boy says, a "more better job" of administration, into thinking through where they have been in their business career, where they are now, and where they are going, and trying to analyze their relationships with other people in the organization.

JOB ROTATION

The fact remains that, no matter what is accomplished in advanced management programs and other off-the-job activities, the richest and most practical locus for contributing to man's growth lies in giving him on-the-job opportunities for growth and development and helping him take advantage of them.

Job rotation, the first of the on-the-job approaches, involves moving men from a responsible position in one function over to a responsible position in another function—not as an "assistant to," but right into the line job, so that he actually has the full responsibility of performing that job. It is important to have that line responsibility—though in some cases, where because of technical reasons the man is not qualified to fulfill the job, it would be valuable to have him there for a time as "assistant to."

Job rotation is practiced in many companies, and it is very difficult to generalize as to when and how it can be utilized. However, I would like to suggest that executives should at least look into the opportunities for rotating people within their organizations. One of the greatest underestimations we make concerns the hidden values or the unexploited and unrealized potentials of people in our own organization. Too frequently, and often to our own detriment, we go outside our companies to find men for top management positions.

JOB PROGRESSION

The second means of on-the-job development, job progression, implies laying out some logical path of progression in the organization, so that as a man is assigned a particular job, some account will be taken of the opportunities for exposing him to several different functions. I have talked to a number of people in business, and have asked them this question, "If you could live your career over again, are there any jobs you would like to have had that you didn't have the opportunity of fulfilling?" And almost without exception each person has answered affirmatively, saying that if he could go back and do it over again, he would like to have more advertising, more promotional work, more accounting, or whatever it is.

Job progression, therefore, has been suggested by some businesses as a method, not of plotting a man's *career,* but of plotting the *paths* up which he might logically move so that at the end of 15 years, with some planning and foresight by the individual, he will have had a great deal of helpful experience. It is very important to distinguish this from plotting a man's career. The company does not tell someone that he is going to be at such and such a level or in such and such a job at the end of any specific period of time. Rather it plans the type of experiences it wants its man to have had by the time he has been in the organization for 10 or 15 or 20 years.

COACHING

The third on-the-job approach to broadening people for general management positions is what is known as coaching. Five years ago I published a small volume, the result of a year and a half of research study, on the coaching concept.*

Completely freed of classroom responsibilities, I had an opportunity to go out and talk with a lot of tough-minded business professionals about what seemed to be the most effective way of helping people to grow and realize their capacities. One of my typical questions was, "How in your own company are you able to broaden and develop your competent, high-potential people?"

Probably one of the less original conclusions of my research is that people learn by doing. The most effective way of learning the administrative process, of learning what is involved in taking broader responsibilities, is by doing it. It is something like acquiring the skills of golf, or any other social skills you may think of.

There are some who believe that it is possible, in fact desirable, to wade through the business literature of all the ages and to extract therefrom a synthesized body of knowledge. Every manager in the

* Myles L. Mace, *The Growth and Development of Executives* (Boston, Division of Research, Harvard Business School, 1950).

organization, they believe, ought to memorize these facts, which would presumably make him a better manager and better administrator. I think nothing could be further from the truth, because the process of administration does not consist of dealing with static units of matter with fixed, known, and predictable reactions. If such were the case, we could all read a textbook and memorize the rules, and presumably qualify as broad-gauge executives.

There is a lot more to the learning process than just being able to articulate a few useful generalizations or principles. Actually, in talking to businessmen about how people grow in their organizations, I heard of very few reliable rules or guideposts. Rather, these tough-minded businessmen suggested that every administrator must have the opportunity to *practice* his skills and capacities if he is to occupy positions of greater responsibility.

The "work situation" is the best possible classroom for a student of managerial effectiveness. We in academic institutions are very envious of the work situation. We try in our cases to construct synthetic equivalents of work situations, to approximate the environment into which our men will be going. And yet so many times we go out into companies and find that they, paradoxically, are neglecting to use the work situation as a real live opportunity to help people to grow, and instead are trying to emulate the school classroom where people go and listen to somebody lecture.

Of course, the extent of the learning and the speed of the learning process depend in large part on a man's immediate boss and the relationships of the two men. It is the superior who has such an important opportunity and responsibility to help his subordinates develop whatever innate capacities they have. The boss's job is called "coaching." This coaching method of helping people to grow into greater general management positions is something that cannot be delegated to the personnel department, thereby absolving line people of all responsibility. What we are talking about is basically and inherently a line responsibility, and that job cannot be delegated to anybody else.

As Professor Fritz Roethlisberger has noted, the concept of "coaching" is basically the same thing as "administration." Both terms refer to getting things done through other people. Coaching is administration, and administration is coaching. This coaching, this process of administration, is going on every day on the job, whether men know it or not. They are teaching their subordinates all the time, and they are learning from the people to whom they report. I think the real challenge to top line officers, if they are going to help their associates to grow and to meet broader responsibilities, is to do a "more better job" of that which they are already doing.

There is a story told about a man with 37 years' experience who went to his boss and said, "Boss, I have had 37 years of experience, and I haven't had a raise, and I want one." And the boss said, "No, you haven't had 37 years of experience. You have had one year's experience 37 times."

An amusing story, but with tragic overtones! Perhaps coaching would have been wasted on this particular man, but his boss had not taken the trouble to find out. The poor fellow had been stuck in one spot for 37 years; it probably was not his fault that he had not learned enough to earn a raise.

DELEGATION

Among the various elements of coaching—which, being also elements of administration, are none of them new or startlingly profound—one of the most important is delegation. Obviously, if people do learn by doing, it follows that the boss or superior must delegate to his subordinates. I would like to quote a few sentences from an article called "The Art of Delegation." This was taken from the National Industrial Conference Board's *Management Record,* and it emphasizes clearly just what is involved in delegation:

> "Delegation is one of the most important and difficult of skills that a manager needs to acquire. Delegation is important because once a man's job grows beyond his personal capacity, the success of what he does is measured largely in terms of work performed for him by other people. The critical point in the career of many an executive is

reached at the stage when he must either learn to delegate or cease to grow in scope and capacity. . . .

"Delegation enables a manager to multiply himself. It makes it possible for him to extend his knowledge and energy and time through the efforts of others." *

Some of the executives I talked to when I made my study admitted very frankly that delegation was one of the most difficult things they had to do. This was particularly true of any man who was a doer or a performer, and who had come up to the top because he was so good. The biggest problem most men had was determining when and how much to delegate. They did not want to assign to their subordinates responsibilities that were beyond them at the moment.

It takes study, of course, to determine how much responsibility a man can actually assume at any one time, and how it should be given to him. I am sure that the boss who really studies this problem will not make the mistakes of what I call the "Americanus Delegatus":

This "Americanus Delegatus" is a new genus of birds which some of my associates and I, through our study of actual businesses, have discovered.

Perhaps the Audubon Society will accept our collection as an official part of their bird organization—it could be called the Business Section of the Audubon Society.

The first delegation bird observed in American business is what is known as the "white-shirted hoverer." He is the boss who gives his subordinate the job and then flaps his wings right over him all the time, hovering around and watching him go down the path, never giving him a chance to run into a stone wall and bump his head and thereby learn something.

Very closely related to the white-shirted hoverer is the "pin-striped whoopster." This bird's habitat is usually a so-called decentralized organization. Here is the boss who gives a subordinate a job, and then as the subordinate goes about doing the work, he "whoops," "whoops," and "whoops" him right down to the completion of the job.

* Louis A. Allen, "The Art of Delegation," National Industrial Conference Board, *Management Record,* March 1955, p. 90.

Next there is the "yellow-bellied credit-snatcher." Everyone knows this bird; I have a model of one in my office. Then, of course, there is the "pussy-footed mouse-trapper"—a rather common species. And, finally, one of my favorite birds is called the "crested crown prince" —the boss who, by habit, lays his eggs in somebody else's nest.

Perhaps this study of the "Americanus Delegatus" will serve the boss as a reminder of the distinction between merely recognizing the concept of delegation and actually practicing it on the job with regard to his subordinates.

COUNSELING

Another important element of coaching is what is known as "counseling." This is not the couch brand of counseling—"Now you lie down there, and we'll talk this over." The counseling I am suggesting is counseling on the "how" of administration. It is the manifestation by a superior of a personal interest in the man that he wants to help do a better job. It means taking time out to give a subordinate advice, whether his problem be one of personal adjustment or acquiring administrative skill. It means that the boss is interested enough to sit down and tell him frankly that there are areas where he can do a better job.

It is not soft-minded or sentimental to help people become "more better" as subordinates. It *is* soft-minded for a superior to neglect his opportunities at counseling, and to deprive people of that little help —that little boost—which they so often need to get them over a rough spot in the road.

What type of concrete results can counseling achieve? Of one point in particular I am sure: men can be changed. Let me recount two experiences:

¶One year we had a man with a Ph.D. in chemistry attending the A.M.P. course at the Harvard Business School. When he learned that everyone was on a first-name basis, he let it be known that he preferred to be called "Doctor." He was a real intellectual snob—the kind of person who, if someone inquired about his health in a polite way, would take two hours and a half to explain that he was not very well, that his temperature was not exactly 98.6, and his enzymes were acting overacidic, etc. He was a little bit superior, and he talked down to the other men as if they were peasants, junior grade. But after just one day of everyone "Doctoring" the merry hell out of him, he snapped out of it. I have seen this man at his job since he took the A.M.P. course, and he is a different person. No one, of course, said to him, "You are an intellectual snob, and it isn't good for you." In this case, it was the man's own self-discovery—brought about by living for a time with some genuine people who wouldn't take any nonsense—that prompted the change.

(Another man who took the A.M.P. course at Harvard was also the patronizing, superior type. He was president of a very substantial and successful enterprise which his father had built. This person was a real "fancy Dan"—he lived in the big house on the hill with his very attractive wife and children, and did not mingle with anyone. He wouldn't engage in any of the social activities in the town; he wouldn't go to the Country Club parties on Saturday nights. He wouldn't become interested in the Community Fund or the hospital drives—that was for the underlings and the plebeians.

I am told that he would call in his three vice presidents on Friday afternoons and say, "We will play golf tomorrow morning at nine o'clock." And, believe it or not, they were there at nine o'clock. This man was a veritable tyrant, and his subordinates hated him with an intensity that is difficult to describe.

It is amazing what the twelve-week program at the Harvard Business School did for that man. Part of the improvement was undoubtedly due to the change he had to make in his living habits while he was there; he didn't have a maid to pick up his clothes, he had to send his laundry out himself, and he even had to make his own bed on Sunday mornings. Most of the changes that came over him, however, were due to the good, rough, abrasive relationships he developed with the other men in the program. The contacts he had turned that fellow around 180 degrees. His traits, his whole personality changed. I saw him after he had been back at work for a while, and he was a different man. A year ago he was Chairman of the Community Fund. And this is the payoff: now even the caddies at the Country Club like him!

Both of these cases, of course, illustrate off-the-job counseling, but the same principle applies to advising in the work situation. It *is* possible for a superior to help a subordinate change his personality traits. Of course, there are cases where counseling of this type is impossible. A Bell Telephone executive confessed to me recently, "One of the most difficult things in the world for me to do is to sit down and chat with one of my people about his strengths and weaknesses. I just can't do it." On the other hand, a straightforward conversation *is* feasible between some bosses and their subordinates, and the results can be most satisfactory.

CREATING A TEAM

Another part of the coaching concept is called "creating a team." By now this is in danger of being a wishy-washy, namby-pamby phrase, which has grown trite over the years. In our glib use of the term, we have forgotten or neglected the deep administrative meaning it has, and what is involved in creating a team of working people.

First of all, it is important for the boss to know his people—just as a football coach or baseball manager must know his men as individuals on whom he can depend to accomplish certain objectives. The "knowing" in business means knowing what a man's aim is and why he behaves the way he does. Moreover, it must be the result of a big, personal, sincere interest in people. It cannot be lip service. It cannot be artificial, because pretense is more quickly recognized and understood by subordinates than most bosses think.

Perhaps this small incident will illustrate what I mean:

> It seems that the president of a big eastern company was one of those hail-fellow-well-met types, who slapped people on the back, called them by their first names, and said, "How is your wife Mary?" and "I understand your child has been sick."
>
> One of the vice presidents, whose personality traits did not include that particular gregariousness, figured if that was the way to be president, he would try it. So he too began slapping people on the back, and calling them by their first names.

But the only effect that all this had on his subordinates was to make them ask each other, "What is the old bastard up to now?" His new approach just wasn't real. They figured he was up to something, and they didn't trust him.

Secondly, if a boss wants to create a team, he must be willing to let his subordinates participate.

There are some people who will say, "All right, let them *feel* that they participate." Here is an illustration of this kind of "participation" which is amusing, but also true:

I was visiting a regional sales office of a well-known oil company, where the regional sales manager prided himself on the extent to which he was able to get participation by subordinates. To demonstrate his talents to me, one day he called in his five lieutenants and said: "Look, fellows, we have two main problems. One is that we have to replace this bulk station over here because the manager, old Jones, died. I sort of thought that Smith or Peterson ought to take the job, and I felt that Peterson ought to have it. What do you fellows think about it?"

And these five men immediately replied: "Yes, Mr. Boss, Peterson is the man. You show such insight in personal evaluations. We were just going to suggest that name."

Then the sales manager said: "And, you know, we had a fire over at the other bulk station here. We have three alternatives. We can rebuild it the way it was, leave it the way it is, or we can expand it. What do you think we ought to do?"

He gave them no clues this time—he was being cute and coy. Well, I have never seen five reasonably responsible business executives engage in that ancient ritualistic practice called dancing on the periphery to the extent that these people did. They waltzed Mathilda all around the place, never quite facing up to the problem until they got a little hint, and then—zoom!—they fell in line right after the boss.

Participation? No! When a boss walks into a conference on the grounds that he is going to get ideas and contributions from his subordinates, when actually he has already made up his mind exactly what to do, he is perpetrating one of the silliest and most easily-seen-through frauds in business. His subordinates know full well what he is up to, and he doesn't fool them a bit.

Real participation, by contrast, has a positive value. There was never a business problem which could not be solved more easily by the addition of other people's points of view. There has never been a business executive, administrator, or leader, however wise or able, who could make a better decision alone than he could by enlisting the suggestions and contributions of his subordinates.

Thirdly, in creating a team, there is need for fair treatment. Many subordinates say, "The main requirement that I make of a good boss is that he treat me fairly, that is, from my point of view." To illustrate this point:

> Some of the subordinates in a company I visited told me: "The only trouble with this company is that if you didn't go to Yale, you didn't live. And if you aren't a Yale man, better you stayed home and stood in bed. We are not getting a decent break. If there is a convention in Duluth in February, we draw it. If there is one at Miami Beach in February, the Yale boy draws it."

All these men wanted from their boss was a fair shake, an equal opportunity for growth and experience in the company. In this case the boss was playing favorites with his fellow Yale alumni. Situations like this exist, unfortunately, in too many companies; you can substitute for Yale any other university background, club membership, or lodge affiliation you choose. And where there is unequal treatment or discrimination of any sort, there can never be any real "team" consciousness.

Another important phase of the coaching concept involves creating a "climate of confidence" or "atmosphere of approval." An executive of a well-known food company, with regional offices in Chicago, has said:

> "If you as an administrator want results and growth from your subordinate, your success will be in direct proportion to the subordinate's belief of your belief in him. If you are able to manifest

by your behavior that you *do* believe in your subordinate's capacity
to do a job, more than likely he will knock himself out proving
that you were right. But if by your behavior you show some doubt,
some real question as to whether he can fulfill a task, more often
than not he will fail, just as you expected."

There is something about the relationship between a boss and his
subordinate that either stimulates or retards the growth of the subordinate. It is by maintaining an atmosphere of approval that the
superior can help his man do things that probably, way back in his
heart, he thought he never could do.

STANDARDS OF PERFORMANCE

The last element of coaching I call "standards of performance." It
might be designated "standards of approval," because obviously a
superior doesn't acquiesce in everything that his subordinate does,
right or wrong. If he did that, his approval would soon have no
meaning at all to the subordinate. Rather, the boss must set up and
publicize certain standards which he expects his men to meet. This
gives a subordinate definite, clear-cut objectives for which to strive.
He knows what is expected of him, and he will do his best to measure
up to the requirements.

The problem of "motivation"—of stimulating people into action,
getting men moving who aren't moving—arises under this concept of
"standards of performance." While some people are self-propelled,
there are others who need a bulldozer in back of them. For instance,
a recent *Saturday Evening Post* cartoon depicts the general manager
of one firm storming into the sales manager's office saying, "Hawkins,
I think you ought to take the pins out of the map and stick them into
that salesman!" Such pin-sticking might be just another way of establishing and demanding certain standards of performance for the people in a company.

Of course a pin is not usually the correct way to communicate a
standard, but the standards themselves should be sharp and clear and
compelling. And a standard is a goad to action; when a man knows

just what his boss desires of him, he is more likely to do a satisfactory piece of work.

Coaching can be helpful and effective not only in superior-subordinate situations but also in the arena of equal-level relationships within the firm. For instance, in many companies there is conflict among the research and development, engineering, processing development, manufacturing, and sales groups who are all working on a new product. The research people say, "This is our domain, and you other men stay out." The manufacturing crew replies, "This is *our* territory; don't bother us." Disagreement between such functions, which are all on the same level on the organizational chart, can fractionate the total objective. This is where some form of coaching is vitally needed.

The "speed groups" which Naugatuck Chemical has developed represent one answer to this need. Such groups are actually project teams composed of a salesman, an engineer, and a development man; these men are responsible, as a team, for the research, production, sales planning, and sales execution connected with the product. Other companies such as Monsanto and Ethyl have found this product group scheme the most helpful way of getting people to forget arbitrary functional walls, to cooperate with each other, to merge their interests.

The speed group, or product team, is coaching in the sense that each man on the team learns from the other. The engineering expert learns what is involved in research, and both the engineer and the researcher learn about promotion from the salesman. Each man begins to realize that he needs the ideas of all his associates. For instance:

A drug company had a great deal of trouble getting cooperation among its employees. Their researchers would come up with a pill that would be bilious purple—no sugar coating on it—just horrible. The salesmen would protest, but the research people would say, "Bilious purple it is, and it is going to stay bilious purple. It isn't going to be changed." Finally the company assigned some of its research men to the road for a month. When these people found out just what the salesman's job involved—the difficulties he encountered in trying to sell a bilious purple pill to a retail druggist—interbranch cooperation in this company rapidly improved.

Coaching, in this sense, is exposure to learning opportunities. Men can most certainly learn from their equals in the firm, just as they can profit from coaching by their superiors.

These concepts of coaching, which I have just briefly touched, do not represent a new mechanical way of doing business. They are not rules that a boss can follow five minutes a day, and then say to himself, "I am going to quit coaching now and start getting the job done." Coaching is not a new management technique. Basically, it boils down to an effort on the boss's part to utilize existing opportunities in the administrative process.

An important part of each superior officer's everyday routine should be the almost unconscious instruction and coaching of his men. In dealing with his subordinates he should always keep in mind his role as an educator. The boss should and can give on-the-job training to his men, thus fitting them for higher positions and broader responsibilities.

The opportunity to use work situations to help the people working for one to develop and broaden and qualify for bigger management jobs is available to every top executive. And whether or not the opportunity is seized depends almost wholly on the boss. It is his individual decision—but it is a most important decision for the future of the company and American business as a whole.

I sincerely hope that business people will realize their chance, and make up now for past errors and lost time. I have outlined here some of the off-the-job and on-the-job ways in which management can develop new talent. Through advanced management programs, by job rotation, job progression, and coaching, businesses can produce from their own ranks men well-qualified to fill the highest positions. It is up to the present managements to do the rest.

PERFORMANCE MEASUREMENT

Russell H. Hassler

IN THIS CHAPTER I hope to point up some of the problems involved in performance measurement.

As Mr. Breech pointed out in Part I, when you start trying to appraise performance, you have to measure it. This means that you have to get a yardstick. Just the very idea of trying to judge how good or how bad, how poorly or how well, implies a job of measuring and also the setting up of a standard. We may measure intuitively or subconsciously, but whenever we say a division has done well or is making an adequate profit, or a man has done a good job, we are, in fact, measuring. We mean *doing well compared to something,* so we have set a standard; and presumably if we have set a standard, we have had to measure it.

A CASE HISTORY

In order to sharpen this discussion, I would like to set down the experience of a very large and successful company that has been

Note: Mr. Hassler is Professor of Accounting, Harvard Business School.

wrestling with this problem now for a couple of years on a really organized research basis.

A few years ago this firm's management was getting a steady stream of complaints from division managers, departmental managers, and so on. They did not know the criteria used in judging how well or how badly they were doing their jobs. "How does management really *know* when it says that we have done a lousy job or we've done a good job?" they asked. "We are inclined to think that the way we are judged has something to do with the color of our ties or how we operate at a cocktail party or something like that. We surely wish the management would tell us how it appraises our performance."

Top management decided that measuring performance really was a topic of importance, worth the expenditure of some money and time. So about three years ago it set up a research group, consisting of scientists, mathematicians, sales people, and financial experts. This was not to be a time-study proposition, nor solely a dollars-and-cents measurement, but an attempt to set inclusive criteria.

The group started out by deciding that there were three steps to the research project:

> 1. Defining the factors involved in deciding whether a job was being done well or poorly which would be applicable not only for the company as a whole but for a division and a department as well, and on which there could be a reasonable degree of agreement throughout the company. (The group members decided at the outset that they were not going to accept any conventional ideas but were going to find out for themselves what was really important about the way in which their people did their jobs. This sounds easy—until you try it!)
> 2. Figuring out how to measure the factors.
> 3. Setting standards of performance.

The factors the group settled on seem to apply to almost any enterprise. This particular company's business covers almost every type of activity from consumer products to heavy industry. Thus the result of these studies may be helpful to the reader.

SIGNIFICANT FACTORS

The group first took the obvious factor which is common to a company as a whole, a decentralized division, or a product line—*profitability*. Somehow or other they felt they must end up with profitability, whatever other criteria might also be considered significant, so that is where they started.

However, when they began using profitability as the single goal, the one yardstick, they immediately ran into trouble. A division manager would say: "Well, my profits weren't so hot this year, but I did a lot of other things that were pretty important. If this company wants to survive, management ought to pay attention to some of these other things that I did. They can't take profits as the only criterion." They decided that maybe the manager was right, and they continued searching.

The next factor they added was *market position*. This seemed to take care of those separate, decentralized divisions that had both profit responsibility and market position to worry about. Also they thought it would cover some of the selling divisions that might not be said to have a clear-cut profit responsibility.

But they had not gone very far when they came up against some thorny problems. Some of their people said: "Oh well, right now we may not be the leader in the market; but, after all, we do have product leadership. That is pretty important, because product leadership is ultimately going to pay off in the market, and consequently it is going to pay off in profitability." So they added another factor: *product leadership*.

Then they faced the problem of manufacturing. Apparently profitability, in some cases, could not be measured accurately if the manufacturing division was selling through another division. Further, the issue of "make or buy"—whether or not the division should expand its manufacturing facilities to make products that could be purchased just as cheaply or even cheaper on the outside—affected the demand of the manufacturing division for more funds and more plant capacity. This activity needed some sort of a yardstick, some standard of performance. They called it *productivity*—meaning effective use of capital, men, and raw material.

Next they began to get at some of the things that are always pointed out when a division manager fails by some of the more tangible yardsticks. "This man," for example, "is doing a good job in his division because he is very skillful at developing personnel." Now they were dealing with a more subjective factor—*personnel development*. Along with this they put *public responsibility,* which is somewhat aligned with it. Next they listed a criterion which, to my mind, is a much more complex one—*employee attitudes*. And the last factor, which I think is extremely important, they called the *balance between long-range and short-range goals*. This one is just full of headaches!

To develop these eight factors took the research group about a year and a half of talking among themselves first and then discussing the matter in the company at large.

This list, which they felt encompassed all the factors of importance in measuring performance in any major segment of the company, points up one conclusion that seems especially significant to me: all criteria except the first actually should be considered as paying off ultimately in profitability. A manager would hardly be interested in being No. 1 in the market just for the fun of being No. 1. Nor would he be interested in the effective use of men and materials if ultimately he did not see it as a desirable way to increase his own profitability. And so it goes with all the rest of the factors.

We can then consider all eight factors as a breakdown of the ultimate goal of profitability. They are all needed for performance measurement over the time span of a year because a year is too short a time to use the single goal of profitability. Too many things, in the short run, come into play.

USE OF FACTORS

The next step was to put these factors into use. Immediately the company had to be concerned with the question of how to combine these factors. How do we add personnel development to product leadership, or public responsibility to productivity, in order to form a total impression? Generally the reaction is that these are qualities, like apples and oranges, that cannot be added.

But inevitably we are forced to the conclusion that the minute we try to decide whether a person or a division has done a good job from an over-all viewpoint, we do, in fact, total these evaluations. We say that a division's market position is good, but its profits are low; or its market position is bad, but the manager has done a good piece of work in personnel development; and then, somehow, we combine all these diverse and dissimilar factors into one judgment. Maybe we do it subconsciously, but we do say, "On balance, I think this man is (or is not) doing a good job," or "On balance, this division has (or has not) performed adequately this year."

The research group was told that adding the eight factors together was impossible, and that once the factors were measured, the rest must be left up to the judgment of the appraiser.

But what did this company mean by "judgment"? For a long time it appeared that, in most cases, what it meant was: "We do not know how on earth we did reach our decision." For example:

> In connection with the personnel development factor, the group used, at one stage of the game, a personnel rating form, with an assigned point system, designed to rate a job and a person's performance on that job. It was also supposed to indicate within what salary bracket a particular position should be classified.
>
> When they started to see how it worked in practice, they ran into difficulties. They would rate a job at, say, $10,000 a year. But when they talked to the manager about it, he would say, "No, I want to give that man $13,000." When they asked him, "Why so much?" he would reply, "Well, I can't explain it, but in my judgment he is worth $13,000."
>
> In short, the manager was either saying that their factors were wrong to begin with or he was mixing in some other criteria which they had not defined.
>
> At this point the group talked with one of the managers who had

been especially vocal in trying to get this whole performance project under way. He had been eager to see in black and white the factors which were used in appraising him and to learn how these factors were measured. But after going through one session with his superiors, when they tried to go along with his idea and applied the criteria to him, he was not so enthusiastic. "This year," he told them, "you should not look at my profitability because unforeseen things have happened. As to market position, well, that is not quite fair this year either because, after all, we have been spending a lot of money on research and we have new products that really won't be out until four years from now." And so it went, through all eight factors.

When they got through, he remarked, "Well, I think maybe after the formal record is set down, you have to use judgment." Then he thought for a minute and continued: "I guess what I mean to say is that I am right back at my starting point. Originally I asked you to put down the factors and your system of measuring them, because I didn't want to be judged on some kind of personality basis. Now that I've discovered what happens in practice, I'm suggesting that what I really want you to do is turn around and use your judgment."

He had made the full circle, starting with a desire to have the criteria defined and ending up with a decision that he did not want to use the factors in the proportion they had set and returning once again to the use of judgment. In his mind judgment involved some balance of these measures.

The company is now reasonably certain on this point: judgment is involved in the way in which these eight factors are mixed together. In one case more weight is put on profitability; in another product leadership and productivity are emphasized; and so on.

MEASUREMENT OF FACTORS

Granting that judgment comes into the adding up of these factors, it still seems the individual items themselves should be subject to some kind of objective measurement. This kind of measurement is obviously indispensable if management is to get any practical value from the list of items. Let us, then, examine the first concept, profitability. How do we measure profitability?

It will be recalled that Mr. Roberts, in Part I, said that he and his company look at return on investment as a measure. On the other hand, Mr. Breech said that he looks at the actual profit as related to his "profit plan"—how much did we decide a particular division was going to make, and how close did the division come to it? Another standard of measurement might be the return on total capital, prorated over a year and for a longer period, with emphasis on the latter. That covers a lot of territory.

The officers of the particular company I have in mind disagreed with return on investment as a measure of profitability because, when they tried it out, they hit apparently insuperable obstacles. One was how to figure investment: do you take depreciated cost, full cost, or replacement values? It happens that this company has two factories —one built in 1938 and the other in 1952—which make similar products. The officers started out by taking depreciated cost, but under this system the return on investment realized by the old factory— the piece of junk, as they called it—was 16%, while the return on the brand new, modern, up-to-date, efficient factory was 7%. Somehow return on investment did not seem to be a fair standard.

Further, they found that if a division manager knows what measure is being used, he will inevitably fit his decisions to the measure. And undesirable results were being produced by using return on investment as a yardstick of performance. For one thing, it was hard to get good men to take over new facilities because the return on investment was not as high. In another instance, a division manager had the necessary capacity to do some marginal business, and the marginal operation was such that it would have brought in additional dollars of profit. However, his return on investment would have been cut from 8% to 6%. Consequently, he refused to increase his *actual* profit because he did not want his record to show this drop in return.

Also, where a company has multiple units making the same product, the product mix is usually set by some authority higher than the division manager. Consequently the return on investment, under such conditions, is not determined by the skill of the manager but rests on company policy. Again sales price affects return on investment, but it is something over which the manager may have no control. A loss might develop because the sales force is not getting as good a price as it could. Can you hold a man responsible for profit when he has to carry the cost but is not charged with the responsibility of setting the sales price?

Then there is the question of a definition of investment. There are, of course, many ways in which it could be defined. This provides us with one more illustration of how difficult it is to get one's hands on the so-called "easy" facts which are involved in all this.

Return on investment, then, is only one of the many measures of profitability, and not such a simple one at that. All of us who have looked into investments on the stock market can see that the various services which analyze the profitability of a company observe many factors: percentage of sales, total gross sales, and so on. As a matter of fact, under modern corporate structure, there is so much variation in percentage of investment that it really means very little.

The difficulty we have in trying to measure profitability—which, with all the records available, one would think would be simple enough—is multiplied as we go on with the other factors on the list. Instead of being less difficult, they are more so. Take market position, for example. The mathematicians on the research team ruled out almost all the ways in which the company had previously appraised market position. Management used to depend especially on weekly reports from a commercial survey service, but this did not seem to be an accurate way of judging market position. So the research group had to start all over to find a measurement for it.

As for productivity, they are still searching for a way to measure that on an over-all as well as on a division-wide basis. So far they have come up with the same kind of device that I believe some of the food processors have used—the idea of contributed value or conversion factor. To try to measure productivity they take sales in dollars, deduct raw materials and supplies, and other factors which do not reflect the productivity of internal operations, and relate the remainder (or residual, as they call it) to profit.

OTHER CONSIDERATIONS

Of course none of this presents a static picture. There is the factor of growth and improvement. A man standing very low on the record in the various categories may have just taken over a factory which has been losing money. His performance, therefore, should be judged on improvement. That is, a loss of 10%, say, the first year, followed by a loss of 5% the second year, followed by a break-even the third, probably indicates better performance than that of another man in a highly profitable post who simply maintains the level at which he started.

Also, the difficulty of the job comes into the picture. A man might be showing up poorly because his competitor was dumping goods at a low price or because of some pressure in some other section of the country. A price war might develop which could damage the entire program. The officers of the particular company I have in mind have decided that they are not going to take such circumstances into consideration. They say they are going to play the cards the way they come up. Executives will be told, "It may not be your fault that your record looks like this, but that's the way things are." Despite the decision, this kind of problem does, of course, impinge on the justice of the measurement being used.

CONCLUSION

One of the most interesting aspects of all this discussion is that in drawing up a list we start with one factor, thinking that it will be *the* yardstick, *the* criterion, for which we are seeking. But when we put this one factor into practice, we discover that it does not take into consideration many other important aspects of measurement, so we draw up a list which seems to be conclusive.

Then we start trying to measure the factors we have listed, and we find that the job gets more and more complicated as we go along. All

this, it should be remembered, is still concerned with the measurement
of the topmost divisions and personnel. We have not reached the point
of even considering finer breakdowns.

Thus, after two and a half years of work on what seems, at first
blush, to be a comparatively simple task, the particular firm I have
been using as an example is still only at the beginning of its attempt
to find out how to fix the standards it has set up. This is a complex
and involved business, and the further we go with it, the less sure we
are that the human element of "judgment" can be refined out of it.

Sometimes this seems like a hopeless area, but actually we have the
same difficulties in any situation when we try to do some measuring.
There is one activity in the United States on which every conceivable
statistic is available—professional baseball. Yet if somebody were to
ask you who is the best player on the New York Yankees, how would
you go about answering the question? You cannot give an answer
that will satisfy everyone. One player would have a fat batting average, another would have a high fielding average, another would be a
clutch performer, and so on. Everything—intuition, judgment, your
own attitudes—are all mixed up in it. But we must—and do—measure
performance all the time, and it is important for us to develop as
objective, clear, and inclusive standards as we possibly can.

THE GROWING NEED FOR GOOD COMMUNICATIONS IN INDUSTRY

Reuben B. Robertson, Jr., and Fritz J. Roethlisberger

DESPITE THE INTENSE INTEREST of businessmen in the area of communications, and all the attention companies have given to the problem, we need to do a better job in this area than any of us have done before. Our efforts have been concentrated on sales, production, research, advertising, cost controls, basic resources, and many other activities necessary to create the products of American industry. We have spent far too little time on the human side of business—the understanding of our people. We have not done enough to help Americans to understand the profit system at work, and recognize how it has stimulated the creation of the standard of living we enjoy.

Note: Mr. Robertson, whose description of his company's experiences forms the main part of this chapter, was, at the time of the National Business Conference, President of The Champion Paper and Fiber Company; he is now serving as Deputy Secretary of Defense. Mr. Roethlisberger, who provides the concluding note as moderator of the session on which the chapter is based, is Wallace Brett Donham Professor of Human Relations, Harvard Business School.

Unless management acquires a much more aggressive point of view and becomes aware of the necessity of doing this job, we are likely to find ourselves in an atmosphere that is increasingly hostile to our free enterprise system.

This is a tremendous challenge. Techniques are being tried and tested in various ways, and all of us are learning as we feel our way in this important area.

One way we can best demonstrate our concepts, philosophies, and practices is to give readers a case history of our experience in the past two years in developing and establishing our new profit-sharing plan. This project covered all phases of communications—employees, shareholders, and the public.

A CASE HISTORY

Our company has a long history of work in communications. The goal of our internal and external communications is to help all groups to work together—management, workers, shareholders, and customers. This is the executive's most important task. Our company is reasonably small, with 9,000 workers and 5,000 shareholders. We are operating plants in three communities, the biggest of which has a population of about 65,000 people, the smallest about 10,000. All of them are "neighbors" whom we want to understand the company's policies and philosophy.

Our biggest job is to make it possible for the people in our organization to work together in the best interests of each other and the customer. We must be responsible, respected citizens in communities in which we live.

There is no single formula or approach to communications that will assure success. It is one of management's most difficult jobs. As Fritz Roethlisberger has said: "In thinking about the many barriers to personal communication, particularly those that are due to differences of background, experience, and motivation, it seems to me extraordinary that any two persons can ever understand each other." We don't presume to know all of the answers.

Over the past 15 or 20 years our company has provided the customary benefits such as life insurance, retirement, hospitalization, and sickness and accident insurance. In addition, we have group incentive pay and what we call time service pay—extra pay for extra length of service. The retirement and insurance programs had certain gaps even though they were well above the average in industry and 95% of our 9,000 employees participated in them. We felt that there were some problems that needed to be solved. We hoped that the profit-sharing approach might be an answer, and, in addition, might stimulate more interest in the company.

Here is a general outline of the main provisions of the former retirement and insurance plans:

1. The employees contributed toward the cost of each plan although the company paid a larger part of the total cost of the entire program.

2. The retirement benefits were approximately ¾ of 1% of the first $3,000 of annual pay and 1½% of pay over $3,000 annually.

3. The weekly sickness and accident benefits were slightly different at each of the plants but in general provided approximately 50% of pay, up to a maximum of $45 a week for a period of 13 weeks.

4. The life insurance was based upon wage and salary classifications. The amount of benefit averaged less than two years' pay, with a maximum of $10,000.

5. There were different hospital and surgical benefit plans at each of the plants.

6. We had no formula for total and permanent disability benefits.

7. We had no benefits payable upon termination of employment.

Here is a summary of the provisions of the new profit-sharing plan which was to be presented:

1. All employee contributions were to be discontinued and employees who had previously contributed to the old retirement plan were to be permitted to withdraw their past contributions without a reduction in retirement benefits.

2. The company would set aside each year 15% of its profits be-

fore taxes. This 15% would be allocated among the different benefits
as follows:

  a. Death benefits equal to two years' pay, less the amount in an
  employee's profit-sharing account.

  b. Weekly sickness and accident benefits of approximately 60%
  of base pay up to a maximum of $50 a week, payable for 26
  weeks.

  c. Hospital, surgical, and medical care benefits designed to pay a
  substantial part of the charges for these services.

  d. Past service retirement and total and permanent disability benefits of approximately 1% of pay times years of service up to
  May 1, 1955.

3. Any balance of the 15% profits before taxes that remained after
paying the cost of the above benefits would then be allocated among
the profit-sharing accounts of all employees, on the basis of their
service units. A time service unit is one unit for each $100 of annual
pay for each of the first 10 years in the plan; two units for each $100
pay of the next 10 years in the plan; and three units for each $100 of
annual pay for each year in the plan over 20 years.

4. The amount in an employee's account in the profit-sharing plan
would be applied as follows:

  a. To provide death benefits. If the amount in an employee's ac
  count exceeds two years' pay then this larger amount is paid.

  b. Provide loans in the event of financial hardship, such as illness
  in the family.

  c. Provide retirement and total and permanent disability benefits
  for service after May 1, 1955.

  d. Provide a severance of employment benefit equal to 10% of the
  value of employee's account, for each full year he has been a
  member of the plan at the time he leaves the company.

Needless to say, this constituted a major change not only in the
amount of benefit provided but also in the method of providing benefits. It is for this reason that it was necessary for us to marshal our
best communications efforts in order to explain effectively the proposed profit-sharing plan. Here is how we went about the job of communications.

DEVELOPMENT OF A PROGRAM

Since the beginning, our company has had, as one of its fundamental philosophies, a determination to maintain a solid foundation based upon:

1. A competitive and equitable wage and salary structure.
2. Steady employment.
3. Growth opportunities for our people.
4. A program for sharing with our people the results of their efforts.

Communications in an organization tend to have a hollow sound unless the foundation is solid. We found we were in a strong position. We realize the fact that being in a stable, growing industry has been helpful in enabling us to achieve these goals.

We took a long look ahead to anticipate the effect of changes we might make in our benefit program. Our goal was to maintain effective leadership and build an even stronger organization. That is the threshold of an effective communications program.

In the development of our new profit-sharing plan we tested every feature by the difficulty of communicating it. Many benefit plans are so complex in their structure that effective communications about them is defeated in the development stage. We chose the profit-sharing approach because it appeared to be:

1. The most realistic method of providing these benefits.
2. The one that would be of greatest value to both employees and shareholders.
3. Consistent with the valuable experience we had gained from working with our cooperative earnings bonus—a form of immediate payment profit-sharing plan based upon quality and quantity of production.

All of this was done to try to find the answer to two questions: (*a*) *Where did we want to go?* (*b*) *What was the best way to get there?*

Unless we had the answers to those questions, it was going to be difficult to communicate our ideas to others. The essence of an effective communications program is not just the *what,* but the *why.* Frequently it is necessary to spend more time on the *why* than on the *what*.

Our ideas were of little value unless they were acceptable to others in our organization. So we reviewed them with Champion people and their families, and our shareholders, keeping in mind throughout who was listening to what we had to say and what difference it would make to them.

Following is the broad outline of the program of communications by which we attempted to obtain the reaction of others and determine the acceptance of our ideas.

After satisfying ourselves that the new profit-sharing program was sound from a management standpoint, we reviewed the program with our board of directors.

We conducted intensive seminars with top management.

We had special meetings with our management people.

We had meetings with all Champions, explaining to them that the plan was still subject to approval by our board of directors, the United States Treasury, and our shareholders.

We presented the new program to our people in this sequence: first, with large groups to whom we explained the background and philosophy of the new plan, together with an outline of its main provisions; next, with small groups, at which trained supervisors discussed the details of the new plan and answered questions.

We felt that the principal effort should be carried out down the line —through the foremen who are responsible for their own people, even though they may have technicians available to help them. Our extensive supervisors' training and policy clearance programs, under which all foremen meet once a month in group discussions, made our job easier. These men were trained in advance so that they had the story complete in their own minds. We wanted these men to be able to answer the individual's specific questions. Each foreman, in turn, met with his own people in groups of about 20, 450 meetings in all.

This effort was supplemented by a booklet for each individual called "Partners in Paper and Profits." The booklet contained the same charts and other visual material which had been prepared for the meetings to help explain the new program. This assured continuity between what the people heard and saw and what they later read. One paragraph in the booklet stated:

> "This book will tell you how the New Idea works. Please read it carefully together with your family, talk it over with other members of the team, and let us know what you think about it. It's a big step, too big to take unless most of the members of the team think it's a good idea and worth a try. So here it is."

We felt it was most important to be specific about the comparative benefits under the old and new plans because each individual is primarily concerned with how something affects him. Consequently, we went to the trouble—and it proved quite a chore—to figure the benefits for each employee under both the old and the new plans. Each man received this statement of his benefits the day before the meeting he attended, so he was in a position to ask relevant questions. The leaders had been briefed to explain the whole program to him, so he could leave the meeting ready to express an informed opinion.

Each person was asked to express himself anonymously about the new program. He was given a card on which he could state whether he considered the new plan satisfactory or whether he liked the old program better, his reasons for feeling so, and any other comments he wanted to make. These cards were mailed directly to the consultants who were helping us with the over-all study leading up to the program, so there was no chance for anyone to feel that we were putting on any pressure, individually or collectively, to accept this new program. The replies were analyzed, and the comments were most enthusiastic, with a 97% response and a 99.7% acceptance. We had agreed in advance that we would tell our people just what the results were, certified by the consultants; and we did so in a letter from the president's office.

We then had the problem of getting the approval of our shareholders. We had already done some groundwork with the Treasury and had very definite indications that legally and taxwise there was every possibility that we would be all right. To avoid the risk of getting this far and then being turned down by shareholders, we had gone to many of the larger shareholders in advance and asked them to give us their opinion. So we had some pretty good indications from about 45 to 50% of our shareholders that this program was acceptable.

But we wanted more than this. We hoped for an enthusiastic response from all of our shareholders. We prepared a proxy statement and called a special meeting so that the proposal would not get lost in the regular annual meeting agenda. In addition we prepared a pamphlet called "Report to Shareholders," which outlined the general concept of the program and its effect, in simple, understandable language. We were very much pleased when we received the largest reply of any proxy statement that we had ever sent out. It was approximately 89%, and of that number 99.6% voted in favor of the program. We sent a letter on the results to both our shareholders and employees, and also put an announcement in *The Log,* our monthly employee publication.

Knowing that the shareholders and workers were in harmony on the program, we were in a position to put the new plan into operation. This involved other types of communication. The next step was an announcement in our weekly paper in each plant of the date for switching over to the new program. Then we had to train our supervisors on the details of this complicated job.

To show how well our advance indoctrination paid off, there was less than a 2% error in the 56,000 signatures required on the forms that the employees and their wives had to fill out because of changes in the existing plans. We prepared another booklet, with more detail on the plan, to accompany the forms.

We then found great interest in the program in the various towns and communities in which we operated, so we felt it would be desirable to explain the new program to our neighbors. We have always been proud of our good community relations and have tried to keep our neighbors informed on all major company projects of community interest. We went to considerable length to make the program public knowledge. We issued explanatory publicity releases and took paid space in every paper in the communities where we operate, in order to avoid any chance of misinterpretation. We tried to tell the story of just what we were doing, the fact that the new program was tied to profits and to profit sharing, and what it would mean to our neighbors. This effort also furthered better understanding among our own people.

We have been working intensively on community communications for many years. Systematically, we conduct open house at each plant: first for employees' families, second for the community, third for graduating high school students, and fourth for teachers and ministers in the county areas. We deal with these primary groups in staggered years. During these open house meetings management has a chance to present the economic facts about what is being done in terms of growth and development, and the role of our payroll in the community. We also solicit questions on such matters as what we are doing about stream or air pollution or conservation of forests. This way we get a feedback. All of this effort has been most helpful in maintaining favorable attitudes toward the company on the part of our neighbors.

Turning again to our own group, we then planned for the future. A good communications program is not a one-shot proposition. It is gradual and continuous. We decided that this program was big enough and challenging enough to require a separate project to improve our communications efforts. We created communications committees, not only at the general office of the company but in each operating division, to guide our communications and administration activities. We wanted these committees to meet frequently. We made a particular effort to have them represent a cross section of all our people. These committees are:

1. An over-all policy committee in the general office, representing the legal, financial, accounting, and industrial and public relations phases of our business.

2. Management committees in the general office and each division responsible for employee communications about the plan, benefit provisions, and costs.

3. Advisory committees of employees on communications to gear communications to the things our people wanted to know and to reflect their reactions and attitudes. These committees constantly keep their fingers on the pulse of employee attitudes.

We then developed specific communications projects, each with its own objective and timing, correlated with the others. We hoped to be able to use a rifle instead of a shotgun in our communications about the new plan. This was necessary if we were to measure our effectiveness. Here are some of the specific projects in the year's program:

1. A statement of account to be given to each employee on the status of his account in the profit-sharing fund.

2. A status report for each employee, giving the status of all of his other benefits under the plan, such as death, disability, health care, and retirement benefits.

3. A booklet to give detailed information about the benefits under the plan and to serve as a reference manual, so everyone has the same information.

4. The president's letter, which is issued quarterly, to tell of the progress of the company and its effect upon the profit-sharing plan.

5. Articles in our house organs to convey specific information about the plan in operation, through human interest stories.

We have a calendar of communications activities about the plan for next year. This is the track on which we will run and hope it will lead us to the fulfillment of our objectives. At that time we hope to be able to measure the effectiveness of our communications efforts and to do so each year. We have tried to measure readership of our house organs and employee attitudes in the past, so the measurement project will not be new, but we hope it will be improved. It is the only way we can assess the value of the many different techniques we will use and shed some light on what we should and what we should not be doing—what does and what does not work.

In order to make sure the communication line reaches to the top, the people responsible for communications from each of the plants come together to talk over with the president the questions that are in the minds of the people in their plants. Initially, we have appointed these committees for a two-year term, but the committee itself is to formulate the best way to select its future membership.

We found that the communications program set in motion for this plan gave us an unusual opportunity to review with our people the philosophy of the company on all phases of our operations and how it related to them, with particular emphasis on the foundations of our human relations program—steady work, good pay, opportunity, and sharing of results. This helped strengthen the feeling of general confidence.

Our philosophy of communications is based upon trying to practice what we preach, not only in communications about benefit plans but in all phases of our operations. This requires:

1. Full disclosure to the organization—to tell them what they want to know, not just what we want them to know. To do this we need to try to find out what it is they would like to know.

2. Continuous training of management people (at Champion this includes foremen and supervisors) on communications. This year we are holding intensive two and one-half day seminars for our management people. One of the major subjects will be communications, and discussions of the new profit-sharing plan will play an important part.

3. Encouraging participation by all employees in all our communications programs. One idea an employee thinks is his is worth a thousand he thinks are yours.

4. Sharing results. This is the most effective way to provide each individual with:

a. A feeling of personal importance through recognition of his individual performance.

b. Recognition of the relationship of his job to the other jobs in the company and to the over-all success of the company.

c. Exposure to company, general, and personal economics and their interdependence.

d. An opportunity and reason for self-expression in his work environment.

We have come a long way, but still have a long way to go. We know that communications is a continuous process of learning what to do, when and how to do it, and what not to do.

We have illustrated here the basic concepts and principles of communications that guided us in developing and establishing our new profit-sharing plan. These same principles are applied, as well, in all other phases of our operations—production, plant expansion, sales, community relations. They are one of the cornerstones of our organization.

Some people ask whether it is worthwhile for us to use company time and money and to stop production just to keep our employees informed. We think the answer is definitely *yes*. Recently we were concerned with how well our own supervisors understood our American economic system, so we had an opinion research poll made. We were distressed by the findings. Our people did not understand it at all, so we asked each of our operating divisions to choose that form of economic education or enlightenment which it would like best to use to improve the situation. There were three or four types available; each was very good, and each division adopted a different one. After our 900 or 1,000 supervisors had been through the course, on company time, we asked them whether we should quit or spend $50,000 to make it available to all Champions. They voted to give the course to everyone, and we went right on through, with a very fine response.

The forces at work to influence the thinking of people have never been more expansive or more intense in their efforts than they are today in all phases of our social and economic existence. They have grown almost in proportion to the expansion of communications facilities and speeds. Management hasn't kept pace. If we do not do our job in this area, others will do it for us and in their own way.

The development of a feeling of confidence in the free enterprise system is one of the greatest tasks and responsibilities of management, and particularly of the head of a company. This feeling cannot be created by full page ads in business publications. Our best chance lies in 10,000 companies working systematically at home with their own associates, making sure that their people know what they are doing, and why. It can be done. The head of each company must carry the fundamental responsibility, making sure that this job is done. This is our real challenge in the years ahead.

CONCLUDING NOTE*

It seems to me that when we are introducing such plans as the one described here by Mr. Robertson, and getting people to understand them, all the folderol we might use may not work unless there is a kind of *basic trust and understanding* between management and employees and between employee and employee as well as between the company and the community.

It is important to note that all the groundwork which Mr. Robertson's company laid developed a relationship of confidence and trust which made this possible. Many of us think there is some easy gimmick that can make an idea understandable or understood, but a great deal of such groundwork is necessary before an idea can be realized in practice.

* By Mr. Roethlisberger.

THE IMPACT OF CURRENT
MARKETING TRENDS

Neil H. Borden

IN THIS CHAPTER I want to do three things: (1) present a pattern which I have used personally to guide my thinking about marketing; (2) explain what we mean by trends and how we use them in planning marketing programs and strategy; and (3) point out two or three important developments which appear likely to have great effect on marketing operations in the future.

But first let me emphasize an outstanding characteristic of business today: we are living in a dynamic world. We are always faced with the problem of discovering where we are and where we are going, and what forces are operating to affect our businesses. We try to answer these questions to make sure that we come out with good figures at the end of our profit and loss statements.

The complexity of today's marketing problems as brought on by a fast changing world was forcefully brought to my attention recently

Note: Mr. Borden is Professor of Advertising, Harvard Business School.

142

during a meeting with some executives of the Salada Tea Company. I listened with these men to a presentation of an A. C. Nielsen survey relating to their business, and what I witnessed illustrates what management is up against now. In these periodic Nielsen reports marketing research has given the Salada people data on various trends. From the data given in the presentation they knew where they were for the period of the survey; what their sales were; what those of their competitors were; what their distribution and that of their competitors was; what advertising and promotion all had carried on. However, their facts for the period were not nearly as important to the company's top men as the data which permitted them to look back and see where they had been and which gave them a basis for planning what to do in the periods ahead.

Some of the trends they examined demonstrate what we mean by a dynamic world. They looked at all these things: a trend line of personal income, market expectations in the light of present economic conditions, the trend of expenditures in grocery stores, the trend of demand for tea as a whole, the trend of demand for coffee (the company's biggest competitor), the downward trend of coffee prices, the trend of tea prices, the trend of Salada sales, the trend of their competitors' sales, the promotional and advertising trends of competitors. Salada's managers had to take all this information, analyze it, and put it to use in guiding their marketing program. This example gives some idea of the complex tasks of market planners today in a dynamic world.

THE MARKETING MIX

In my own job of teaching Marketing I have found it helpful to think in terms of the marketing mix when dealing with marketing problems and the planning of strategy in a dynamic world. Businessmen are sometimes too prone to think about only one element of a marketing program when adjusting their operations. They center thinking on management of sales force, or advertising, or price, and fail to think of the interdependency of the various marketing functions. Sound management thinking requires consideration of all the elements so that when change is made in one area, desirable changes may be made with other elements of the mix.

In the following paragraphs I shall list the important elements of the marketing mix, and the important forces which bear in on the marketer in his operations and to which he must adjust the elements of his mix if he is to have a successful operation:

> First in the "mix" list, there are the problems of product planning or *merchandising*. Management must always adjust its product line to the market, keeping in mind product changes that must be made to meet changing conditions. Shall we add a product or line? Shall we drop an item? Must we change quality or design to meet or surpass competitors who are bringing out improvements?
>
> Next, there is the important element of *price* as a part of the marketing mix. Is our price where it ought to be to meet changing conditions? Is our pricing strategy good? Where do we stand with regard to margins?
>
> Next, there is the element of *personal selling* in the mix. Is the push of personal selling important or relatively unimportant? Are conditions changing to render greater or less stress on personal selling?
>
> Closely allied is the element of *advertising*. What is the burden that is to be placed here? With changing conditions of competition, should more burden or less be placed on advertising?
>
> And so I might go on down through this list, pointing out the interrelationship and interdependence of one element and another which must be well molded into a total marketing program—*branding, channels, promotion, packaging, display, servicing.*

Here are the forces bearing in on the marketer to which he must continually adjust the elements of his program:

> First, there are the forces generated by the *consumer*—his attitudes, habits, buying power, numbers, and environment. The facts of the consumer as they bear upon the marketer are subject to constant change.

Next, there are the forces generated by the *trade,* its changing character, attitudes, and methods of operation.

Next, there are the forces generated by *competition,* which are in constant flux. Competition is continually changing, in amount and in intensity. In the changes of competition and the other forces bearing in on the marketer, we look for the trends—the subject of this chapter.

At this point, the term "trends" ought to be defined. Now, when we speak of trends in demand, we usually refer to an industry sales curve, such as will appear in a Nielsen chart of industry sales. But, in laying marketing plans, we have to go back of these demand curves to find the underlying forces to which we must adjust. We look for changing consumer characteristics, numbers, attitudes, and habits that are affecting demand; or we look for trends in competition and trends of forces generated in trade channels. We must keep digging from one series of phenomena to another to gain understanding of the forces to which we must adapt our marketing operations, if we are to be successful.

To make more explicit what we mean by trends, let me quote a few paragraphs out of my book, *The Economic Effects of Advertising.* When I tried in that study to measure the effects of advertising it became quite evident that I could not come up with very accurate answers because there are so many factors influencing the demand for a product. It became clear to me that anyone who wanted to evaluate advertising methods would have to study the forces generated in our society and become a student of social behavior. Indeed, every marketing man has to be a sociologist. Here are some of my conclusions on this subject:

> "An appraisal of the reasons for demand changes requires an understanding of human behavior and of the effect of sociological forces upon behavior. Consumption patterns flow out of people's ways of living and out of attitudes that are developed by the whole complex of forces that shape society and its mode of living. Advertising is but one force involved in molding consumption attitudes and in guiding consumer expenditure. Advertising enthusiasts would

be naive to claim too great credit for this force in shaping people's consumption habits. Successful users of advertising do not make this mistake, for they have learned that when they seek to mold people's viewpoints they must be careful to shape their own merchandising and promotional efforts to meet clearly defined consumer wants and preferences. . . .

"In any quantitative study of demand it is essential to have a clear understanding of consumer living habits and attitudes that relate to the consumption of the specific product. Any changes in the rate of consumption of the product must be interpreted in the light of possible operation of basic demand trends, which are attributable to changing living habits and attitudes. It is beyond the compass of this study to trace or appraise all the underlying causes for such demand trends. To attempt to do so in particular cases leads only to speculation, for these demand changes have their roots in the intricate play of forces that form the character of our free society, a mobile society little hampered by traditions of class or caste. The products whose trends of usage are investigated in themselves represent one force affecting society's form and people's behavior. For example, the growth in automobile usage helped bring improved roads, but improved roads in turn have been a factor in increasing automobile usage. What have been termed the 'causes' of changes in demand more properly in many cases should be looked upon merely as phenomena accompanying such product trends. The various changes are related, but it is impossible to disentangle cause and effect." *

TWO CASE STUDIES

So much for what we mean by trends. The important problem of the marketer is to keep his marketing mix adjusted to these changing forces bearing in upon him. Let me illustrate what I mean by drawing on two examples which appear in my casebook—cases from the flour and meat-packing industries. In these cases, gathered some years ago, executives of both industries were faced with the problem of a sharply declining trend in the consumption of their products.

* Neil H. Borden, *The Economic Effects of Advertising* (Chicago, Richard D Irwin, Inc., 1942), pp. 194–195.

Both groups had to consider whether or not they should add industry advertising to their marketing mix. In seeking an answer to this question they had to study the market forces bearing upon the demand for their products. In effect, they had to become students of sociological trends. Then they had to appraise the probable effect of alternative courses of action. In particular, in these instances they had the task of appraising the value of advertising to lick the downward trend.

They learned from the government's *1939 Yearbook of Agriculture* that there had been a marked change of diet in America during the last two generations. For many years there had been a practically continuous trend upward of some foods; a trend downward of others. Relative consumption of dairy products, sugar, and miscellaneous fruits and vegetables had greatly increased, while the proportion of meat and grain products consumed had gone down. These were the demand trends, but back of them were sociological trends accounting for changes in food consumption.

Men in the flour and meat industries were, of course, desirous of changing or counteracting consumer attitudes toward their products which had brought the decreased demand. A first step, therefore, was to find an explanation for the downward trends.

Analysis of the situation indicated that changes in food demand were closely connected with changes in consumer living habits. General economic statistics showed that a larger proportion of the population was at that time found in the older age groups, and the food requirements of older and less active people differed from those of younger men and women. The shift of population away from the farms and into the cities had altered the conditions of labor. More people were earning their living sitting at desks. Mechanization had reduced the exertion of those people still performing physical work. Labor hours had decreased with every passing decade. These changes helped explain the lessened demand for high-calorie energy foods, including meat and wheat products.

There were still other developments that were significant in the analysis of food demand curves. Better housing, a wider use of central heating, and a consequent smaller exposure to cold had probably affected the need for heat-producing foods. Results of research in the clothing industry may have had similar effects. The so-called authorities on diet had preached the virtues of vitamins and minerals. Food habits had probably been as subject to fashion influence as had consumer tastes in clothes and automobiles. And now doctors are telling us to "eat less and live longer"; medical experts as well as fashion leaders put a premium on the slimmer figure. It is interesting to note that today practically all soft-drink manufacturing concerns now emphasize the low-calorie content of their beverages—"Refresh Without Filling," for instance. Advertisers in the malt drink industry are likewise adapting their propaganda to an increasingly calorie-conscious population.

As for the problem faced by the meat and flour industries in the 1940's, another significant factor was that the availability of certain foods had undergone a distinct change over the years. Improvements in transportation and refrigeration had put fresh fruits and vegetables on many more tables than previously. Remarkable developments in canning and freezing processes had made such foods, once to be had only during short seasons, available throughout the year. And, of course, dietary experts had emphasized the importance of including fruits and vegetables on the daily menu.

Of special significance to management in the flour industry was the trend away from home baking. Women were no longer willing or able to spend as much time in the kitchen as they used to, and the "hot stove rebellion" was one reason why people were eating less bread, fewer doughnuts, and less pastry than formerly.

From what I have said, you can see that research indicates numerous social trends, many supportable by series of data, that explain the industry curves.

After the planning strategists had analyzed the basic social forces behind the decreasing demand for grain products and meat, they were in a position to try to better the situation. An issue faced was: Could they increase consumer demand for their particular products by advertising?

In the case of the flour manufacturers, it was unlikely, I think, that consumer-directed advertising could do very much in the way of stepping up consumption. People had become so worried about their health and had been made so aware of the undesirability of excess weight that many were avoiding fattening foods. Nowadays it seems that no woman, no matter how skinny she is, can eat a pecan roll without at least saying, "Well, I really shouldn't, but . . ."

Moreover, all of the forces operating against high-calorie foods, generated by the social changes occurring during the transition from a rural to an urban society and from a heavy-labor to a light-labor society, were still in operation, and advertising would not touch those forces. In short, advertising was not a promising tool to employ in light of the social trends operating against flour products.

The flour people and their counsel decided to undertake advertising in spite of these adverse conditions, but I think their decision was ill-advised.

More likely to check the downward trend of flour products were other marketing strategies which milling companies put into their marketing mix. These moves were better designed to deal with the forces that were operating against their industry.

One move was to find means of getting more appetizing baked foods on the table. One milling company gave the bakery industry the "brown-and-serve" roll. People reach for good hot rolls on the table although they will pass by less appetizing bread. Moreover, "brown-and-serve" rolls fit in with another trend, namely housewives' constant quest for ways to lighten their household tasks.

Then came the development of the new cake, cooky, waffle, and pie ready-mixes which are now having such an upward spurt in the market. They make baking infinitely easier and less time-consuming. Lots of the ready-mixes, moreover, produce better "home cooking" than many housewives can produce by their own mixing. The greater taste appeal that home cooking offers over store-bought food helps in the effort to stop the down trend in flour consumption.

The meat people had a different set of forces operating against them. People were not avoiding meat because they wanted to stay slim, for meat, unlike flour products, is not fattening. Analysis indicated that other social attitudes accounted for the decrease in meat consumption.

Marketing research indicated that a substantial group of people felt that meat was not healthful, that it might lead to rheumatism or other ills. Some thought it bad for children; others looked askance at it for the aged. The same studies indicated a widespread ignorance of the healthful properties of meat. Such attitudes probably were responsible for part of the sales decline of meat.

The most important source of trouble in the meat industry, however, seemed to be consumer income limitations—many people felt they simply could not afford to buy meat regularly. It is interesting to note that as incomes began to rise just prior to World War II, meat consumption also began to increase; many more people were earning enough to permit them to have meat at dinner.

When the meat-packing industry started to include advertising in its marketing mix of 1940, the prospects for increasing sales by this means looked good. The advertisers had to contradict the notion that meat was not healthful and prove, on the contrary, that the dietary merits of this particular food were great. They had to demonstrate that meat was the best available source of vital proteins, minerals, and vitamins, and that it should be served at least once a day on every family table.

Also, people could be encouraged to eat more meat if they could be taught how to prepare inexpensive cuts in an appetizing way. Therefore, much of the industry's promotion work took the form of culinary advice to housewives. Colored pictures of budget-wise meat casseroles were featured in the advertising sections of women's magazines, and low-cost recipes were printed on cellophane wrappers for the retail sale of meat.

Today the meat product sales curve is rising along with the upward trend in personal incomes. Industry advertising has probably spurred the increased consumption of meat; and since the cost of this advertising is not large when related to industry sales, we can assume that it has been a good addition to the industry's marketing mix.

I have included these examples of decision making in the flour and meat industries because they demonstrate the practical applications of the study of demand trends and of the social forces behind market behavior. Obviously, it would be impossible for me to go into great detail and try to explain all the forces applicable. Often it is hard to judge what social trends are applicable. Each individual case demands the use of the businessman's own intelligence and imagination. He must analyze his industry's market curves and try to see the forces lying behind them. In short, he should attempt to isolate the more important and significant social forces affecting him and assemble data that might help appraise their strength in his situation.

IMPORTANT CURRENT DEVELOPMENTS

I should like now to mention a few rather general developments or trends that will inevitably affect marketing strategy in the immediate future.

First of all, marketers are always dealing with people, and therefore they must keep a weather eye out for population trends. Forecasters continually have to change their market estimates and realign them with significant changes in the population. Changing age distribution, the movement toward the cities and away from farms, the size of families, and geographical distribution—all of these have important bearing on demand and must be followed.

Secondly, market strategists have to watch income statistics. Today the national income is rising, and wealth continues to be spread more widely throughout the population, as people have had more money to spend. What have they done with it? Where has their income gone—into houses, automobiles, appliances, clothing, food, or entertainment?

In this connection, businessmen might well peruse *Fortune* magazine's study, *The Changing American Market,* which is now available in book form. This is an interesting statement of the changes in various consumer markets due to changes in the national income and other social forces. As the study points out, there are today 60 million more Americans in the middle-income group. These people are fostering a lush new suburban market, an insatiable demand for housing, and fabulous sales opportunities for clothing and new gadgets of all kinds.

Another valuable book for those interested in sociological trends is the new and recent study of The Twentieth Century Fund on *America's Needs and Resources.*

Another area which business strategists ought to watch and think about concerns the whole question of leisure time. In less than a century we have moved from working 72 hours a week to about 40. What effect will such an increase in free time have on the demand for travel, for luxury goods, hobby equipment, and so on?

The changes which important innovations produce in the population are also of great significance in planning a marketing mix. Product innovations have a tremendous impact on the way people live and what they want most to buy. The automobile, for instance, has revolutionized people's lives during the past 30 years and has consequently influenced the demand for innumerable products. Or take television at the present; everyone is aware of the changes this invention has made in the way people spend their time. Atomic energy is another development that is going to cause vast upheavals and greatly affect the habits of the consuming public.

Now, let us look at a few of the specific trends in trade—in their methods of operation and attitudes. Here again it is useless to try to give a complete list since there are so many of these trade forces, but some key trends in the retail field are fairly easy to see. Take, for instance, the trend toward suburban shopping centers. This change calls for a continuing reassessment of the elements of the marketing mix, particularly as regards distribution channels employed. Or consider the trend to self-service: manufacturers, in formulating their promotional strategy and in planning point of purchase displays, must adjust to new trade methods and attitudes.

More recently, there is the advent of many new products and a resultant increasing trend in competition for shelf space in stores. This development has caused many important retailers to limit the brands they will stock. Here is a force arising from competition and, related to it, a trade attitude which are both of utmost importance in the manufacturer's operations.

At this point I am thinking especially of the grocery store. Producers are finding it increasingly difficult to keep their old products on grocers' shelves. Many companies have already felt the squeeze on their products, and others are going to feel it very soon. Let us take cereals as an example: if a new cereal comes in at the top, some other breakfast food will have to go out at the bottom because this is a bulky product which takes up a lot of space. Retailers are limiting the brands and sizes they will stock. The manufacturer whose brand standing puts him at the bottom of a retailer's list is in danger of being pushed out in the cold unless he can do something with his product to hold it on the shelf.

Supermarket managers especially, after studying their return on shelf space, are becoming increasingly aware of the need to select items carefully. One consequence is that it now costs manufacturers a great deal more than it used to, in advertising and other introductory efforts, to get new products onto the grocer's shelf. It is necessary to enter with heavy brand impact, particularly if the company is in a keenly competitive field.

Looking ahead, I think we can predict that the battle for shelf space will be intensified, since every year the large retailers are placing more emphasis on study of shelf return. At the same time, supermarkets are having more and more new products shoved at them. The economic implications of these trends are interesting, because they are bearing down harder on the small companies than on the big ones. The burden of carrying a new product onto the market and spending enough to keep it there until it is established tends to squeeze out the little fellow, although the large firms may not necessarily want it that way.

ADJUSTING TO THE TRENDS

What are some of the ways that market planners can adjust to this continual advent of new and differentiated products and this pressure for shelf space? What are some of the implications of this trend? First of all, there is the importance, even to small businesses, of continuous research to improve the quality of their products and to bring out items to meet and compete with others' new products. I find that too many companies have taken their research on a catch-as-catch-can basis in the past, turning out something that appeals to their newest vice president merely because it was a pretty successful product in his last company. Now these firms are setting up formalized groups to study products and product policy with an eye to assuring the company a more stable market.

Unfortunately, I find that even many companies with good management fail to keep a continuous check on their competitors' quality in order to avoid being caught short. Research should, of course, keep a firm step ahead of its competition, but there have been too many instances of well-established companies being overtaken for us to ignore the defensive purpose of such studies.

Other suggestions whereby small companies may meet the challenge coming from the onrush of new products have been offered from time to time, and I present them here not as a definitive list, but rather to stimulate the reader's imagination in relation to his own particular situation.

  1. Build up a small but strong regional position. With a good product and a lot of imagination and drive, a manufacturer can make a place for himself locally. One example is the firm in a hard-water area that developed a coffee which was especially suited for these hard-water conditions.

  2. Develop such an outstanding product, in a new and needed area, that no market can afford to ignore it. This, of course, takes a combination of ingenuity and good luck.

  3. Work out really skillful promotions. Big companies tend to become inept in their promotional programs, partly because they launch so many of them and also because they may become far removed from the needs and desires of the ordinary retailer and his customer.

  4. Devise effective methods to insure the retailer better service, fresher products, more flexible delivery schedules, and so on.

5. Concentrate on building brands and labels in soft spots, giving retailers promotional advantages on these. Develop specialty items which will attract the attention of enough consumers to give you a good business.

There is one final trend in trade I would like to touch on, because it is receiving so much publicity. That is the trend toward low-cost selling operations, particularly the operations of discount houses. The development has assumed such proportions that it is forcing manufacturers to make radical changes in the mix of their marketing elements: in pricing, channels, and the role of advertising and of personal selling.

We are still too close to this trend in low-cost selling in so-called discount houses to know just what the full implications are. But one thing is certain: it is not a brand-new phenomenon. In this free economy of ours, the one thing we can always count on is the perpetual attempt of man to make a profit. In so doing, he exercises all his powers of ingenuity, trying to find new ways of doing things. These discount house fellows are, for the most part, people who have just found a way to get merchandise into the hands of the consumer at a much lower cost than the traditional operator. They have found means of coming up with amazingly low costs of operation in competition with department stores and specialty stores with far higher costs. They have been able to sell large items with terribly impressive discounts, and most consumers are quite willing to go out of their way to save a dollar!

What has happened to make this possible? For one thing, so-called service retailing on many of these items has ceased to have much significance. The consumer often may not get any servicing from these discount stores, but he has discovered that he does not really need any service or guarantees from the retailer. If he buys something good, with a well-known brand on it, he can always go back to the manufacturer with his complaints. And he knows he can turn to a local repairman or rely on the manufacturer's service organization.

Another explanation is that the element of personal selling in the marketing mix has declined in importance on these items. Formerly, the mix called for a large degree of selling on these large ticket items by the manufacturer, the distributor, and the retailer. On new lines a great deal of personal canvassing was frequently put in the mix. But such heavy reliance on personal selling is no longer needed, for the products are wanted and brands are known. There has been a decided shift, with advertising taking much more of the burden relatively than it used to take in the old marketing mix. The discount houses have taken advantage of this change and are forcing a realignment of marketing plans and strategy.

I want to emphasize that this advent of low-cost retailing is not a new development. For instance, the same phenomenon occurred when the chain store appeared on the scene and forced manufacturers to abandon long-established and firmly fixed ideas about trade discounts. Manufacturers vowed that they would not sell to chains or, at least, would not sell at a discount—but they did. Manufacturers will just have to continue adjusting to these basic trends and changes as they come along.

The point I am trying to get across is this: We should all be students of social behavior and trade behavior and competition and keep alert to indicators of change. We must look for the emerging drifts and trends, such as may be discovered through our own observation and analysis and our reading. There have always been trends, and there always will be. The problem is to identify them, recognize their relative importance, and adjust our businesses accordingly.

LABOR RELATIONS, 1955: A YEAR OF INNOVATION

James J. Healy

TO LABEL 1955 "a year of innovation" in labor relations is to produce a masterpiece of understatement. The AFL–CIO merger and, particularly, the guaranteed annual wage (GAW) issue, aside from other developments in the field, present management with many new and pressing problems. In establishing new dimensions in long-range planning, they force us to re-examine some of our previous programs and practices.

The Ford Motor Company's settlement with the United Automobile Workers and the negotiations which led up to it seem to me to be almost an ideal example of the kind of planning which we need to be doing in labor relations today. These negotiations were, without question, the most sophisticated we have ever witnessed; they were extraordinary. Both parties had been thinking through all the problems relating to the proposals, not for a period of weeks or even

Note: Mr. Healy is Associate Professor of Industrial Relations, Harvard Business School.

months, but for years. Furthermore, when they reached the bargaining table, they did not meet in an atmosphere of animosity and hostility; they met, instead, with the joint desire to work out some type of amicable formula.

It is true, of course, that the fact that both parties were disinclined to engage in economic warfare had a great deal to do with that constructive attitude. Nevertheless, such a climate of reasonable harmony, constructive thinking, and intelligent exploration was significant.

Looking at the resulting bargain, the long-term planning which preceded it definitely paid off from Ford's standpoint. For the finally accepted settlement of the GAW issue is primarily a creation of the Ford Motor Company, not of the United Automobile Workers. The union proposal was set aside, for all practical purposes; and Ford, after making its preliminary stock purchase proposal, placed on the table what were to be essentially the final terms accepted. Further, from the standpoint of negotiations, it is important to note that there were only four substantive changes from the Ford proposal as it was first put forward.

But while the settlement is really an instrument of the company's creation, the principle is not. Ford resisted the principle and did its utmost to defeat it in these negotiations. But once the company recognized that the principle of some form of supplementary unemployment payments was going to prevail and had to be worked out, from there on in—unlike so much bargaining characteristic of large-scale enterprise—it was Ford that took the initiative, not the union. A major implication is that the final plan was not a zero-hour improvisation, born in tension. For these negotiations, unlike perhaps three-fifths of those which have occurred since the war, did not fall into the neat pattern of the ditty attributed, somewhat apocryphally, to Dryden:

> He leapt upon her
> And would have robbed her of her honor
> Which, thanks to her timely acquiescence,
> She prevented.

Judging by Mr. Breech's observations in Part I, Ford had this exact proposal or some variation of it in its back pocket before the negotiations even started. It is obvious, the more carefully we look at it, that a plan such as this just could not have been formed in a few months. As a matter of fact, it is very probable that, instead of wearing pants with the usual two back pockets, Ford was wearing a pair with seven or eight, and the company had something available in each one of those pockets. That is the way industry should negotiate. It is this ingenuity and the capacity for flexibility without sacrificing basic convictions which should always characterize the approach to collective bargaining.

MANAGEMENT'S PLANNING

To bear out my point, let us take a closer look at the Ford program, for its real ingenuity has not been sufficiently explained in the press. Basically it is one of the safest, one of the simplest, and, if I may say so, one of the most moderate plans which possibly could have been worked out consistent with the principle which the union sought to establish. I am referring, of course, to the current period and the first three years, not to the enlargements upon the plan which, inevitably, will take place at the next negotiations in 1958.

First of all, it is of some concern to us to know the exact amount of the basic wage increase. It comes to approximately seven cents. That amount was derived by taking the six-cent improvement factor which was agreed upon and which will go into effect now, plus the special allowance for skilled workers which the last time it was given averaged a little below one cent. So in the main it can be said that a seven-cent immediate wage increase was granted. One of the interesting features was the fact that the improvement factor, which formerly was a flat five cents, has now been changed to six cents or 2.5% per annum, whichever is the greater. Thus a pattern is established for all those companies which, up to now, have adopted the improvement factor principle.

Turning to the so-called GAW aspect of the program, I want first of all to emphasize that it should not be given the title of "guaranteed annual wage." It is *not* a guaranteed annual wage. It is properly and exactly what it is referred to in the agreement: a Supplemental Unemployment Benefit Plan. Secondly, it differs sharply from the program which had been originally promulgated and placed on the bargaining table by the union in one important feature. The Ford plan calls for benefits supplementing state unemployment compensation to be paid only for the same period as the state unemployment compensation benefits themselves are paid, that is, 26 weeks.

By such an arrangement—and this is most essential—Ford has relieved itself of all the administrative headaches which would arise if it tried to extend payment of benefits from a private fund beyond the limitation period prescribed by state law. To illustrate, if the benefit period were to be extended beyond the state's period of only 26 weeks up to 40 weeks, in line with the earlier union proposal, the company would then have had to face up, as partners, with the union to all the administrative problems which would arise in the period between the 26 weeks and the 40 weeks. As it is now, all such decisions are the state's and the state authorities'.

The key points in the program are:

1. The company contributes, effective June 1, 1955, five cents per hour for every employee's hour of work until the fund has reached $55 million.

2. Employees are going to get benefits out of that fund no earlier than June of 1956.

3. By adding benefits from the private fund to those of the public fund employees will get 65% of their after-tax wages in the first four weeks of unemployment. Following that period, benefits drop to 60% of after-tax wages.

4. The duration of benefits is coterminous with the state Unemployment Compensation Law.

5. The amount of private benefits can never exceed $25 per week.

A reasonable guess is that the average supplemental payment from private funds to employees under this plan will be no more than about $10–$12 per week—and even that may be an exaggeration. It may be closer to $8 a week. Based on average direct wages in the auto industry (obviously only direct wages are involved) of $2.10 per hour, weekly pay comes to $84 per week. Without making exact calculations, let us assume that after-tax wages are $75. If we apply 65% to that figure the allowable benefit will be around $48. Under the Michigan law an employee with a wife and one child would receive $42 from the state. Therefore, for the first four weeks, the private fund will pay some $6.75. After the fourth week, the figure will be $3.

One of the peculiar features of the news reports is that they always list a man's average earnings at $100 weekly. I suppose from the standpoint of a press release it is easier to compute on the basis of a nice round $100, but the average earnings of the Ford employee are not $100 per week except during periods of overtime activity. So the actual average per week benefit is more likely to be in the vicinity of $7 or $8.

The Ford program is not geared to dependents. Moreover, it overcomes one of the most serious disadvantages of our various state laws: the fact that the worker gets a flat amount no matter what his earnings. The private benefits are, of course, tied to prior earnings.

Finally, the private fund does not become operative until after the one-week waiting period, if such exists in the state. In this way, and all other ways except for the time element, it is administratively tied to the state regulations.

COSTS AND FINANCES

As for the fund itself, Ford has protected it most carefully. First of all, the fund is strictly administered by the company and by no one else. The agreement gives the company the exclusive right to designate where the money is to go, with the exception of the special provision applying to certain U. S. Government securities. Also, the company chooses the trustees, and the union plays no part in that choice.

In addition, employees receive only a quarter of a credit unit for each 32-hour workweek between June 1955 and June 1957. This was one of the major points bargained out. The company's plan, when first laid on the table, provided for a 39-hour base week. Walter Reuther plugged for 28 hours. A 32-hour week was the final compromise. Thus for this short workweek a man will receive a fourth of a credit until June 1957; after that date, the weekly credit will be increased to a half unit.

Now, not one penny can be paid out of this private fund during the first year—until June 1956—so the fund is being currently built. And, of course, even by June 1956 the plan will not have become fully operative. Here is the way things will be handled in the interim:

> An employee who worked all 52 weeks of the year beginning June 1, 1955, would accumulate 13 credits during that time. In other words, if he were suddenly laid off as of June 1956, he would be entitled to only 13 weeks of benefit. He could not possibly have accumulated the maximum 26-week benefit during this first year.
>
> If his employment continues through 1956–1957, his rate of credit accumulation still is a quarter unit weekly because the half-unit credits do not begin until June 1957. This means no worker can possibly get up to the full 26 weeks of benefit until June 1957, when those now employed have accumulated two full years under the program.
>
> Let's carry this a step further. Suppose a man is laid off when the fund is only 40% to 48% of the maximum amount initially determined by the plan—$55 million. Suppose he has less than five years of service. For every week he collects a benefit, that man will be charged two credits or what would take him eight weeks to accumulate during these first two years.

Other interesting arrangements have been incorporated into the fund plan. To guarantee that extensive unemployment would not leave senior employees—who would be the last to be laid off—without any benefits because of the depletion of the fund, junior men are charged more and more as the fund position drops. Thus, during a period of serious unemployment, a junior worker's supplementary benefits may be cut off at the end of 10 or 8 weeks instead of being continued to the full 26-week period. But no such larger offset or charge is made against 20-year or 25-year men's credits. Their charge, normally, would be one for one until the fund gets down as low as 39% to 30%. And, finally, if the fund should drop to less than 4% of the maximum amount, no benefits would be paid.

Now, what about the cost of all this to Ford? To make a rough calculation, 140,000 employees working 2,000 hours per year (with overtime) at 5 cents per hour comes to $14 million. That is Ford's annual contribution to the fund until it reaches $55 million with the aid of accumulated interest—somewhere short of four years. (This cost does not include the 7-cent increase that we discussed earlier, or any of the other benefits besides the SUB.)

Once the fund reaches $55 million, the company's 5-cent per hour obligation ends. From that point on it must only replenish the fund to maintain it in full force. Even at 10% unemployment, which would really be severe, an average pay-out of $10 per week for 26 weeks would represent a cost no greater than 1% of total payroll. In other words, from a practical standpoint, once the fund is built, the drain on it will be only a fractional portion of the total, and the cost to Ford will correspondingly be reduced.

The question arises, of course, as to what share the company pays through taxation to support the state fund. It is very difficult to determine this figure, and we have no idea at all of the additional cost to Ford of an increase in benefits from the state. But we can assume that the cost is likely to be fairly minor, largely because the reserves of the state fund are already in good shape, and also because of the merit-type program which favors a company with stable operations. A company like Chrysler or American Motors might be very badly hit, but Ford is in a safer position.

FUTURE TRENDS

We cannot really predict labor relations trends. Recall the story of two caterpillars who were crawling along munching on a blade of grass, and having an interesting time chatting together. One of the caterpillars happened to look up and saw a butterfly flying overhead. Turning to his friend, he said, "They'll never get me up in one of those things!"

Some very extreme predictions, which would appear to be outrageous at the moment in this supplementary payments field, come to mind. And yet I think of where we began on pensions, and where we are today, particularly with the Ford plan.

For the pension provisions in the Ford settlement are the real fly in industry's ointment, not the Supplemental Unemployment Benefits scheme. I do not believe that the pattern consequences of the latter are going to mean much in the foreseeable future, but the new pension arrangement will have an effect right away.

Under this agreement, Ford has increased its pension benefits by approximately one-third. When you are dealing with pensions, of course, your cost of benefits and improvements is closely correlated with the cost of the payments, so that to get a one-third increase in benefits you can just about count on a one-third increase in costs.

Not only have payments been boosted, but there has been a breakthrough on pension principle as well. In previous programs, a worker stopped accumulating credits for the purposes of higher benefits after 30 years of service; under the new Ford plan, he continues to accumulate in relation to the years he has worked. In other words, his benefits continue to grow, proportionately, beyond 30 years of employment with the company, rather than reaching a plateau at that point. An even more startling pension change was the application of improved benefits to those already retired. In effect, this retroactive feature tended to make the union the bargaining agent for retired employees as well.

One of the first general effects of the Ford SUB settlement will be that the point of political pressure will change during the next three years. Initial attention is going to be given to the state legislatures and to Congress, and we are going to see the companies hammering away at an increase in the benefits while the unions hammer away at extending the length of time of the benefits. The companies will want to increase government benefits because that is where they are hit in terms of the cost of the fund. The unions want to get beyond the

26 weeks so they can say to the employers: "O.K., it's now going to be increased from 26 to 40. Now with a new contract we'll increase the SUB to 40 too." What was done with old age security will be done here.

The interesting thing is that from now on in, for both large and small enterprises, we will see unions acting in concert with management to seek improvement of the unemployment compensation laws —and this is a good thing; they should be improved.

It is true, of course, that industry has not taken this position in the past, any more than it did with old age security until the unions came along and hit management between the eyes. But management must not behave in a reactionary, "nothing new is good" manner this time. It must assume the responsibility of going to the legislatures and getting improvement, because individual companies should not be burdened with what ought to be a social cost.

Another probable trend for the future is that the unions in the next few years will try for a shorter workweek. In effect, management bought out the unions on this issue by offering substantially increased benefits. Having now got these benefits, the unions may shift their efforts back to their desire for shorter hours, or they may keep the idea of a 30-hour or 32-hour week open for bargaining for a while in order to use that to secure more fringe benefits.

In any event we ought at least to envisage the possibility of a 32-hour workweek when planning for the future. Whether such a shorter week is a good thing is another question. Certainly the reduction to 40 hours did not bring the dire consequences that many predicted.

This 32 hours would be paid for at the going rate, remember. You cannot reduce take-home pay. How, then, can the company recover the increased costs of production? Sometimes selling prices can be raised. Or perhaps the way out is through automation and the acceleration of technological improvements—what we have been hearing so much about. This latter possibility—exaggerated though it may be for the immediate future—illustrates one of the most interesting and, on the whole, most desirable phenomena of American industry.

This kind of bargaining sets in motion peculiar, vicious circles (but not vicious in the moral sense) which out of necessity force you to get up in that airplane you thought you never would get into. To cover the increased costs of a packaged deal like this one, which probably amounts in total to 20 cents per hour, you have to make more. So you go to automation if you can (and Ford can, because it operates on a two-production-line basis, which makes automation feasible, whereas American Motors and Studebaker-Packard can adjust less readily because they do not have a two-production-line operation). So you cut costs, and the American public gets the same product at roughly the same price (or a little more because of the built-in inflation), and the workers work less hard or under better conditions.

And then, because there is in our society the countervailing power of the unions, pressures arise for some new benefits for the worker. So you are saddled with another cost package, and you work that much harder to improve efficiency and get your costs down so you can handle the new package. And as fast as you do that, something else is going to come up. We must expect that, however difficult it may seem in each instance, and on the whole it is gratifying that the process never stops.

All in all, this Ford settlement is a very, very progressive document, and in more ways than one. I think it can be said that, while it favors the unions, giving them a victory on principle—in addition to very substantial immediate gains in terms of pensions—and a more realistic approach to the improvement factor, each one of us should also regard this document as somewhat of a victory for the Ford Motor Company and for American industry generally. I know the costs involved, and I appreciate the seriousness of the cost factor. But if we are going to have this type of principle adopted, I can think of no better way than in this form.

Part Three

NEW VIEWPOINTS AFFECTING STRATEGY

OPERATIONS RESEARCH & SYNTHESIS IN MODERN BUSINESS

Melvin L. Hurni

IF ALL OF US were convinced that economic activities are a strictly rational phenomenon, there would be little need for a discussion of Operations Research & Synthesis. We would be utilizing it to its fullest extent now, much as we utilize engineering, for example, without particular argument as to what it is, whether we should employ it, or how it should be integrated into a business.

Even though most of us, as business executives, would be identified as men of action rather than philosophers, and hence not given to objective and critical examination of the social scene, we recognize, instinctively perhaps, that business is not wholly rational.

Most of us would subscribe to the view that business contains at

Note: Mr. Hurni is Senior Consultant, Operations Research & Synthesis Consulting Service, Management Consultation Services, General Electric Company. Robert O. Schlaifer, Associate Professor of Business Administration, Harvard Business School, acted as moderator of the session on which this chapter is based.

least an element of the fleeting, the uncertain, the not easily or completely defined, and that it requires the intuitive judgment, if not an almost artistic sense, of men with particular endowments. These endowments make it possible for them to sense opportunity, even when it may not be fully understood, and give them the courage to proceed even without complete understanding.

It is with this view of business activity that we consider Operations Research & Synthesis—a rational process presuming that research may be done on a business and its environment, and that hypotheses or models for action may be synthesized and pretested for their effectiveness as an aid to decision making.

The most thoughtful writers on the subject admit that it has its origins in the scientific method of inquiry, which presumes a basic and, in some fashion, determinable orderliness in the phenomena under study, an orderliness not readily apparent to businessmen as far as business is concerned.

Most examples of Operations Research work published so far are mathematical in content and hence highly logical. Moreover, these examples take a mechanistic approach. Certain relationships are maximized, minimized, or balanced as though they were absolute and immutable, and decisions are made on highly abstract planes.

Unfortunately there is no description of the relationship of this type of research to a business operating in various free markets where there is no single body of integrated knowledge or connected reasoning with respect to the whole market and how it functions. This, I believe, explains the doubts experienced by even the most thoughtful business executive when he considers the published case histories of Operations Research & Synthesis work and ponders its validity for use in his own business.

DEVELOPMENTS MAKING IT POSSIBLE

However, the skeptical executive overlooks three important developments that have made possible Operations Research & Synthesis. These developments have emerged from the study of business as a phenomenon rather than out of the practice of business. They are not new, but influenced and aided the work of Frederick W. Taylor, even though he did not specifically refer to them. They are inferred in the monumental writings of Harry Arthur Hopf. They received expanding if perhaps accidental recognition and use during the recent war years.

There is sufficient evidence of their reality to make the business executive ponder if they do not represent a new opportunity to find out more about what goes on in his business and why, thus strengthening and reinforcing his decision making.

These developments are as follows:

1. People are realizing that business management is not just feel, intuition, or experience resulting in inspired decisions which even the executive himself cannot explain. Rather, to a very significant extent, it is the result of rational action. Even though the business executive may view a market as uncertain or unreliable or not completely comprehensible, once he decides to take action he proceeds on a rational basis.

This means that the manager focuses on specific objectives, be they the reducing of price levels, the changing of production schedules, or the expansion of facilities. He bases his thinking on assumptions regarding the environment and the resources available. He appraises risks and weighs them against attainable benefits. He attempts to identify alternative courses of action and selects the one that seems to offer the most favorable balance among effort, risk, and likely result. He has expectations regarding the outcome of the course of action chosen, thus establishing a basis for measuring results and for revising and changing his decision if circumstances change or if the results prove the decision inappropriate.

A manager may now have to "guess" or "play hunches" with respect to every one of these elements. In fact, there may always be a degree of uncertainty or irreducible ignorance in making decisions. However, if he does reason rationally and is not acting on mere inspiration, it should be feasible to make these notions of the nature of the business, the market, the resources, and the effect of action more precise through systematic study. Continuing research should uncover important details about each of the elements in decision making.

2. Systematic study of these elements in a number of business situations has already brought to light a basic and significant orderliness in an expanding range of business phenomena. In other words, business and economic life is not entirely haphazard. It must be admitted that we are not dealing with immutable patterns of order similar to those of the physical world, but rather with dynamic and shifting patterns. However, these patterns do have a reasonable life span, and hence may be utilized for the attainment of economic or social purposes.

While the idea of rational action may come easily to the experienced business executive, the notion of an orderly and rather reliable pattern for business phenomena may be more difficult to accept. Yet we admit of this orderliness, even though we do not overtly recognize it, when we build a new plant and expect that basic conditions will remain sufficiently unchanged to permit payoff in from 5 to 20 years. We redesign our products and retool with the same type of expectancy. We count on an essential order of long enough duration to assure payoff. When a manager goes into automation, he is expecting the ultimate in a durable pattern of business life.

Similarly, we promote people on the basis of their past experience and performance. This presumes that what has happened in the past has significant validity for the future. We instinctively recognize these patterns of order without being too aware of them. What is important is that we not only develop such an awareness but also define these patterns, both in terms of their actual content and in respect to their tendencies to vary and shift. With such knowledge, we can decide and plan with greater assurance for both present and future.

The discovery of patterns and relationships already covers a great range of situations for particular businesses. An examination of the literature will disclose investigation of such things as the relation of cost and volume, volume and price, machine failure and volume, profitability and product mix, to mention a few. Here again the objective of the research is a crisp, understandable, communicable description, not just a feel or sense for the situation resting on the judgment of a single individual. One can see a close kinship between these relationships and the characteristics and properties of materials and mechanisms which are familiar to the physical scientist and engineer.

3. There is a growing recognition of the applicability of investigation methods from the physical sciences, mathematics, and logic. Business phenomena and managerial problems can be defined and described in simple and often in quantitative form. This in turn makes possible systematic analyses of situations, intelligent anticipation of consequences through the synthesis of hypotheses or models of situations, and a high degree of measurability and communicability also.

These three developments must be grasped by business executives who wish to understand or apply Operations Research & Synthesis, for this research is founded on them and is informed by them. It is not a fire-fighting procedure, a means for solving spot problems, or a collection of canned methods. In its processes, methods, and outlook, it is in an important sense analogous to physical research as conducted in industrial laboratories.

WHAT TO EXPECT FROM IT

The major aim of Operations Research & Synthesis is to disclose and at the same time to strengthen the rational system underlying the business enterprise. It does this principally through discovering, wherever possible, facts, actual relationships, and characteristics to replace opinion, vague generalities, or lore. It does this further by developing hypotheses, models, or analogies that describe how parts of the business fit together and how the whole business works. It thus provides a basis for the prediction of performance or consequences, at least within the range of expected conditions. It provides means for developing better understanding of the system in operation and foreseeing and pretesting possible improvements.

To many experienced business executives, this latter aim is by no means new. Because in most businesses the facilities are operated by organizations of people, there must be a measure of clarity in procedure if the enterprise is to have any sense of unity and coherence of purpose. The familiar and currently popular work on organization structuring, position design and description, reservation, and the delegation of authority and responsibility for policy making are a part of this aim. In fact, I have heard the comment that this is really just an old lady fitted out in a new dress. In that this is the scientific method applied to business, I suppose the statement is a fair one.

What is unique about Operations Research & Synthesis is its purposeful and directed application of the scientific approach, which allows greater precision and detail in description, the possibility of testing over ranges of circumstances, and predictability of performance, measurement, and communication.

We might then expect from Operations Research & Synthesis work four specific things:

> 1. Increasingly precise knowledge of how things behave under a range of stated conditions.
> 2. Tested ideas as to why they behave in this manner, and ideas as to how this behavior may be utilized to meet specific objectives.
> 3. Valid suggestions for changing this behavior, consistent with specific business objectives.
> 4. Increasing insight into the nature of the business and its characteristics.

One example of the fourth expectation comes from a major railroad which began its work in Operations Research & Synthesis with the study of individual problems:

> It studied paper work procedures, such as freight billing, with an eye to cutting costs. It studied operating problems, such as freight car allocation, to relieve bottlenecks. It examined individual capital investment decisions, such as the capacity of a new switching yard. In all these problems, Operations Research & Synthesis provided information that enabled the managers to make better decisions or to make vital improvements in their mode of operations.

> But at the same time, these particular studies and others like them led to a general insight regarding the nature of the business and the kinds of major changes required to relieve such symptomatic and

continuing problems as the aforementioned high costs and bottle-necks. It led to a *hypothesis of the business;* namely, to the hypothesis that a railroad is a whole economic process rather than, as had always been assumed, a series of individual job-shop operations. The hypothesis implied that the basic economic problems of a railroad are the rate at which it utilizes its capital equipment and the "yield mix" between different kinds of "products" put through the total system.

This insight in turn led to important improvements and to significantly better decisions. But at the same time, it also indicated the need for further research in specific functional areas. One of these areas was that of organization, particularly the question of whether the traditional "building blocks" of railroad organizational structure were really adequate. Another study area was the proper classification of the railroad's business as to economic characteristics and profitability, aimed at the development of a purposeful marketing plan based on an optimal "product mix."

Another area of study uncovered was the design, capacity, and location of equipment in light of this new-found knowledge. While each of these studies is a long-term project in itself, already further insights into the basic hypothesis of the business have been developed, and managerial decisions in all areas and on all levels have been sharpened.

Let me cite an illustration from our experience at General Electric:

Just after the war one of our departments was having a great deal of difficulty recapturing its flexibility. It seemed that we would not be able to beat competition unless we took terrific inventories. Consequently, we tried various systematic solutions, but nothing happened.

Now this was a multiple product business with some 10,000 active items. As we got into the problem, it became apparent that there were certain key models, forming the hard core of the business, which moved with a fair degree of constancy. We tried to develop a relationship between these and all the other products. Ultimately the simple conclusion became apparent that we actually had a parts business, and then an assembly business, with the two related only by the fact that the parts were used to make a variety of assemblies. This new insight finally changed the entire strategy of that particular business.

We thus find Operations Research & Synthesis work performing three major functions:

First, it transforms lore about business into concrete knowledge. For example, incoming orders for certain types of businesses are described not as distinct and separate events, but as a continuing activity in time which has a typical rate and an expected range of variation about this rate.

Second, it replaces feel or intuition about what goes on within the business, its markets, and its environment by tested or testable knowledge. The establishment of the relationship between all parts and subassemblies to all finished models of a product is an instance.

Third, it provides insights that help the manager to develop a rational and systematic hypothesis regarding his entire business. This enables him to integrate individual functions and specialized operations with the whole business and the business with the whole economic process of which it is a part.

WHY IT IS NECESSARY

As practical business executives, I know the question must be in readers' minds, "Why do I need all that?"

Perhaps many of you do not. This is a decision you must make for yourselves. However, I do wish to call to your attention certain situations that you might well ponder before you come to a conclusion.

By way of introducing these situations, I would like to recall a bit of history that is probably not unfamiliar to you. Approximately 70 years ago, Frederick W. Taylor ushered in the era of modern management simply by refusing to take "Work" for granted, to accept it as so many others did as a matter of either talent or of time exposure, and a thing which everybody knew all about. Work had been performed for ages. Yet until Taylor, no one had bothered to look at it systematically. The results of the seemingly simple and so obvious question, "Precisely how do people work?" are familiar to all of us.

Today we are still finding new answers, and we still have utilized only a small part of the answers we have found. With Operations Research & Synthesis, we start out in the same way with another simple question: "Precisely what is the nature of a business?"

We begin with this question at a time when business executives are experiencing the effects of phenomenal business growth. They are facing important technological developments such as automation that have had and will increasingly have great impact upon our traditional notions of engineering, manufacturing, marketing, and even accounting. Businessmen are operating out of more mature markets and under pressure of the increasing demands of our society.

We start out in the face of a growing realization of the inflexibility of the modern production system and the resultant increase in business risks.

We ask this question with an awareness of the smaller effect of variable cost control as a managerial tool, both because of its increasing social unacceptability and because modern production systems reduce its significance so markedly.

It will not be possible to discuss each of these factors. I would like, however, to highlight a few of them to bring your own problems and experience into focus.

Growth, for example, raises many questions that are well known to you. It has resulted in the decentralization of numerous large companies into components that may be larger and more determinate in character than many separate corporate entities. This type of business is presented with several new problems for which there are no traditional solutions. For example:

a. How do we get corporate information to the general manager and the functional managers of such a decentralized component? Likewise, how do we get information from such a component to the corporate officer without, in the process, lessening the effectiveness of decentralization?

b. How can the headquarters or executive office in such a corporation provide the plus value that corporate size and strength should give to customers, to our economy, and to our country? What must such an office provide so as not to be just an overlay and check upon the type of managing required at the component level?

How do we go about solving problems of this type when there is no storehouse of tradition, no long experience on which to draw? In these instances we are literally forced to synthesize knowledge based on our understanding of that simple question, "What is the nature of the business?" How well we synthesize depends in turn on how complete and penetrating our understanding of the answer to this question is, and how well we use the logical and rational tools available to us to build an operational system and to test it. This is a problem of growth that may even now face many of you.

A more general result of growth is the increasing complexity of business information and business organization. Every day the executive finds the areas of basic importance more difficult to discern. The raw information required to deal with such areas is voluminous, complex, and diversified in nature to the point where it defies the capabilities of the unaided mind. At the same time, decisions come to have greater impact than before.

How shall we discover the simple facts and principles that underlie this mass of detail so that correct decisions can again be made with assurance?

These new problems will not be solved quickly or easily, to be sure. However, there are two kinds of solutions available. *One* is to play our hunches, to experiment at a cost which no one can determine. The *other* is to recognize that we can find patterns of orderliness, that we can study and determine the nature of a business, and that we can use the tools and approaches available to build solutions logically and rationally.

Modern production systems are another example of an area in which we have no tradition to fall back on. As we all know, one never gets anything for nothing. We purchase the advantages of these systems by accepting the restraints and inflexibilities they impose and the risks that result, except in the simplest businesses. These inflexibilities and rigidities make themselves felt not so much in the production system itself, which is apt to be tied together in some form of mechanical sequence, but in marketing, in engineering, and in risk assumed.

Each of these new production systems is built logically and rigorously around the expectation of an average situation in respect to volume and product mix, and is usually designed for a fixed and predetermined range of products. It is also usually based upon the notion that product design will not change markedly during the period of payoff.

In making a decision to attain the advantages of such a system, the business executive is confronted with a variety of serious questions, including the following:

1. Will the range of products remain adequate over the life span of the system?

2. Can volume be expected to remain within a sufficiently narrow band during the period to make the system profitable?

3. Will product demands remain sufficiently constant to maintain the limited range of product mix combinations that this system will take?

All of these and others are but subquestions to the more fundamental one—is the business suited to a modern production system, and at what probable risk will the system be adopted? And behind this question lies another, of course, "Can I discover before my competitors that my business is so suited, or can I discover before my competitors what I need to do to make my business so suited?" These are questions that demand more precise answers than we can give by relying on our usual tradition and our typical experience. These problems must be tackled with an uncommon amount of rationality, and the decisions cannot be based on sketchy information or mere preference.

This perhaps can be illustrated by a simple example. In a modern production system, it is not unusual, in order to attain certain economies, to install a battery of single-purpose machines designed to perform certain operations for a specific design of product. In a more traditional shop, however, this work would more likely be done on multipurpose machines equally applicable to other types of operations should it become necessary to change product designs. The element of risk is less in the traditional system, since the opportunity for flexibility is greater. The impact of managerial decision is also less for the same reason.

How can we employ the modern systems with any degree of assurance unless we discover the basic patterns of business phenomena, form some concrete notions of their life span, and get some measure of their rate of change?

There is still one more reason why the business executive today needs Operations Research & Synthesis. This need stems from the increasing demands and expectations of society. The negotiations we have witnessed between the automotive industry and the union should be ample evidence. It is not appropriate to examine this issue here, but I wish to point to it objectively as one example of the growth of social expectations and demands. It is possible that such benefits may reduce the resilience of an enterprise. They will narrow its permissible margin for error in risk taking, if nothing else. Demands from our society of this sort require the business executive to make even sharper and crisper decisions. The question I leave with you is "How?" unless we come to know more about the fundamental nature of our business.

ORGANIZATION FOR IT

It seems appropriate to make some comments on how the business executive should organize to do Operations Research & Synthesis work, if and when he sees and understands the need for it in his own business.

It is not my intention to present a canned organizational pattern but rather to state some of the general criteria for successful application of the work:

1. The objectives of Operations Research & Synthesis are the disclosure of knowledge about the business for the benefit of those concerned with operations.

2. It is a type of work which requires time to reflect, to test, to re-evaluate away from the pressure of day-by-day operations. Operations Research & Synthesis demands, then, a specific attitude: the scientific, objective, research attitude.

3. Operations Research & Synthesis is a continuous activity. The work cannot be done on a sporadic "study and learn" or "task force" basis. There are three reasons for this:

   a. Insights gained in one study furnish the foundation for the next. They might become lost without a permanent organization component and men to carry on the work.

   b. Economic life is not static. Much of its characteristic change is a slow drift, or creep, imperceptible at the beginning, gradually gathering cumulative significance. This means there needs to be a continuing organization capable of feeding back results of one study into the conclusions reached in an earlier study and of projecting them forward to the assumptions of the next.

   c. The results of any work must become a part of the intellectual and emotional character of operations people. The conclusions must be interpreted, and translated into practical understanding and use by operators. Neatly bound reports are not enough. It takes time and constant effort to translate nicely phrased principles into applicable guides for day-to-day operating activities. Truly, I think we do not yet understand that O.R.&S. is not a system working in a vacuum, but one that must be closely related to the managers involved.

4. Operations Research & Synthesis workers need to be able to see and identify the over-all problems of the whole business. Hence a cross-functional view is required, since the important problem of balancing functions and identifying the common relationships among functions is becoming increasingly difficult. Thus, Operations Research & Synthesis itself represents a primary functional field of work at the over-all level of the "business"—whether a decentralized business component or a separate corporate identity—rather than an activity to be located within one of the other functional areas or components.

5. Operations Research & Synthesis workers will be available to devote time and attention to the study of situations within a function

and to individual operating problems when requested by the functional managers concerned. Indeed, such functional situations may quite frequently be the starting point of work. But real results will not be obtained if Operations Research & Synthesis is confined to such operational studies, nor is understanding of these narrower situations usually the greatest need of managers.

The study of such individual situations should bring out plainly their impact on other areas of the business. Indeed, the results need to be projected beyond the localized problem and on to the entire business. Operations Research & Synthesis work, therefore—when required in a particular business—needs to be organized to engender the understanding, teamwork, and confidence of the managers and staffs in the other functional areas, and to avoid any suggestions of functional partisanship, except that partisanship—or more properly, partnership—which is directed toward the common interest of the business as a whole.

6. Operations Research & Synthesis workers have a unique relationship to the business and to its functions. They do not manage. They do not make decisions. They do not control. They are producers, and they supply a finished product to managers and men in all other functions of all levels—a body of organized knowledge and information which *all* these others need in making their own decisions in their respective jobs.

Organizational arrangements need always to be made in light of these fundamental criteria.

CONCLUSION

In summary, Operations Research & Synthesis work is addressed to that constantly recurring question—"What is the nature of a business?"

It is founded on three insights: *first,* that managers do manage rationally; *second,* that a significant orderliness can be found by systematic study of business phenomena; and *third,* that methods of inquiry from other areas of human endeavor such as the sciences are applicable and useful in transforming unsubstantiated beliefs about business operations into understandable, teachable, and usable knowledge.

Operations Research & Synthesis is concerned with providing more and better information and knowledge, which will permit executives to manage increasingly from and by consciously selected objectives with a growing understanding of the alternatives available in making decisions to meet such objectives and of the risks involved in doing so.

CONDITIONS THAT SHAPE CORPORATE GROWTH

John G. McLean and Robert W. Haigh

THERE ARE SEVERAL WAYS in which corporations commonly grow. First of all, there is of course simple expansion of sales volume. Secondly, growth can be achieved by horizontal integration, either in sales (such as the merger of the Hilton Hotel chain with the Statler Hotels) or in manufacturing (as demonstrated by some of the recent automobile mergers).

Another possibility is vertical integration, which can go in either of two directions: backwards toward raw materials or component parts as in the case of Chrysler's acquisition in 1953 of the auto equipment business of the Briggs Manufacturing Company, or forward toward market outlets as in the case of the Sunray Oil Corporation and the Mid-Continent Petroleum Company merger (in which Sun-

Note: Mr. McLean, who makes the introductory observations, is Professor of Business Administration, Harvard Business School; Mr. Haigh is Assistant Professor of Business Administration, Harvard Business School.

ray, largely a producer of crude oil, acquired Mid-Continent's refining facilities and wholesale and retail outlets). Finally, a common form of corporate growth is product diversification, which is well illustrated by the merger of the Borg-Warner Corporation, an automotive parts manufacturer, with the Byron Jackson Tool Company, an oil field supplier and electronics manufacturer.

As a corporation faces these various possible methods of expansion, a host of decisions to be made by management immediately arise. For example:

Which of these many avenues of corporate growth should we pursue?

If we are going to embark on one of them, how far shall we pursue it?

If we are going to integrate backwards, do we go merely to the component parts or behind the component parts to the raw materials that are used in making them?

What balance shall we establish? If we are going to make steel, shall we meet all of our requirements or only part of them?

What should be the timing of our expansion moves?

How should we accomplish them? By merger? By building our own facilities? By acquiring the assets of other companies?

How should we go about financing the successive steps in the process?

How should we go about providing adequate manpower to handle the enlarged organization?

And these are only a few of the many questions which must be answered.

The decisions that are made on these problems of growth and expansion are important for a number of reasons. Let us begin with a very simple, fundamental idea. We live in a nation with a rapidly expanding population, one growing at a rate that continually outstrips our best statistical forecasts. Therefore, if we are to maintain our standard of living merely at its current level, we must continually expand our industrial plants and our output of goods and services.

But, from an economic standpoint, our national requirements for industrial growth and expansion go somewhat beyond that point. Despite a high average standard of living, there still are people in this country who are unable to obtain the necessities of life. If we are to provide *all* of our population with a reasonably satisfactory standard of living over the long run, we must expand our output of goods and services at a rate which will do more than keep pace with the growth of population. In other words, we must insure a steady increase in our national productivity per capita. And to secure that increase is a very real obligation and responsibility of professional management. It is one way in which industrial managers can make an enduring contribution to our modern society.

Furthermore, if our programs of growth and expansion are not properly motivated and soundly conceived, we are fairly likely to have legislation enacted which may restrain the initiative for industrial growth and expansion and encumber the processes by which it is accomplished. We are all familiar with the recent investigations of the Federal Trade Commission, the Antitrust Division of the Department of Justice, and the Senate and House Judiciary Committees into mergers and consolidations. These have been thoroughly reported in the press. The implications of such studies, and of the attendant publicity, can be drawn fairly easily.

Looked at from another point of view, the decisions on these matters of expansion are important because they provide one significant means by which management may discharge its responsibilities to stockholders, to employees, and indeed, to management itself. Through such growth, management provides its stockholders with a chance to share in the nation's steadily rising standard of living. It likewise protects its stockholders from the hazards of long-run inflation. For employees, a soundly conceived program of growth and expansion means continual opportunities for professional advancement, for promotions and higher salaries. Finally, a well-directed expansion program provides an outlet for the creative instinct which is a native trait in all mankind.

With these thoughts in mind, let us go on to consider some of the determinants of a *sound, long-range* program of growth and development.

DETERMINANTS OF GROWTH *

Using the oil industry as a case example, let me begin by discussing some of the things Professor McLean and I found important in influencing corporate growth in that industry.† Our primary purpose was to find why it is that large, vertically integrated companies occupy such a prominent position in the oil industry, whereas in some other industries the majority of the business has remained in the hands of companies that are small and nonintegrated.

We found, essentially, that business growth in the oil industry results from a vast mixture of different types of economic, business, and personal considerations such as:

1. Company policies with respect to growth
2. The economic climate in the oil industry
   a. Behavior of profit opportunities
   b. Character of physical facilities
   c. Expanding markets and capital availability
3. Personal considerations
   a. Influence of personalities
   b. Reflection of business interests
   c. Nonbusiness problems—family, health, and tax
   d. Managerial competence
4. Investment and profit considerations
   a. Analysis of capital equipment proposals
   b. Capital budgeting
5. Competitive pressures
   a. Defensive
   b. Offensive

* By Mr. Haigh.
† The results of Mr. McLean's and Mr. Haigh's three-year study of the determinants of growth and expansion in the oil industry have been published as *The Growth of Integrated Oil Companies* (Boston, Division of Research, Harvard Business School, 1954).

6. Changes in economic, legal, and political conditions
   a. Temporary shortages or surpluses
   b. Tax laws—income, inheritance, and chain store
   c. Prorationing laws
   d. ICC regulations

Most of the companies we studied had certain general policies with respect to growth. These policies might have been along the lines of maintaining a rate of growth consistent with that of the industry as a whole, or perhaps obtaining and holding a certain portion of the industry's market. Moreover, most of these vertically integrated companies had certain policies with regard to the balance of operations that they believe should be maintained among the primary activities in which they were engaged. There might be, for example, some general policy as to the amount of crude oil that they should refine. Within the framework of these general policies, these companies worked out their growth programs in response to various other factors.

We found that the economic climate in the oil industry generally was especially favorable to growth through vertical integration. One of the forces that influenced such growth was the behavior of the profit opportunities at the various levels of the oil industry. The gross margins and the profits that are available are constantly changing. Moreover, fluctuations in profits at one level of the industry do not correspond with the movements at another. The refining margin may be going down, for example, while the wholesaling margin may be holding steady or moving up. The companies found, therefore, that they could do much to stabilize their earnings ability by spanning two or three levels in the industry.

This was particularly important from the standpoint of the refiners, who found they could offset the violent fluctuations in their profit position by integrating either backward into producing activities or forward into wholesaling activities. This motivation for vertical integration, based on the behavior of profit opportunities, is not greatly different from the motivation for product diversification in many other industries.

A second general factor for the oil industry has been the character of the physical facilities and the risks associated with them. Often the risks are very large, and vertical integration has constituted one way of reducing such risks. This point can best be illustrated by considering a modern oil refinery:

> An average size plant of 20,000 barrels per day capacity would represent a capital investment of some $20 million. The companies naturally want to do everything they can to protect such a large capital investment.
>
> They have found that protection of these capital investments has rested upon three things in particular—the maintenance of a high level of throughput at the refinery, the continued maintenance of a good supply of crude oil at competitive prices, and efficient transportation. Crude oil is a very important cost to a refiner, often representing as much as 80% of the value of the products sold in the plant. Transportation costs are also significant, sometimes representing 25% of the value of the products sold from the refinery.
>
> Integration forward into the market provides the best assurance possible that markets will be available at the time that products are in surplus supply. Likewise, vertical integration back into crude oil processing activities gives the soundest guarantee that crude oil will always be available at competitive prices. Finally, integration into pipelines and other transportation media provides the best possible assurance that transportation is always available to the refiner.

Integration and growth generally in the oil industry have also been aided by the fact that oil companies have usually enjoyed steadily expanding markets and fairly good profits. Consequently, capital has been available to finance growth.

We found that personal considerations and personalities were important in all the companies that we studied. This is particularly true in the case of the smaller businesses. In many of them we found that growth, or lack of it, was heavily dependent on family and health problems, inheritance taxes, income taxes, and economic conditions. In both large and small companies we found that the particular interests of the key executive people and the effectiveness with which they argued their cases was very important in determining the way in which their companies grew.

Many of the firms prepared payout and return on investment analyses of the specific investment proposals that would give direction to their growth programs. We found that varying degrees of importance were attached to the investment analyses and capital equipment analyses, and likewise varying degrees of care were exercised in preparing them. Consequently they assumed different degrees of importance in different companies. But one factor that was important in all of the companies was the competitive pressures to which the various companies were subjected. Countermoves, often of a day-to-day nature, were made to offset moves made by competitors or to gain some sort of advantage over them.

Finally, we found that changes in economic, legal, and political considerations have been very important in influencing growth in the oil industry. Temporary shortages and surpluses of both product and crude oil motivated certain vertical integration moves. During the 1930's there were very great surpluses of crude oil which caused many companies to turn to refining and marketing to find an outlet. Likewise, after World War II many companies engaged in the marketing of refined products found they were in short supply and integrated back into refining activities. Often these reasons were transitory in character.

The tax laws have been very important. Inheritance, income, and chain store taxes were factors that loomed large. Finally, the administrative control that the government sometimes exercises over common carrier pipelines has influenced the amount of money that some companies have been willing to put into this activity.

TWO CASE HISTORIES *

Samuel Groves (Executive Vice President, United-Carr Fastener Corporation) : Our company is a medium-size one operating in a service field. We have tried in general two main courses of expansion. First

* Taken from the open discussion which followed Mr. Haigh's observations.

of all, as a service business, we want to keep pace with the general economy and have tried to meet our customers' wants; as the number of our customers has grown, we have tried to increase production.

We have to anticipate such growth by providing various facilities and services to better our position. Personnel must be trained for advancement within our own organization. Consideration has to be given to the decentralization of the operation, bearing in mind the availability of markets. There must be a continuous effort toward what we call external expansion—the acquisition of companies previously not competitors whose products will be suitable as additions.

An important factor in such acquisitions is the personnel acquired with them. Preferably the acquired firms should be operated by the original personnel without too much interference by the parent company. Such use of the same personnel continues until everyone has become acclimated and the parent company has had a chance to learn about the new business. This preserves the personnel's sense of independence—we supply the capital and leave them alone.

[*From the floor:* Of course, that is not always possible. Sometimes the merger is made for purely financial reasons, and the personnel of the acquired company is fired immediately—with plenty of headaches and heartaches. Some companies have had to make a deal in the course of the merger by which they put one or more people on a retainer for five or ten years, with the explicit understanding that they stay away from the business. But under these circumstances you need a tremendous amount of confidence in the basic product that you are taking over.]

Our financial policy is to function without borrowing. Hence we usually expand externally either by exchange of stock or cash. However, if some major acquisition can be made where the line of product, profit margin, purchase price, and so on, are especially good, we are willing to finance by borrowing. We also have made it a policy to expand horizontally, rather than vertically; our experience has been that this is more advantageous.

Our growth in foreign countries has been guided by the following principles:

1. We have operated in English-speaking countries only.

2. We have attempted to manufacture the product itself abroad, thus capitalizing on American development and research.

3. We have attached some foreign subsidiaries to augment our production with other products suited to the particular countries where we are operating. These we call environmental products.

4. We have attempted to operate our foreign subsidiaries with native personnel.

James Robison (President, Indian Head Mills, Inc.): The textile field, which is a soft goods industry, is a very hard business indeed. Recently some of my Harvard Business School classmates were comparing notes. Some of the men asked a friend in the brokerage business how things were going. "Well," he said, "for the last couple of years we have just baled and weighed it. We don't bother to count it any more." I assure you that things have not been like that in the textile business over the last few years!

To call our current operations a "program of growth" dignifies a process which has really been more a matter of opportunism, expediency, happenstance, and an attempt to salvage something out of chaos.

I am the president of a medium-size textile manufacturing company, with total assets of $9.5 million and annual sales of about $20 million. We started out over two years ago as a spin-off from Textron, which company has since been merged with American Woolen. At the time of the spin-off, it was obvious to me that some elements of the Textron business were going to fall out of the back of the wagon, and I thought it would be fun to try to keep the Indian Head business going as a separate company. The resulting story was sufficiently interesting to be used as a case at the Harvard Business School, and I have had a chance to see some of the comments of the students about our situation. Here are a few:

⫗ "If we don't solve the immediate problem, there may not be a long-run future to worry about."

⫗ "Obviously the company needs capital, but how can it get that capital at this time in the textile industry unless it borrows from banks or sells common stock? A buyer of common stock will look with a wary eye on any common stock issue."

⁅ "There is no doubt that this company is in a precarious position. You could almost say there is much more evidence it will fail than succeed."

Those men were almost right! To outside observers it would appear that we have had an interesting growth in a very difficult business and with practically no starting capital. About a year after we started up we had an opportunity to reduce part of our debt, which started at $5 million. A few months later we carried out a merger with the Naumkeag Steam Cotton Company, which had been in serious trouble, had lost a great deal of money, and, as a matter of fact, is still in the red. This merger, made on the basis of a new issue of preferred for an old issue of common, gave us control of enough capital to move us from a standing start two and one-half years ago with practically no net worth, to a net worth of about $6 million today.

Ours is an industry with real opportunity. The sheer vastness of it and the obvious need for its products lead me to believe that it has terrific possibilities. But to take over the management of a textile company demands a long purse and a stout heart. Also, for the long run, I would urge careful attention to some personal philosophies which I think were promulgated by that incomparable pitcher, Satchel Paige:

⁅ "Avoid fried meats—which angry up the blood."
⁅ "Never run if walking will do as well."
⁅ "Never look back; something may be gaining on you."

OTHER POINTS *

Of course, not all growth is constructively planned. Some expansion is strictly defensive—to keep up with the rest of the industry. In the past 10 to 15 years many major oil companies have expanded

* From the discussion

their oil and refining activities faster than crude oil production, but almost to a man they say they would like to have a higher ratio of crude oil production to balance marketing. Then, why in the world have they been expanding their marketing so fast? Just to keep pace with the industry!

When a company is expanding at less than the industry rate, it is considered to be backsliding, and real trouble breaks loose. The questions come hard and fast. "Why are we falling behind?" and, indeed, "Why aren't we a notch ahead?" I think there is a difference here between the oil industry, which produces a common product, and, say, the pharmaceutical or chemical industry, where there is a vast range of products and a small incremental growth in one line may be less profitable than going into new lines.

It must be remembered that the goal is more than just increase in sales volume. The stockholder does not profit from that. Also, the stockholder's goal is not just greater dollar profits; it is greater earnings per share. So the objective should be to achieve the rate of expansion that will provide the greatest growth of profits, of earnings per share, rather than simply to grow for the sake of growth or to "keep up with the Joneses."

CONCLUSION*

It seems to me that one of the first essentials for a corporation in finding its way through these complex problems of growth and development is the harmonious blending of three very different management temperaments. I use the word "temperament" deliberately, because I think successful growth is to a considerable extent a matter of temperament as much as anything else.

These temperaments, which I am sure you will all recognize, fall into three categories, which I shall term: the advocates, the sea anchors, and the judges.

    1. The *advocates* are the dreamers in an industrial corporation, the men who can see beyond tomorrow, who are perpetually discontented

* By Mr. McLean.

with the here and now. They are the source of the new ideas and the initiative, the aggressiveness necessary to get things off dead center. Frequently they are distinguished by the way they use figures in analytical studies. To them figures and analytical studies are the means of convincing less imaginative souls that the course they have decided on is correct, not the means of picking out the right course of action in the first place. These advocates are a rare breed, and their talents, I think, are to be cherished.

2. Those of you who sail small boats know that a *sea anchor* is an article something like a canvas bucket which you throw out behind your boat in stormy weather. It keeps you on your course by *pulling on your stern*. The sea anchors are often the professional managers in an industrial corporation—the really good operating people. They are men who are pretty well convinced that the grass *is not* greener on the other side of the fence. They believe that the way to make an honest dollar is to get the costs down, to turn out a better product, and to do the job they are already concerned with in a better fashion —instead of jumping into a dozen new areas.

3. The *judges* are the fellows who have to listen to the advocates and the sea anchors and reach a decision on where to go and how to go about it. These judges have one qualification above all others: namely, the ability to distinguish clearly and surely between *business opportunism* and *business administration*. There is a vast difference between a program of growth and expansion which springs from picking the best of the prospects that come along in the stream of the day's work and a program built of projects which you yourself have generated and planned in an orderly fashion.

There seem to be, then, four jobs for management to do. First, it must assemble the cast to play each of these three roles, and to play them effectively and forcefully.

The second responsibility of management is to create the stage on which each of these three roles can be played—to establish committees, administrative machinery, and so on, to give each of these groups a chance to speak its piece and exercise its influence on the others.

Further, management must help each of these groups to understand each other's role and appreciate its importance. The differences in philosophy and emotional temperament among the three groups are such that there are all kinds of opportunities for bloodshed unless each can come to recognize the proper and legitimate function that the others play.

Finally—and here is the toughest responsibility of all—the top man himself has to make the transition in thinking which is necessary when he moves up the line out of the advocates' or the sea anchors' group to the judges' group. I think one of the common causes of misfortune in growth and expansion occurs when a man reaches this judges' level in the organization and fails to realize that he has made the change. Before he may have been an advocate and the sea anchors were his adversaries, or vice versa; now both groups have become his staunch allies, and it is his task to strike a balance between the two.

MANAGEMENT AND AUTOMATION

James R. Bright

IN THIS CHAPTER I have attempted to raise some questions and explore some problems, rather than provide any formulas or complete answers. It is unfortunately true that business, in many cases, is moving into automation without examining these questions or considering the implications of the changes which they are making. Furthermore, many executives do not realize the extent to which the decision to automate forecloses other choices which they have been free to make in the past.

Therefore, if you start this section of the book hoping to read that automation is just the greatest thing that ever came down the road, I am going to disappoint you. Automation is not going to solve all our problems—nor is it going to drive us all out of work. There will still be room for men and for human judgment. I am reminded, in this connection, of what the jet pilot said.

Note: Mr. Bright is Lecturer on Industrial Management, Harvard Business School.

He had been taken to a famous laboratory and shown its latest achievement—an automatic pilot for pilotless planes. The scientist then decided to needle the pilot a little. "See this, Bill?" he said. "It looks as though you are about washed up; you won't be needed any more!" "I don't know about that," replied the pilot. "Where else can you find a machine that has five senses; responds to smell, taste, light, touch, sound; is completely self-powered and self-contained; weighs only a hundred and fifty pounds; and can be so readily reproduced by unskilled labor?"

CONCEPT OF AUTOMATION

What, actually, is automation? That is the immediate question.

The word was coined in 1947 by D. S. Harder, Vice President of Ford Motor Company, to describe the automatic handling of work-in-process. However, it is such an apt expression—so spontaneously descriptive—that it has been used in a hundred ways to describe new levels of mechanization. To some it means *automatic handling,* to others *automatic processing,* to still others *mechanization of paper work, automatic control, self-regulation, feedback control, automatic work feeding,* or simply *the art and science of manufacturing as automatically as is economically feasible.* Even the man who originated the word redefined it in 1954. "A new philosophy of manufacturing," he called it.

Regardless of the meaning you favor, management and industrialists in general are using this term to mean not the last word in mechanization but, rather, the *latest* word. It seems clear that we have had a semantic void in our technical life, and "automation" has rushed in to fill it. I find that most industrial executives use the word as meaning a significantly higher level of mechanization (embracing a noticeable amount of automaticity, of course) than previously existed in a particular phase of production or distribution. It does not denote an absolute or static level of automatic operation, but something relative, dynamic.

"What is the difference between the things you've called automation and just plain, everyday methods improvement?" I once asked a prominent automation engineer. "Nothing," he said, "but it does get management wholeheartedly behind the program, and that's why I like it!"

You will find violent disagreement with this on the part of economists, editors, and many other "nonusers" of automation; but such argument is pointless. To the extent that common usage defines a word, automation means, to most executives, a vigorous effort *toward* more highly automatic operation.

From what I have seen going on in many industries, I wonder if this is not the major value of the expression? We now have a word which we can use to get across an idea, a program, a philosophy of progress. It is an expressive word, under which an aggressive, company-wide (not just methods department-wide) program can be launched to achieve higher levels of mechanization.

This concept is significant enough, without bringing in all the sensational claims advanced for automation. People have said it is going to usher in the "Second Industrial Revolution," "the push-button factory," "the automatic factory." It will produce "an unemployment situation, in comparison with which the depression of the 1930's will seem like a pleasant joke." Let us look at the concept realistically.

In a study of some 15 so-called "automated" plants over the last year, I have identified 17 levels of mechanization (see *Exhibit I*). Step-by-step a process can be plotted against these levels, and thus what I call a "mechanization profile" is created.* In brief, this approach reveals that mechanization has two distinctly different qualities: "span" (or spread over the plant) and "level" (or degree of mechanical achievement). Neither is anywhere nearly as great as is generally implied or assumed.

With the exception of the oil industry, I found scarcely a single plant in which more than a few individual operations were on the levels of "performance control," where the response is *action* rather than simply a *signal* (on which manual action is to be taken). In fact,

* For a detailed description, see James R. Bright, "How to Evaluate Automation," *Harvard Business Review,* July–August 1955, pp. 101–111.

Exhibit I. Mechanization Profile—Rubber Mattress Unit

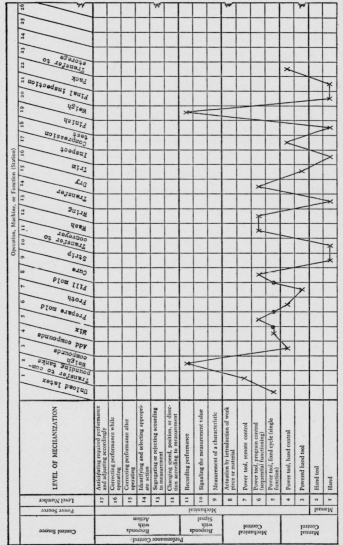

Note: Dots on lines between operations represent the level of the materials handling device.

the most advanced plants, like Ford's Cleveland engine factory, are basically at the levels of mechanical control or "program control." On that particular highly automatic production line for engine blocks, operation after operation falls near the bottom of the chart. Every time inspections are made or assembling is done, there seems to be a reversion to hand operation. I do not mean to cast any unkind reflections on Ford's very fine accomplishments. I merely want to establish the fact that processes called "automatic" are not nearly as automatic as we believe. This can be seen in mechanization profiles of later engine plants: each one is more automatic than the previous one, and there is more mechanization of formerly manual jobs. Even in these later plants, however, there are still many hand and hand-tool operations in the line, and the over-all level of the profile is far from high.

AUTOMATION AT WORK

Although automation has not yet produced the "push-button factory" (and I doubt that such a plant will appear in the foreseeable future), my study of several of the most advanced plants did point up some general trends connected with the new philosophy. Here they are:

1. Processing and handling equipment are being integrated through new levels of conveyer technology. More and more production machines are being built around the conveyer, rather than vice versa, and it is becoming the heart of the factory.

2. Work feeding and removal devices for production machines are becoming much more common. Thus mechanization is spreading out on both sides of the machine in little—or large—"islands" of automation.

3. There is a shift from making bulk material products in batches to making them through continuous weighing, mixing, and blending operations. As a matter of fact, a great many batch operations, themselves, are being performed automatically.

4. Programed controls are being applied on a much wider scale to processing machinery, so that the machine will automatically proceed

through a series of timed and otherwise controlled operations. Punched-card and tape control of machinery is appearing in isolated instances.

5. Remote control is more common. This enables operations to be controlled from a distant point and is encouraging much more so-called "push-button control."

6. Instruments and controls are being applied more widely to sense a variable, compare it to a standard, and pass, reject, or shut down the operation. There is some *slight* increase in the use of self-regulating control, or feedback. There is much talk of (and, probably, effort toward) introducing more of it.

7. The mechanization of assembly operations is slowly gathering momentum. This is probably the most fruitful area of all at present.

8. Combination machines, tying together several functions on one machine base, are being built to perform the operations of a series of machines.

Taking the bird's-eye view, two major developments are under way in industry with regard to the new processes.

First, a number of individual functions not formerly mechanized to any appreciable degree—such as inspection, design computations, commercial paper work, materials handling, and assembly—are now being mechanized or given higher levels of mechanization.

Secondly, but if anything more significantly, the factory is becoming one big machine—a master machine or super machine, if you will—either rapidly, as in a radically new plant, or slowly, as when equipment is gradually being "automated." This usually occurs in "islands" of automation created, in the total process or plant, through (*a*) compounding—i.e., coupling a group of machines together into a master machine; or (*b*) combining—by building a single machine to perform a number of operations; or (*c*) integration—the use of handling equipment to join production machines or areas.

The parts of the super machine are highly dependent on one another. Material supply depends on the preceding machine, and demand for the product of the operation depends on the next machine, since the elimination or reduction of in-process inventory is implicit in the continuous process. With little provision for slack in the system, the rate of flow must be constant or within narrow limits of permissible fluctuation. And not only must every machine in the plant be geared to run at a speed consistent with the supply and demand on each side of it, but like the Deacon's wonderful, one-hoss shay, everything must be made so that it can be stopped or serviced, or will wear out, at the same time and *only* then. Individual element breakdowns cannot be tolerated, for any one downtime occurrence will multiply lost production by the number of operations that are shut down by the failure.

IMPLICATIONS FOR MANAGEMENT

The further we move toward the automated factory along the above lines, the greater become the implications for management— and the more serious the situation if management does not recognize these implications.

For instance, under automation performance information must be gathered, transmitted, and acted upon much more rapidly than in the conventional plant because of the cost factors. Cause of a shutdown must be located and corrected as quickly as possible. Faulty materials or faulty products must be detected, rejected, and the trouble corrected rapidly, since their cost multiplies at the rate of the production.

Moreover, this super machine must be carefully planned. Since it can produce efficiently only what it was designed to produce, we must:

1. Fix the size, shape, and construction of the product.
2. Fix the rate of production and probably the product mix.
3. Anticipate and allow for changes in design, in materials, in processes, in raw material supply, and in the rate of output required.
4. Build a machine that can be amortized over the commercial life of the products that this machine can produce.
5. Consider the impact of competition, so that the machine will be flexible enough to meet the changes—or the costs—which competition introduces.

6. Anticipate and allow for the possibility of radical technological developments, economic changes, or fashion trends.

7. Plan the relationship of men to machines. The required skills must be available. Training and the time for training must be planned.

8. Break-in time, practice, correction of troubles—all must be anticipated and provided for.

In short, the automated factory is a problem in planning and in design. Everything must be in harmony with everything else—the output with the demand, the raw material supply with the quantity and quality requirements, the machine elements with each other, and the people (for the factory is really far from automatic) with the machine.

It takes great design skill to create such a machine, and more than mechanical skill, for this is more than a mechanism. It is a device to serve mechanical, economic, and social ends.

And who is the designer? It can be none other than *management.* Management makes the over-all decisions in the sphere where these three elements overlap. Because everything has been made absolutely interdependent, management no longer can leave production people alone to go their own way. Furthermore, automation will raise the price of mistakes. This super machine provides cost and quality advantages in exchange for greater rigidity.

Here are some illustrations of the grief that can result from faulty planning:

⟨Let us look first at a bakery which decided to create a highly automatic plant. Under the new system, flour was received in bulk cans and unloaded through pneumatic tubes. The plant itself worked beautifully, but when the bakery people checked on their suppliers, they discovered that only two out of the six were able to fill their bulk hopper cars. In effect, automation had cut their supply sources from six to two.

⟨Then there are the men in a Pennsylvania coal field who set out to mine by remote control. By using automatic cutting and transportation equipment which carried the coal from the mine face into the waiting trucks, they were able to mine "automatically" a thousand feet from the entrance. They intended to use television cameras so they could control operations from outside the mine. There was every promise that this system could be developed to work perfectly. Finally, however, it became necessary to move to another vein. Unfortunately, in this new area the coal structure was different, and timbering was needed. This proved to be the case in most of the rest of the mine field, so this particular mechanized system had to be dropped. The effect of automation again was to restrict supply.

⟨[A foam rubber plant introduced a new "automatic" system for the production of mattresses. When the plant was put up, the management told its technical men, "You will have to make about 15% foam rubber seat cushions on this line." The technicians objected that the system was set up for mattresses, that the density of the rubber would have to be varied, and that there would be a loss in production. But since an additional system was out of the question, the line was installed and began turning out 15% seat cushions. Then orders for cushions increased to 20%, 25%, and finally 30%.

When I was at the plant a few months ago, the finishing end of the factory was bogged down—you could hardly walk through it. The storage conveyer was stopped, and the place was piled high with foam rubber cushions. What had happened? The manager explained that seat cushions entail a lot more finishing per pound of foam rubber than do mattresses, and it takes a lot more people to make the repairs. The plant's new automatic system, however, did not allow space to do repair and assembly work properly. Demand had changed, and had partially nullified the excellence of a very fine mechanical system. Automation is likely to require continuity of the product line.

⟨[At another plant a production manager asked me, "How do I get fractional runs?" "Just run the machine a couple of hours," I suggested. "No," he answered, "we are booked solid. Suppose we get in an order for just a certain number of items. It doesn't fit into one shift. If we are already running six days a week, two shifts, how can I get two more hours of work out of the system? Overtime is too expensive for the whole plant, yet I can't run the system in pieces!"

⟨[Recently a friend of mine, who is an inspector in a plant which makes a rather complicated piece of machinery, took me on a tour of his outfit. "Say," he said, "I have a question for you. Down here at this point, we inspect automatically. How can we get the report of an inspection that doesn't meet our standards to the engineering department in time for them to do something about it? Just to start with, our telephone is way over there. Then, the reports are rather complicated, and we need our data sheets, so we have to carry them over to the phone, too." I pointed out that the trip was only 400 feet. "Sure," he replied, "but remember, this thing turns out a product every three minutes. What do you do about the kind of fault that requires time to analyze? Shut down?"

¶[And then there is the automobile manufacturer who has a highly automatic engine line. He wanted to install a new type of water pump on his 1955 model car. However, it would have cost him at least $500,000 to make that little change in his product; he would have had to rip apart his whole automated assembly line in order to get two small holes drilled for the attachment of the pump. As a result, he had to forego this installation until enough improvement ideas had been collected to make alterations in the production line machinery economically feasible. Again, inflexibility!

OPERATIONS PLANNING

If under automation mistakes are so much more costly and if changes are so much more difficult to make, what must be done?

First, there must be much, much more planning. Fundamentally, we must search for order, we must maintain order, we must create order. We must know exactly what to make, and how much. This requires more accurate forecasting and shrewd analysis on a scale not dreamed of before. The marketing man is going to have to be *very* right or else he may have nothing to eat but a stream of unsalable products. He must not create a machine to make a product that cannot be sold, nor must he sell a product he cannot make economically.

The more superbly conceived as an automatic super machine, the more inflexible it is likely to be. Some of the worst boners are going to result from merely dropping a very fine mechanical solution on what appears to be a production problem but what in fact is a tridimensional problem which also includes marketing and social factors.

Furthermore, management will find that it is inheriting exactly the same problems as its own machine designers face, but on a larger and more consequential scale. To design the super machine, management must, as I have said, fix a desired character and quantity of product. But almost inevitably there will be some changes sooner than anticipated, with corresponding shortcomings of the machine. The first machine probably won't work perfectly, so a second one will be built quite differently. Further, this machine will take longer to construct and longer to get running than expected, and it will probably cost more than allowed. There will be unexpected failures, and a further period of "debugging." And finally, if luck holds this far, maintenance will assume a new significance (and just this can make or break the operation).

Also, there is a new need for quantification on both the production and the marketing fronts. Automation means, perhaps, the end of what General Electric's Melvin L. Hurni calls "Golden Gate Bridge engineering"; no more beautiful, one-of-a-kind engineering masterpieces. Design will have to be controlled by manufacturing and sales disciplines, rather than sheer mechanical perfection.

Multifamily products must be analyzed to find common parts so as to create opportunities for automaticity. This, too, calls for redesign to create parts usable in many products, and ones that are easy to manufacture. Perhaps we will have two kinds of factories, in effect; we may manufacture only parts, and then assemble products to order.

The problems on the sales front are even tougher. What happens, for example, when an adverse sales trend sets in sooner than anticipated? The breakeven point is higher, the time to change is longer, the cost of changing may be staggering if not impossible. Will we have to plan on new levels of sales promotion and marketing effort to *support* the super machine until it is amortized?

How shall we encourage sales over the automated part of the line?

By selling the customer through price reductions, through technical education in the advantages he gains? Probably we can't do this until we train—and sell—the sales force first.

In fact, not only sales but all elements of management must adjust to the new machine. Proper records must be developed so that trouble spots can be identified and dealt with in order of importance. Throughout, the need is for quantification. Since this entire machine must run smoothly, or not at all, trouble-detecting and trouble-correcting mechanisms must be built into the whole organization. We need signals that tell management promptly what is wrong.

Management must measure as it never has, and it must create control systems that are as responsive and automatic as possible—either for adjustment or trouble correction. Time now is a more valuable commodity than ever.

Obviously, the smart thing to do is to build the plant so as to minimize all the rigidities connected with automation. How can this be done? Again, only by more careful planning.

Does this mean that management by exception will decline? I believe so, for we cannot permit many exceptions. Exceptions bring the automated plant to a halt. Management's job will become twofold: (1) it must plan imaginatively, aggressively, and shrewdly, upon sound data, and (2) it must be the control mechanism—the sensing device—between the super machine and its technical-social-economic environment. By control I mean that executives must be sensitive to changes and be swift to modify the super machine or its performance as needed. This, of course, requires that every person in every phase of the business be more conscious of the other fellow's problems. It looks as though management will spend more of its time creating teams and fostering teamwork.

Automation, then, necessitates extensive planning of operations within the plant if costly mistakes are to be avoided. But the new mechanization also poses considerable problems in the field of industrial relations. In dealing with these questions, I do not want to give the impression that the figures come from a comprehensive census. My study of automated plants has been an exploratory one, and only to the extent that these firms were typical do my conclusions have some validity.

SIGNIFICANCE FOR LABOR

Too many over-all generalizations, based strictly on hypotheses, have been tossed out on this subject. To make an accurate appraisal, we must divide the labor question into several parts:

More jobs or fewer jobs?—It is foolish to deny that one of the principal aims of automation is to replace the human labor content in manufacturing activity. These machines do replace people. However, there seems to be universal agreement among management, economists, and even labor leaders that, *in the long run,* technological advancement creates jobs far more rapidly than it destroys them. We have dozens of industry experiences to prove this. Ford, for instance, employs today about 40% more people than in 1947 when it first formed an "Automation Department."

Nevertheless, the short-term technological unemployment accompanying the introduction of automation worries both labor and non-labor people. I have no all-inclusive nationwide statistics regarding the effects of mechanization on the work force, but there are some significant examples I can cite to suggest trends in employment.

For instance, in 12 out of 15 of the particular plants I studied, the number of people employed today is higher than it was prior to automation. In some cases the automatized plant was brand-new, having been created to meet new market demands. In other cases there had been a temporary decline in employment right after the plant adopted automation, but the volume of business soon grew to such a point that more employees had to be hired—this in spite of the fact that productivity per worker often increased enormously. In still other instances, management had made a definite point of delaying expansion programs so that they could be timed to absorb displaced labor from the automation program.

In a number of cases I found displacement figures grossly exaggerated. In one plant, for instance, displacement was quoted as being 50% of the working force. However, on checking the figures closely, I found that it really amounted to 50% of the people in that particular operation—who represented only 16% of the total employed on this item's production line. Further, this production line was only a piece of the entire plant's activities, and the number of displaced employees showed up as actually about 1½% of the total working force! Again and again I found that the drastic percentage figures so widely quoted had been applied to very small segments of the total production activity. With one exception, the amount of displaced labor could not be considered as significant.

More skill or less skill?—What about the character of labor? Does automation mean that we will have an enormous retraining program on our hands? Remember that we are dealing with two kinds of labor —operating and maintenance. Will we have to re-educate both types?

Let us look first at operating labor. In spite of automation there are still large numbers of machine operators, patrollers, and inspectors left in the production system. On the whole, training requirements for this operating labor appear to be *less* in the automatic factory than in the conventional plant. In the plants I studied, I found that the machine had assumed most of the skill requirements of the job, and the production systems were easier to run and required less skilled labor than before. There literally was nothing for the worker to do but "push a button" or "monitor" the machinery. The clearance of stoppages, an occasional shoving of the material into the machine, the pulling out of faulty parts, and so on, is all the job amounts to. In two plants, management advised that one of its major mistakes had been to overestimate the technical requirements of certain jobs. In several instances, a primary motive for automation was, in fact, to create jobs so *simple* and *easy* that unskilled labor could handle them.

There are exceptions, of course. Where intricate setup work is required, a very high-caliber, highly skilled operator is needed. What happens when tape control of machine tools comes in? Engineers in this development work tell me that the tape will be prepared in the methods department and "anyone" can then set up the machine for operation.

The total impact of automation will vary with the nature of the industry and the particular production activity. The proportion of jobs "simplified" to jobs made "more difficult"—requiring significantly higher levels of skill—is unknown. In the particular plants I saw, however, automation seemed to lower training requirements for the *majority* of the workers.

We should not confuse "skill ratings" with "caliber of people to be employed." From the manager's viewpoint, his problems are:

a. Can I run my remodeled plant with the same people?
b. Will I have a terribly difficult retraining problem?

In the plants I observed, the answer to the first question was "yes," and to the second, "no." I feel reasonably certain that the general effect of automation is to lessen the skill qualifications and training requirements of the remaining production line workers, rather than add to them. Look at it this way: Is today's car, with all its automatic assists, harder or easier to start and operate than the old Model T?

What about maintenance labor? Automation eliminates operating workers and requires more maintenance workers (or at least a higher percentage of them). These maintenance workers apparently must be highly skilled. Will this have the effect of upgrading the skill requirements in the total work force?

Again I do not have nationwide figures, but I did find that, although maintenance requirements in the automated plants I visited tended to go up, the increase was not nearly as great as most people believe.

For instance, in one plant the maintenance force doubled; that is, it went from 20 men to 40 men in a plant employing a total of 600. This was hardly a sensational alteration in the total work force. In some plants making electrical parts, it was hard to see any significant percentage increase of employees in maintenance. What evidently happens is that while the number of maintenance employees goes up, the expansion of the business also necessitates additional workers for nonautomated activities. Therefore, the new percentage of maintenance workers to the total work force is often not startlingly different. Usually the change is surprisingly small. In some automobile plants the effect of automation is to reduce the number of production workers but to require the same or a slightly larger maintenance force.

Automation has one notable impact on the character of the maintenance force—to wit, the new skills demanded of plant electricians. Highly automatic machinery is so loaded with electronic devices and has such elaborate control systems that the ordinary plant electrician needs advanced training before he can maintain it properly. Indeed, it seems we need a new class of plant electricians—"electronic technicians." This was almost a universal complaint among the plant managers I talked to. I do not mean to say that enormous numbers of such men are required in an individual plant. Rather, there will have to be several electronic experts—maybe several dozen—in the larger plants and at least one such man on the maintenance crews of smaller factories.

As for millwrights, machine repairmen, carpenters, welders, etc., a few more such men are needed. However, this problem is not so much *different* as it is quantitatively *greater*. Here it is more a matter of experience than of skill.

There is no doubt that the manufacturer who introduces a highly automatic system would be wise to assign his maintenance force to work with the contractor during the installation and break-in periods, even though it may seem expensive. I ran into half a dozen manufacturers who were sorry they had not adopted this policy.

Although this may seem hard to believe, I found definite indications that *maintenance costs in some kinds of plants will actually drop under automation.* This is possible because automation had reduced the total amount of machinery in the factory. It is true that automation usually means more maintenance per pound of cubic foot of machinery. But highly automatic machines usually combine a number of functions, replacing four or five other pieces of equipment. In other words, although there will be more maintenance per machine in the automated plant, there may be fewer machines. If the total equipment reduction is great enough, *total* maintenance requirements will be reduced also. This phenomenon has occurred in some of the advanced oil refineries.

As a matter of fact, exactly the same thing *may* happen regarding the cost of automation as a whole. Pound for pound, automatic machinery is more expensive than ordinary equipment, perhaps 30%–50% more. However, less of it is needed, and it will fit into a smaller building. As a result, the total plant *may* be less expensive than a conventional plant. Of course, this does not happen unless almost the entire plant is highly advanced. Simply dropping in an exceedingly automatic machine at one point in the plant will not produce this happy result. Nor will it happen as quickly in those plants that are, in effect, unique machines where each piece is especially designed, as in automobile plants. It is more likely to happen in plants that are unusual combinations of standard components, like oil refineries.

SIGNIFICANCE FOR SMALL BUSINESS

The small businessman will have to be alert and ingenious in adopting as much automation as he can possibly handle if he is to compete pricewise with the large firms. There is a tremendous cost advantage—cost reduction—once automation is properly installed and operating.

Most small concerns cannot afford to automate as extensively as the large plants; they cannot hope to realize the savings which big business will gain through the wholesale mechanization of production. However, again there are exceptions. Unique combinations of standard machinery have been applied by small businesses and are well within many budgets. New degrees of automaticity will become "standard."

I can only speculate on the following points, but it seems to me that the small businessman's salvation lies in the fact that he will retain a certain flexibility while the large manufacturer—the highly automatic manufacturer—is likely to lose it.

The small manufacturer will be able to build specials, handle custom work, meet deadlines, do rush jobs and a host of things that require the ability to shift production output on a few minutes' notice. The large automatic plant simply will not be able to do this. Thus automation may very well prove an actual blessing to the small businessman who is fast on his production and sales feet. When a new product, a new material, or a new idea comes along, he can develop it and have it on the market before the highly automated plant can even draw plans.

On the other hand, it is doubtful if the small businessman can exist by making a conventional product, in a conventional way, to distribute through conventional outlets, at his old conventional price, if there is an effectively automated production system in competition with him. Rather, he will have to make his living by producing the fastest or the finest, not by direct competition. His situation parallels that of the independent cobbler, who cannot compete with the modern shoe factory, but who may make a nice living on custom-tailored shoes.

The severity of automation's effect on the small businessman will be tempered, to some extent, by the nature of the market. Those people who manufacture and sell locally need fear only the particular automation that can produce for the same local markets. Where the costs of transportation prevent national distribution of the output of a highly automatic plant, the local businessman can breathe easier. Only to the extent that automation facilitates production through small units that are easily dispersed geographically need he anticipate trouble.

CONCLUSION

Having looked at the mechanical and social problems connected with automation, let us just summarize some of its possible advantages. Labor reduction, greatly increased output, improved quality, and a reduction in scrap are almost certainties. Some plants will find a great benefit in reduction of lead time. There are likely to be other reductions in material costs and inventory. Probable benefits to labor are higher pay, better working conditions, and improved safety conditions.

Management will get its machinery into a lot less space, and in a few instances plants will actually be cheaper to build and run. The total amount of equipment will be substantially reduced by automation, though each item will be more expensive. This factor, together with smaller total plant area, will mean cost reductions for some manufacturers.

One word of caution—generalization of any kind, either as to benefits or problems of automation, is dangerous. *By no means do all the comments I have made in the preceding pages apply to every case.* Each executive must study his own plant to see if they do. In planning for automation, there are nine factors which management should consider:

1. *The degree of automation.* As indicated above, there are some 17 identifiable levels, and the difficulties in moving from one to another are not equal.

2. *The nature of the industry.* Automation means one thing for automobiles, another for bread, something else again for chemicals.

3. *The starting point.* Problems are more complex in moving from a high level of mechanization to an even higher one; on the other hand, the first stages of automation do not create the same kind of difficulties.

4. *The materials being processed.* It makes a difference whether the raw materials are foodstuffs or jet engines, single continuum products or discrete parts.

5. *Technical maturity of the process.* Is this the first time a machine to perform this particular operation has been constructed—or is this the tenth refinement of the original model?

6. *The kind of product line.* Multiproduct factories present far more difficult conditions than do single-product operations.

7. *Product stability.* Some items are always in demand and remain constant in form; others have to be changed continually to fit shifting consumer needs. What flexibility can be retained?

8. *Management's approach.* Are the motives, objectives, and bene-

fits of automation clearly pinned down or is management just doing a lot of wishful thinking?

9. *Sales situations.* Organizations that have a set geographical distribution without significant national competition have different problems from those which must consider changes taking place everywhere in the country.

One point is clear, I think. Although there are many production advantages as a reward, automation means much more time, work, and worry for management. This is particularly true in the early stages of development. The final question, then, is: "Shall we buy this much trouble, and shall we buy it *now?* Shall we pioneer this thing, or wait until it is perfected a bit more? Do we want to go through the sweeping self-analysis of our business and make the basic changes this will demand? Can we do it? What is it worth to be first?"

I cannot give any answer to that kind of question, of course, because each management group will have to decide for itself. But I can offer you the comment of one topnotch manufacturing research man: "The firm that rushes into this thing blindly is going to lose its shirt. The firm that doesn't go in at all is going to lose its market."

SOME DEVELOPMENTS IN
BUSINESS DATA PROCESSING

Robert N. Anthony, Edward L. Wallace,
and Peter B. Laubach

INTRODUCTION

JUST ABOUT A YEAR AGO the spirit of a discussion similar to the one we are about to present here could best be described as enthusiastic. Recently I read over the chapter incorporating that material * and noted my own conclusion: "The 'revolution' . . . is upon us, and it

Note: This chapter is based on a panel discussion by three members of the Harvard Business School's research project on data processing. Mr. Anthony, who served as moderator and is responsible for the introductory observations, is Associate Professor of Business Administration; Mr. Wallace is Assistant Professor of Research in Business Administration; and Mr. Laubach is Research Associate in Business Administration.

* Robert N. Anthony, *et al.,* "Effective Delegation and Control by the Controller," *The Management Team,* edited by Edward C. Bursk (Cambridge, Harvard University Press, 1954), p. 98.

will be a stimulating and exciting period." I think now that this was, at the very least, an overstatement.

The somewhat overdone enthusiasm that I, and others concerned with data processing in business, displayed has been tempered by disappointments encountered in four major areas:

First, those of us involved in a Harvard Business School research project on business data processing have found that some installations, which a year ago gave promise of being pioneer installations capable of showing the way of business, are not working out as satisfactorily as we initially thought they would.

Second, some companies appear to believe that the important problem they should investigate is the problem of adapting automatic equipment to an existing accounting or control system, whereas the area that should really be investigated is the system itself. In other words, there has been a tendency to mechanize existing procedures without giving much thought to the adequacy or efficiency of these procedures.

Third, we found very little effort being applied to the development of integrated data processing systems. Automatic equipment is being used in specific areas, such as payroll or inventory record keeping, but few, if any, attempts are being made to develop systems and related equipment that will process all the company's data in an integrated, coordinated, and unduplicated manner. It now appears that our original expectations about integrated data processing were unrealistically optimistic. The job of analyzing a company's total need for quantitative data, and of developing the most efficient mechanism for supplying this need, is a fiendishly complicated one. We must now admit that the solution of this problem lies far in the future.

Fourth, and finally, we found that there are only a few instances so far in which automatic equipment is being used to provide better management information. There is, on the one hand, a considerable amount of theoretical work being done in this area in academic institutions, and a great deal of talking and writing about what *might* be accomplished is going on. But, on the other hand, examples of *practice* are hard to find. There is an unfortunate emphasis on accepting the *existing* end product of a system as being the *desirable* end product. For example, payrolls are being mechanized without concern for labor cost control—the management problem that stems out of the payroll data.

There are indications, however, that two important developments with management implications, as distinguished from the routine processing of data, may soon become significant: (*a*) certain kinds of low-level decisions may be made directly by automatic equipment, and (*b*) information available to management for other, higher level decisions may be much more powerful than before.

Inventory control is an example of an area where low-level decisions may soon be made mechanically. In the inventory area there is a whole class of decisions which are of a routine nature. For instance:

> A branch warehouse sends an order to a central inventory control point asking for more of a certain part. Somebody at this center must then make the decision whether to ship the part from another warehouse that has it, manufacture the part, or buy it. For certain items, such a decision involves the application of well-defined rules. There seems to be no reason why such a set of rules cannot be put into the program of a computer so that the computer can proceed to make the decision. Such decisions, of course, will be subject to human veto.

There are a number of decision areas of this kind where automatic equipment has real possibilities. Production control and scheduling, credit management, and such special questions as the blending problem in refineries have already been worked on by computers. Decisions of top management importance, such as judging performance, probably never can be made by machines, but even here the possibilities of helping management with more powerful information on which to base a decision need a much deeper exploration.

GENERAL PURPOSE VS. SPECIAL
PURPOSE EQUIPMENT*

Before embarking upon this brief discussion of the relative merits of general purpose and special purpose automatic data processing machines, it seems worthwhile to review certain of the more important contributions which have led to the design and construction of this equipment. There are three technical innovations which in combination one with another have been responsible for all recent advances in data processing and the emergence of the automatic digital computer. Without these innovations progress would have been impossible; between them they fully explain the present state of the art.

These innovations are:

1. The development of a system of automatic control permitting indefinite sequential processing of information without human intervention.

2. The use of electronic and electromechanical circuits to perform arithmetic and logical operations at speeds roughly equivalent to the time required to change the state of a vacuum tube, transistor, or electromechanical relay.

3. The development of mechanical techniques which permit the storage of large quantities of information in a highly condensed form.

Automatic control is the principal factor differentiating the newer types of equipment from their punched card predecessors. It has removed the economic limits upon the number of operations that can be performed on a selected set of data without human intervention, and has made feasible fuller utilization of electronic or electromechanical processing speeds.

In combination with speed, it is also responsible for the popular but fallacious name—"electronic brains"—now being used so extensively to describe such equipment. No name for these machines

* By Mr. Wallace.

could be more misleading, for automatic control to be effective requires the presence of specific and detailed instructions regarding both the type and the timing of the operations to be performed. There is only one way such instructions can be prepared initially. Some individual must analyze the processing requirements of each situation, convert these requirements into a code intelligible to the machine, and introduce these coded instructions into the processing system. Once this has been done, automatic control will direct the machine to perform the operations in accordance with these instructions, whether they are right or wrong.

The third innovation, condensed storage, is a necessary adjunct of the other two, for without it input and output speeds could not be balanced with the optimum rate of internal processing and the entire system would be less efficient than certain of its individual components.

These three innovations and their importance to every system of high speed automatic data processing can best be illustrated by means of a diagram. In *Exhibit I* the major components of a general purpose automatic data processing system are set forth schematically. These include input and output, internal storage, control, and various arithmetic and logical components. They are tied together into a complete and homogeneous system by the number buses and connecting circuits (solid lines) which transmit information from one part of the system to another.

The control mechanism is the coordinating device for the system as a whole. It directs the type and sequence of operations as well as the transfers of data within the machine. These results are accomplished by means of the control circuits (dashed lines) which convey information from the control register to the gates (arrowheads on the dashed lines). By opening and closing the proper gates at any given moment of time it is possible to direct the transfer of information from component to component or to perform a desired arithmetic or logical operation within any one component.

The opening and closing of gates throughout the system reflects instructions being received by the control register. These instructions are derived from internal storage where they have been placed and are retained for this purpose. Processing in any general purpose system is primarily a problem of preparing the proper coded instructions and introducing them into the system along with the data to be processed. As these instructions are received in the control register, they are interpreted as directions for opening and closing gates throughout the machine, thereby permitting information to flow from input to internal storage; from internal storage to the desired arithmetic or logical components; from such components back into storage; and finally from storage to output. By virtue of the instructions and the control mechanism the entire process from input to output is automatic.

For our purposes, the important concepts to be gleaned from this brief description of a general purpose system are (1) that it is a grouping together of various components capable of performing the full range of possible operations, and (2) that the operations actually performed depend upon instructions given the control mechanism. By virtue of the variety of components included in such a system, general purpose equipment has been made a highly flexible device. It can perform whatever operations are desired in any sequence that is required. This explains its success for scientific purposes and the advantages it possesses for business data processing where the operations required vary considerably from situation to situation. Conversely, these same attributes point to the type of situation where it may be less than optimum. Where the objectives of processing are certain and only a few arithmetic or logical operations are to be performed, many components of a general purpose system may not be required. If, in addition to this, the volume of such processing is large, then another system which incorporates only those components needed to accomplish the desired processing is likely to be both more efficient and more economical.

Another limitation of some importance is the fact that most general purpose systems are flexible only insofar as the main frame (i.e., arithmetic and logical circuits, control mechanism, and internal storage) is concerned but are quite inflexible as to input-output. This

Exhibit I. Schematic Diagram of General Purpose Automatic Data Processing System

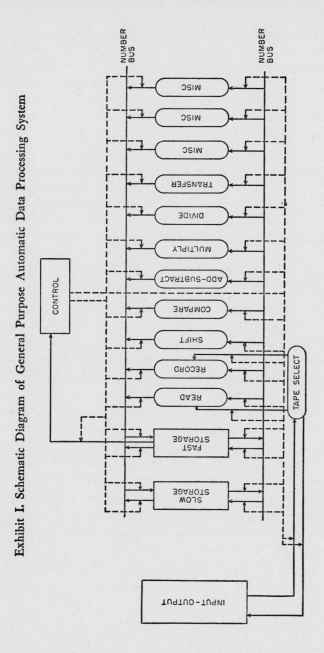

is a serious restriction, for one of the facts we have learned is that in business input-output flexibility is as important, if not more important, than flexibility of the main frame.

This inflexibility of input-output is illustrated by the fact that most general purpose systems make use of magnetic tape as an external storage medium. Magnetic tape has tremendous advantages for this purpose since its storage costs per unit of information are low, the packing density of information is high, and its speed for input purposes is great. There are, however, certain disadvantages to magnetic tape, and under particular conditions these may more than offset its more favorable attributes. For example:

> In the case of a public utility, if customer billing is to be done electronically, the meter readings which now are received on written reports must be transferred to punched cards and from such cards to tape by means of an automatic converter. The difficulty with this procedure is that it is slow and it costs a good deal of money both for the equipment and for the personnel needed to carry out the various steps required in the preparation of magnetic tape.
>
> If, however, the system had a greater flexibility as regards inputs, much of this cost of equipment and labor might be saved. The meter reader could punch or mark-sense a tape which could be fed directly into the machine without intermediate transfers of data. In this way considerable cost savings would be possible without reduction in the speed of the processing operations. All that is required is the relatively inexpensive tape equipment for the meter reader and an input device which could handle punched or mark-sensed tape. Both of these are available at present, and one study of a public utility has indicated that the labor savings alone from this type of input would amount to approximately $100,000 a year.

This same lack of flexibility of general purpose equipment presently exists on the output side. Again, magnetic tape is the usual storage device, and its disadvantages as a single output medium are the prime cause of this inflexibility. For example:

> Where a variety of reports are to be prepared on automatic equipment, it is necessary to prepare instructions for each of the various

report types wanted. The preparation of such instructions is both a time-consuming and costly proposition. Consequently, once the form of a report has been established and instructions for its preparation developed, there usually will be a great deal of reluctance on the part of one and all to change that report.

Since the majority of business reports involve sorting and summing basic information, another alternative is available. Where it is possible to derive output in the form of punched cards, these can be sorted on an electric sorter and summed on conventional punched card tabulators. Then, if the form of the report is to be changed it involves only the relatively simple procedure of rewiring a plugboard rather than complete reprograming of the general purpose system. Changes in reports will be more frequent, and new or special reports can be tested under this system—a result which is far less likely to occur when the reports are prepared within the general purpose system.

In this respect there is still another factor which needs to be considered. Where a report is the result of sorting and summing, the general purpose system is performing what is for it a very inefficient operation. This fact, coupled with the inflexibilities introduced by magnetic tape as a form of output and the reluctance of persons to revise instructions for a general purpose system once they are prepared, indicates some of the benefits derivable from having available a multiplicity of output types on a general purpose system.

There is considerable evidence that the business machines manufacturers are aware of this need for input-output flexibility. Some of the equipment recently announced either incorporates or has made provision for the inclusion of such devices as card readers and punches, readers for punched paper tape, mark-sensing readers, and the like. When this type of input-output flexibility is coupled with the extant flexibility of the main frame, the result is often a machine whose processing capabilities are far greater than the requirements of the situation to which it is applied. In scientific work flexibility is a necessity, but in business repetitive rather than varied processing is frequently the case.

This leads us to an interesting and important tentative conclusion. In business, the extreme degree of flexibility embodied in the general purpose automatic data processing system may not be required in a given situation. Only certain of the input-output and arithmetic and logical components may be required. To use a general purpose machine in such a situation means that many of the components purchased as part of the system may in fact never be used. If this is the case, another alternative is possible. Why not analyze the situation and determine what components will be needed, design a system which is in effect a grouping of the necessary components, and evaluate it to see whether or not such a system will do the required work more economically and perhaps more efficiently than the general purpose machine? To illustrate, let us take a simple example—a situation which requires classifying and summing for inventory purposes:

> In this instance the only components required to perform the necessary processing would be the selected types of input and output (probably punched paper tape and direct printing) and the main frame components of read and record, add and subtract, and compare. There is no need for either a multiplier or a divider, both of which are quite expensive, or for some of the special components, such as a shift register, frequently found in the general purpose system. With fewer components the likelihood is that the equipment will cost less and the processing may even be accomplished quicker than on a general purpose system. This latter result may be obtained because of the possibility of inserting data directly into the components where it is to be processed rather than routing it through some type of central internal storage.

There are certain limitations upon special purpose equipment which must be understood as thoroughly as its advantages if it is to be properly applied.

First, the objectives of the processing must be clearly defined. Experience seems to indicate that expression of these details in commercial rather than technical terms is the best procedure, because this shifts the burden of detailing the technical specifications for the equipment to the engineering representatives of the manufacturer.

Second, the objectives of processing must be fixed. Since control for special purpose equipment is most economical when it is wired into the equipment rather than obtained through a control register, processing details must be fixed and remain that way for some period of time. Otherwise, considerable additional costs of rewiring will be incurred each time processing procedures are changed.

Third, the volume of data to be processed should be large. Special purpose equipment lacks the flexibility of general purpose systems; therefore, volume is necessary to compensate for such specialization. An interesting adjunct to this factor occurs in those situations where either type of equipment would not be used to its full capacity, but it must be ready for processing at any time. In such cases special purpose equipment may have an advantage over a general purpose machine because the general purpose equipment assigned to such processing could not be used to handle other types of data. Switching general purpose equipment from one type of processing to another is an involved proposition which may not be economically possible where the need for a particular type of processing occurs sporadically throughout the available operating time.

This brings us to the question of how successful have been those companies which have acquired special purpose equipment. Have they successfully spelled out their requirements in sufficient detail to permit the development of useful equipment? The answers to this question are mixed—some have and some have not. There are companies which supposedly analyzed in detail their situations and set forth specifications for equipment to meet their needs, and after such equipment was built found they lacked the proper capacity or circuitry to perform some of the analyses they needed. This equipment is now standing idle. (Much of the early special purpose equipment which received considerable publicity has unfortunately suffered from this deficiency.) On the other hand, there are a number of special purpose machines which have proved highly successful. These are found in those situations where the processing volume is high, the procedure repetitive, and the preparatory analysis done with care.

In summary, one point should be brought out. We have learned that it is both difficult and dangerous to generalize on this question of general purpose vs. special purpose equipment. There is no such thing as a general type of business data processing. Each firm has problems which are different in one respect or another from those of other firms. The question of what is the proper type of equipment has to be approached from the viewpoint of the individual firm. Each situation must be analyzed in detail and the applicability of all types of equipment studied to find which best fits the needs in the particular case—a general purpose or a special purpose system. Where management itself is uncertain of its objectives, the solution is likely to be a general purpose system initially and then a special purpose system once the objectives have been determined.

TECHNIQUES FOR INVESTIGATING*

Generally, the approach to the field of automatic data processing taken by various companies has been a two-stage proposition.

In the first stage, the company personnel, usually drawn from the methods and procedures department, have made a survey of the field of automatic data processing in order to find out what computers can and cannot do, and to discover how other companies have gone about evaluating electronic equipment for their own purposes. Company personnel, in these cases, have gone around to various computer manufacturers, training schools, academic institutions, and other users, and potential users of electronic equipment, to pick up information concerning the field of automatic data processing in general.

The second stage is an internal survey to determine the applicability of electronic equipment and methods on the company's own data processing system. In some companies this stage is pressed more intensely; in some companies the first one.

The influence of top management on the company's data processing projects is sometimes very significant. In many cases, top man-

* By Mr. Laubach.

agement has initiated the study, occasionally keeping very close control over the direction of the projects and even specifying the exact step-by-step procedures to be used. But most often top management has left the company's methods and procedures people to determine the selection and sequence of moves leading up to installation.

The time involved in such preparatory studies varies considerably—from six months to three years, with a tendency to become shorter as the availability of electronic equipment and the experience with its use increase.

A great deal has been written about the question of personnel —who is going to work on a company's data processing project. In general it comes down to the fact that it is a lot easier for a company to train its own accounting and methods procedure personnel in programing than it is to train an expert programer and an electronic technician in a company's particular data processing project and system. It is important to point out, however, that there have been several very successful examples where accountants from a company and the manufacturer's electronic technicians have worked harmoniously together in the development of special purpose equipment.

It is also important to mention that the systems procedures analysts of the future will probably have to take a top management viewpoint in much of the work that they do. It was mentioned earlier in the chapter that there are going to be greater needs in the design of new data processing systems to provide better information for management. And these new systems procedures analysts will probably have to take a much broader viewpoint and be policy-conscious.

Touching briefly on the use of committees, we found they could perform several useful functions. Possibly their main service is to gain interdepartmental cooperation for the data processing project team in gathering information for their study. Another function is to direct and appraise the work of the project team. They also can help to sell top management on the idea of adopting the electronic equipment.

Consultants are often called in to advise on equipment selection, to help devise a plan of attack to guide the company's data processing team, to make economic analyses as a basis for evaluating the various alternative methods of data processing, and (particularly in the case of general purpose systems) in preparing personnel for programing and supervisory requirements. There is much to be said in favor of having consultants come in to train company personnel. It should be kept in mind that sending company personnel away to a formal training program run by a computer manufacturer or an educational institution entails expenses for travel, room and board, and sometimes tuition, and the cost can easily outweigh the fee paid to a consultant for coming in and training the company's personnel.

Computer manufacturers' representatives have know-how and experience to share, and can be useful so long as it is remembered that they tend to be sales-minded and, unfortunately, a few of them have gone so far as to talk a customer into believing that the brand of equipment they are interested in is the only type to consider.

Whatever assistance is employed, management itself should keep four points in mind in selecting equipment:

1. Alternative input and output equipment, like punched cards and other mechanical devices, should be considered *while* you are selecting electronic equipment.
2. Special purpose equipment can have as much flexibility built into it as you want—and no more.
3. When an application takes up the full time of a general purpose computer, it becomes, in effect, a special purpose computer.
4. When a company wants flexibility of equipment to perform special arithmetical operations, there is always the possibility of taking advantage of the facilities offered by service bureaus.

As for the kind of applications that justify the use of the computer, the following points are considered important by a number of companies:

1. A large amount of data should be involved.
2. The operation should be common to many departments, so that there is fuller use of the equipment; this also makes the project easier to "sell" within the company.

3. Customer relations should not be affected, so there is no danger of loss of goodwill in the event of breakdown. (Only a few companies feel this way.)

4. Initial applications should be simple, as in payroll accounting rather than production control, to enable the company to gain experience with the equipment and make it pay for itself as soon as possible.

THE ATTACK ON BIG BUSINESS

John D. Glover

SOME YEARS AGO a number of us at the Harvard Business School came to the conclusion that there was not really a great deal known about big business. There were all kinds of books about it, to be sure, but the hard body of irreducible fact in this field did not amount to much in total, especially in printed form.

In the course of discussions some of us had, it became apparent to us that, as an early step in the development of this field, we would have to take a look at the widespread hostility to and criticism of "big business." This attitude is part of the environment in which business, all business, operates; and business must take account of it.

First of all, I would like to point out that the branch of business

Note: Mr. Glover, who served as moderator of the panel session on which this chapter is based, is Professor of Business Administration, Harvard Business School. His remarks summarize some of the points he made in his book, *The Attack on Big Business* (Boston, Division of Research, Harvard Business School, 1954).

which the critics of big business have in mind is perhaps quite different from the "big business" most businessmen have in mind. You, perhaps, are comfortable in the thought that the attack on big business is an attack on somebody else, because your definition of big business is really *very* big business or that part of the business community described by some other term like "mammoth corporations," and not many people look at themselves as "mammoth corporations," "giant firms," "corporate empires," "massive concentrations of corporate wealth," or "entrenched economic groups." These are some of the terms used by the critics of big business.

The fact remains that, most of the time, the critics are actually talking about ordinary businessmen, about plain business, about people like *you*. It is not just the 100 or 200 largest corporations in the United States that their attack is focused on. This becomes clear when we take a look at the kind of things they hold up in contrast to "big business," the kind of things they favor instead. They use terms such as "little workshops," "little establishments," "petty employers," "the millions of farmers," "tiny individual economic units," "resident proprietors beholden to no one." Terms like this rule a lot of people out of the category of business acceptable to the critics. I think we must accept the conclusion that the brunt of the attack is directed at the bulk of *ordinary* business and that it therefore includes the majority of individual businessmen. The chances are that you are not connected with any form of business which meets the ideals of most critics.

At the moment, I think, there is not quite as much general hostility toward big business as there was, say, in the early 1930's. I believe this is due in large part to the fact that we are in a period of prosperity. If a period of depression should come, the attack would certainly become much more intense. If I must make a long-range prediction, I expect we will have a lot of criticism still with us in the year 2000.

In looking at the criticism of business and trying to understand it, it seems to me that there are three separate phases to it. There is, first, an attack at the economic level; secondly, there is a social and political attack; and, thirdly, there is an ethical and moral attack on business.

ECONOMIC ATTACK

The economic attack, I would guess, is the one business people are most familiar with. Just before World War II, the hearings and monographs of the Temporary National Economic Committee represented a high point of this kind of attack. Boiled down, this attack holds that big business is (1) inefficient and (2) monopolistic.

On the first score, the contention is made that big business cannot be managed efficiently. This argument, by the way, goes back in a direct line to no less an authority than old Adam Smith. Critics have argued that big business does not owe its growth to efficiency, but to predatory, price-cutting attacks on competitors, to the withholding of inventions, to disparaging the activities of small business, and such like. And when big business does appear to operate somewhat efficiently, it is generally claimed that this is because of monopoly profits and the bludgeoning of small suppliers and consumers. It is said that the apparent efficiency of big firms—those which appear efficient because they are profitable—since it is the result of antisocial causes, produces no *net* economies at all from the point of view of society as a whole.

The second part of the economic attack, that big business is monopolistic, is primarily a highly developed theoretical argument which contends that big business invariably ends up with higher prices, smaller output, and an inferior product. The charge of monopoly has been put forward for the past 50 years; it is a familiar contention in the halls of Congress.

The economic attack is undoubtedly a matter of concern to businessmen. It would be imprudent for them to shrug it off. However, I think the two other levels of attack—the social and political and the ethical and moral criticism—may be truly more important in the long run.

People, it seems to me, will be making this type of complaint against business long after the economic attack is turned back—if that should ever come to pass. The second and third levels of attack are important also because they have a rather widespread public acceptance throughout the nation as a whole.

Although we do not actually know a great deal about what people in general think of big business, a number of studies indicate that something like three-quarters of the population think big business, on the whole, has done a pretty good job. But when we start looking behind these figures, we find some important reservations. Even among the people who think big business has done fairly well from the economic standpoint, about 60% believe that it is probably bad for the country in the realm of politics, ethics, and morals. And certainly among the one-quarter who believe that big business is not good for the country economically, the overwhelming majority also believe that it is not good in the political and social dimension.

POLITICAL LEVEL

On the political level, the main theme is the charge that big business runs the country; that it has bought or insinuated itself into governmental agencies; that it controls the national administration. This charge has been made continuously since the time of Grover Cleveland—even concerning the administrations of Franklin D. Roosevelt and Harry S. Truman. And now more and more frequently we hear again the assertion that the Eisenhower Administration is a "big business administration." This puts our present government in the same category with every other administration all the way back to 1885, not counting what a lot of people have had to say about Ulysses S. Grant.

There are those who say that big business is incompatible with the economic basis of democracy—that it represents a concentration of economic power, which leads to the concentration of political power. It is argued that any such concentration of power undermines the democratic principle that all power shall be widely and equally dispersed among all the people. We have in big business, so critics say, an institution which holds vast power but is not responsible to the people.

Another extension of the "antidemocratic" charge is that big business is incompatible with the *social* basis of democracy. This theory has three principal lines of argument:

1. Democracy, according to some, presupposes a nation of individual entrepreneurs, of self-employed men. Obviously, big business is not made up of self-employed people. It is made up of large numbers of interdependent employees—including the officers of corporations, who are also employees. With the growth of big business we have millions and millions of people who are not self-employed but are called, by critics, "wage earners," "white-collar workers," "clerks," or "mere hirelings."

2. Big business, by its very size and power is—some say—driving out of society those small business units which *are* compatible with our political and social doctrines. It is driving them to the wall. Through various and devious means it operates to undermine democracy and bring on an undemocratic state.

3. Some say that big business controls the press, the schools and universities, and even the churches of America.

Just who are the people who are thus attacking business and businessmen? They cannot be dismissed as just "reds," "fellow travelers," or even naive socialists. Actually they include people of all political complexions. They also include people of great responsibility. Theodore Roosevelt, for instance, was certainly one of the most active—and effective—foes that large-scale business ever encountered. T. R.'s arguments were not appreciably different from some of those cited above. There is a large and entirely home-grown body of American critics who have political ideas of this kind.

ETHICAL AND MORAL LEVEL

However, it is on the ethical and moral planes that, in my opinion, the most significant—that is to say, *practically* important—criticisms are leveled at big business. From such a respectable and respected source as the church—not just one, but all American churches—come denunciations of the methods and aims of business. Prominent among the critics, also, are many of our poets, playwrights, novelists, and essayists; and their words, I believe it is fair to state, express with great emotional impact the feelings which many people have. J. P. Marquand's *Point of No Return* is a recent example of implicit moral and ethical criticism of business and business practices that has become a "best seller."

To digress for just a moment, perhaps as a people we aren't fully aware of the role which big business, for better or worse, has actually played in shaping the character of this nation. America is different from other countries. We buy different qualities of merchandise, wear different kinds of clothing, use different productive techniques, ship by different methods of transport, sell through different types of stores, and so on. We use all these goods and services in larger quantities than other nations. The material basis of our civilization is different from, and greater than, that of other countries.

Whatever advantages may inhere in the differences—and I, personally, believe there are many—are not because of "little workshops," or "tiny economic units." Those aspects of material life in America which are unique are largely the consequences of large-scale organization and production. More than any other people, we have organized our economic life in large-scale units. These economic units, in our private enterprise system, are largely business corporations. And when I say "large scale," I mean business corporations—*units*—employing 500 or more people, or perhaps even 250 or more people. In much of the rest of the world, and in comparison to what we have known historically, even an organization of 250 people is *large*-scale.

There are critics to whom it appears that we live in an "Age of Anxiety"; that we are a "Beat Generation," spiritually and morally bankrupt, with no "Peace of Mind" and no "Peace of Soul." Essentially they are arguing that only material values matter to us today; that economic advantage is the one and only thing which counts, and, for the business community, any means to that end is completely justified. It follows that all other values such as justice, charity, fairness, and responsibility of the individual have gone by the board. This is a picture which many critics paint of a single-valued system in which all of the Western World's traditional ideas of good and evil are overlooked and forgotten, a "corporatized" system in which all individual responsibility for individual actions is neglected.

Some of the critics are willing to admit that there is prosperity. Indeed, quite a number charge that the fact we do prosper is one of our troubles. They say we are *too well* off. They insist America has a *bad* system and a *bad* society because our *values* are wrong, because we deny the significance of the individual, and because we deny the importance of, or neglect, religious duties. Some say that "the Factory" itself is basically an inhuman means of organization, and that for the sake of maximum production techniques all considerations of human dignity and individual worth have disappeared. They also say that "the City," built up by and around large-scale enterprise, represents a poor way of life as compared with the traditional agrarian, small-town, highly individualized way of life. The criticisms of business extend, even, to what is said to be the standardized, low level of taste of the articles produced in factories.

CHALLENGE TO BUSINESS

What does all this criticism add up to? What do such statements about big business mean? There are a few facts that emerge rather clearly. Certainly there is evidence, in the "best selling" appeal of some of these critical attacks, that criticisms of big business, especially on the political and social plane and on the ethical and moral plane, reflect, if they do not engender, widespread feelings of hostility or misgiving. It is also evident from a lot of things, I think, that we—all of us Americans—have hopes and aspirations beyond the desire for mere economic advantages and security. We want a *good* society—a *democratic* good society. And many Americans have doubts, at least, as to whether business enterprise, as such, shares those aspirations.

We are all interested, of course, in a rising standard of living—not just within the borders of our own continental area but all over the world. We make no secret of this particular economic aspiration of ours. Only a few are ashamed of that aspiration. But the attacks on "big business" indicate that we are also interested in a more perfect democracy, in greater opportunity for individual growth. We have had these interests from the time this nation was established, and we still have them. We want a better tomorrow, with a maximum of opportunities for our people to make use of their individual talents and to realize themselves as responsible human beings. All this is very important to us.

How can big business help us realize *all* our hopes and aspirations? How can our economic system aid us in achieving the *good* society we so desire? Such is the problem we face. As I have said, on the first plane, the economic level, the majority of people think big business has done a good job. Most people do not complain a great deal about the wages big corporations pay or the prices they charge. The bulk of complaints, it would seem, center on social and ethical matters, grievances real or fancied which have little to do with the *economic* performance of business. Big business in the minds of many people has not made very good grades at the political and moral levels. This critical attitude may not be well founded or fairly taken. But its widespread existence is a fact.

Now, what is the prescription for action? First of all, I might say most critics have no prescription for action. In our nation's progress toward a better tomorrow, most critics do not visualize any active role for the businessman. There isn't anything they really *want* him to do. The critics, generally speaking, would have some group *other* than the business community deal with our problems. But in the United States businessmen are action-oriented, and I think it is appropriate here to take a look at some of the things they can do.

First, probably the most obvious thing business can do is to continue what it has been doing to increase the efficiency of our economic activities, to make the most of all our resources at hand. Business enterprise can continue to strive to be technically competent, imaginative, enterprising, and risk-taking. All this seems to me a permanent responsibility of business and a task which, in the years to come, will play no less a part in the challenge to business than it has done in years past.

Secondly—and this point is a little harder to put in tangible form —I think businessmen themselves have got to clarify *their own thinking* about the nature and objectives of business enterprises. All too many times, businessmen, when they write or talk about business, sound—of all things—much like their critics. They say or imply, along with their critics, that business has one sole aim, one sole value: to make a profit. But in so doing they understate their own objectives and their own criteria of decision and action. Actually, the research that has been done at the Harvard Business School over the years and the thousands of cases we have collected indicate that business is a multivalued system. A lot of things get taken into account in business policies and actions besides profit making.

Business *is* multivalued. Decisions are made on very complex criteria, and whether a profit is achieved or not is only *one* of the important ones. Nobody wants to work for an organization operating at a loss. Unprofitable operations don't hold out much promise of security for anyone. But we find that business balances profit considerations along with ideas of what is the fair, proper, responsible thing to do—fair to itself, fair to management, fair to its employees, fair to the stockholders, fair to the community, and fair to competitors. This is what we at the Harvard Business School, as observers, find when we watch business decisions being made. We see a multivalued system at work. Theoreticians and doctrinaire individuals on both extremes of political Left and Right may find this hard to believe. But clinical facts from the field speak for themselves.

One of the principal jobs of managing large concerns consists precisely of assigning proper weight to the variety of considerations which always have to be taken into account.

Thus, we can count on the fact that the values of business form a complex pattern; that they create multiple responsibilities for, and put multiple pressures on, the administrators of big business. I do think businessmen *can* do much more by way of becoming explicitly aware of *all* the values they hold important and the values, especially the nonmaterial values, they wish to promote by their policies and actions.

In some companies, I am sure, the range of values taken into account, the objectives of business enterprise, probably *are* too narrow to meet all the aspirations of Americans, and, I would say, they will certainly have to be broadened in the years ahead.

There are several areas, as many people have pointed out, where the business community generally has been a little slow in picking up responsibility. However, it is heartening to observe the increased awareness and sense of obligation in business leadership over the years.

For instance, there are probably students at the Harvard Business School nowadays who could scarcely believe that business people could make the type of statements which are found in some of the testimony given in 1899 before the Industrial Commission of Congress. Not only did many of these statements reflect an attitude of total irresponsibility toward the community at large and toward labor, but also toward stockholders—the owners of the companies. These are the kind of remarks which, if anybody made them today before a Congressional committee, would make our hackles stand on end. Yet they were made and are a phase in our history. For example, this interchange took place between the chairman of the Commission and the president of one well-known company:

Q. Did you pay the last dividends out of the earnings or out of the surplus?
A. I did not mention that.
Q. Do you mean to say you would not like to answer that?
A. I mean to say that I did not mention it.
Q. Do you refuse to answer that question?
A. I think it had better remain as it is, Mr. Chairman.

In June 1899, as some of you know, there weren't even many public statements wherein stockholders, or anybody else, could find out if a corporation had any earnings or what its assets and liabilities were.

We have come a long way from the time of *no* public statements to the time when very full statements are published by virtually every large corporation.

The old attacks on business have undoubtedly served a purpose, and I believe in the 50-odd years that have passed since then there has been a growing recognition of the responsibility which goes along with business enterprise. The fact that leaders like Owen D. Young of General Electric and Frank Abrams of Standard Oil, New Jersey, have advocated widening the avowed objectives of corporations and increasing their stated obligations is a good indication of this trend.

The next point in my prescription for action is that businessmen must make sure their broad policies get translated into reality down at the working level. For instance, not long ago some members of the Harvard Business School faculty had the good fortune to study at close range the operations of a certain well-known company, which illustrates the difficulties involved:

> This company had an expressed management policy that its dealers and distributors were to be treated as independent businessmen—to be treated with respect. They were definitely not to be pushed around or pressured by company salesmen. Price and other policies of dealers and distributors were not to be dictated by company salesmen; rather the company was to offer its ideas and suggestions, and the dealer or distributor, on his own, could decide from that point on.
>
> Such was the policy at the level of top manager. When our faculty people looked around and saw what the salesmen were doing, however, it was found that this policy was far from being carried out at the dealer and distributor levels. Actually, many of the salesmen *were* using a heavy hand in their relationships with dealers and distributors, telling them what they must stock and must not stock, what their margins should be, and so on.
>
> The company management was interested in what its dealers thought, and in soliciting their opinions it received, as might be expected, all sorts of complaints about the way it did business. Get-

ting top-level policy put into effect at the working level may be difficult in any circumstances, but somewhere in that company communications had gone completely amiss. The management went to work on this problem with renewed energy. This is the type of occurrence business must work to prevent.

As my last recommendation for action I suggest business must promote a better understanding of business itself. Thus, business should continue to sponsor research into the nature and structure of the business entity, as it has in the past. I hope that this type of investigation will not be overlooked in the midst of many and great pressures on *technical* research, so that the public can come to know better what the large corporations in our midst are like and to understand their operations more clearly.

It seems to me that business can and should agree to make many, many opportunities available for people, and not just scholars and researchers, to come in and learn at first hand what is going on in business. College groups and clubs, ministers, school teachers, and so on—companies ought to let them come in and see for themselves what business is and how it operates, and to ask any questions that they like.

It is practically impossible to realize how many people in this country have never even been inside a factory. Even among students of business subjects, many have only a vague idea of what an assembly line looks like. A still greater proportion of public school teachers have never had an opportunity to talk to businessmen about their problems or see them at work.

I have failed to mention outside public relations programs—on purpose. Programs of this sort have a place. But reliance upon them is not the way, to my mind, to make the processes and problems of business enterprise better known to all of us. Indeed, if such programs take the form of self-serving pronouncements, I can think of nothing more surely destined to be self-defeating, more likely to furnish new material for the critics of business. I am sure in my own mind that there is no substitute for understanding based on firsthand knowledge.

QUESTIONS ABOUT THE ATTACK ON
BIG BUSINESS*

From the floor: Do you think that the very, very big businesses' policy of buying up small town plants and making them part of a large organization has aggravated the criticism of business? Of course, there are two methods of operation when a small plant is purchased by a large organization—the local management can be thrown out and the plant becomes part of a highly centralized concern, or the local management can be retained and the plant can be run much as it was before but with improvements. But my impression is that there have been a lot of acquisitions handled in the first way.

Mr. Glover: According to the critics, the small local enterprise in America is rapidly giving way to the large national business organization, and this phenomenon, they say, is bad. Certainly mergers have been going on in recent years, and the merger tendency will undoubtedly provide future ammunition for the critics.

From the floor: Isn't there evidence that big business tends to act with more discretion and perhaps is better behaved than many small businesses?

Mr. Glover: Certainly there are many notable cases where this is true. Whether we can make a substantial generalization out of this, I don't know. Large industry, I am sure, is responsible for many instances of improved working hours, holding the price line in face of inflation, adherence to price lines, recognition of labor leadership, reducing racial discrimination, and so on. But I am leery of a generalized answer to your question.

From the floor: To carry this question of the attack on business one step further, isn't there a new protagonist in the fray—namely, subversive activity? I have in mind the local struggle between communism and capitalism. Don't you think that much of the criticism of business practices is communist-inspired—that it is a deliberate

* Businessmen present at the panel discussion summarized in this chapter raised certain questions which brought about the interplay of ideas reported more or less verbatim in this section.

maneuver in the class struggle? With big business out of the way it will be easier, the communists figure, to take over small business.

Mr. Glover: That assertion would obviously be very difficult to prove, and we had better not make too much of it. On the other hand, I think it possible that there is something to it. I have felt in my bones that some of the material I have read was conceived by the Kremlin, so to speak, but I still say this idea should not be over-emphasized. The war against big business long antedated serious communist activity in the United States. This is still primarily a home-grown problem, and is as much American as apple pie or William Jennings Bryan.

From the floor: What about government help to small business-men in bidding on certain government contracts? Do you think such aid is economically desirable or justified?

Mr. Glover: It seems to me that on occasions this practice has been made a political plum, and it has no doubt interfered with war efforts. However, it may very well be that small business could have produced effectively in cases where the government procurement agents, who are conscientious and diligent in their work, simply found it easier to work through larger companies, so that small com-panies didn't get contracts they could have handled. Blanket legis-lation isn't the answer, and unless the government men who are sup-posed to help small business are responsible and competent, such practices can be uneconomical and perhaps dangerous.

From the floor: Cannot large corporations help bring about a better understanding of business problems through more widespread own-ership of stock?

Mr. Glover: To the extent that more people own a few shares of stock and take a look at their company's annual report to see what business is doing, that suggestion is certainly valid, I would say.

From the floor: In regard to stock ownership by the employees of a company, I would like to add this thought. I happen to work for a firm with 17,000 employees, and I regret that we are not trying to get an employees' stock ownership plan into effect. It seems to me that in a corporation of our size such a plan is very important. Employees are certainly part of the general public; and if a company encourages them to buy an interest in the business, they will also know that it is thinking of their own welfare. This ought to encourage them to do a little better job, too.

From the floor: It was mentioned that clergy and teachers are among the most influential critics of business, especially on the ethical level. Are you familiar with what the National Industrial Conference Board is doing in sending information to 50,000 teachers and churchmen? The Board sends, on request, pamphlets of information every few weeks, and letters from recipients indicate that they are making good use of them in the classrooms.

Of course, the problem of moral criticism is a big one. Our company has tried to face up to this problem. We made a survey and found that many of the clergymen in our plant areas believed we were making over 25% profit on our sales. We didn't think this situation was good for our operations, so we devised a very simple program. We brought in 26 representatives of the clergy, gave them a brief tour of the plant, let them talk to management people and union leaders, and then gave them a chance to find out anything they wanted in a two-hour question and answer period. This program was the start of good relations with the churches in that area. I don't offer my idea as an all-embracing solution to the problem, but we did find in one place at least that clergymen could be brought around when they were presented with realities.

INCREASING THE EFFECTIVENESS
OF CONFERENCES

Robert F. Bales

THE TOPIC OF DECISION-MAKING CONFERENCES has only taken on great significance in the past five or ten years at the most. Before then one didn't hear much about decision making, the term "small group" was seldom used, and there was no very general impression that anything was to be gained from comparing decision-making meetings in one context with those in another. Times have changed. There is a field now recognized in the academic disciplines as "small group research," or research in social interaction and decision making, and results are beginning to be available. It is in this area that my colleagues and I have been working.

It is true, of course, that our research has not been primarily directed at assisting executives to meet problems which they face in conducting conferences. Participants in our experiments have never

Note: Mr. Bales is Lecturer on Sociology and Research Assistant in the Laboratory of Social Relations, Harvard University.

met before, have no responsibility for the decisions they make, are officially leaderless, and operate in an organizational vacuum. But we are reaching some findings, nevertheless, which management may find helpful.

SIZE OF CONFERENCES

One of the problems we have been concerned with is the size of group conferences. A good deal of decision making is done in comparatively small groups, and it may very well be that decision making on important, complicated issues always tends to gravitate to a small group center. If so, I think this has something to do with the characteristics of interpersonal communication. It is impossible for a large number of persons to think in agreement for any length of time. None of us can calculate, for example, exactly what is going on in the minds of even four to eight people, but in a small group like this we have a better chance of guessing probable reactions. Keeping track of the thought processes of five, six, or seven individuals is apparently about the best that the human mind can do. It must be this fact that underlies the tendency for decision making to gravitate into the hands of small groups.

In the past few years, we have run tests on a series of group sizes from two to seven people. From these tests, and other research, we have obtained some idea of what happens in the group when the number of participants varies.

In the first place, groups in sizes up through seven, according to our experience, allow each person to speak at least a few times to each other person. But when we come to groups of eight or more people, empty relationships begin to appear, and the people who talk least in the group do not talk to each other at all. There is a kind of time limitation, you might say, which influences the way communication channels can be set up. Above size seven it becomes increasingly more difficult for everyone to interact directly with everyone else. Below size seven this is easier, and the smaller the group, the more complete the interaction of minds.

Different group sizes below seven have special characteristics. For instance, two-man groups are different from all others in that they have significantly lower rates of antagonism and disagreement but higher rates of tension and anxious, nervous behavior. Size two groups also usually show high rates of information-giving and low rates of suggestion-making. In a two-man group it would seem that the participants have a power problem which they are trying to keep at arm's length. It is not possible for them to appeal to any majority, for the majority is two people and anything less than the majority is a lost cause. Since there is no third person to whom they can turn, each participant is dependent on the free and willing cooperation of the other. Generally, therefore, a pair tends to handle their problem gingerly. They avoid disagreeing and they avoid getting entangled in quarrels. They steer clear of suggestions, but rather just give and ask for information.

Three-man groups also have a unique character, which is again related to the problem of securing a majority. In these groups there is a strong tendency for a combination of two against one to appear, and in this case the majority is inordinately strong. If you are in the minority in a three-man group, you are all alone and a lot of pressure can be brought to bear on you. Apparently people tend to take advantage of this, and it is hard to avoid the snapping shut of a two-against-one coalition. You get on the safe side, if you can, and get yourself a pal, and you hate to give him up because the poor fellow who is left on the outside is really holding the bag. Thus a group of this size tends to run into difficulty because of the personal insecurity of its members. You either get caught in the majority coalition or out of it! In other words, political maneuvering tends to interfere with the logical requirements of the problem.

Groups size four and six usually have significantly high rates of disagreement and trouble. A group of even size, if it is split on an issue, tends to break into two equal factions, and no majority can be brought to bear on the decision. It is an old and probably wise adage in administration that committees should be appointed in odd sizes so deadlocks can be broken. We now have specific evidence that groups of even size are indeed more prone to discord and antagonism, and they do in fact need tie-breakers, both to facilitate decision making and to encourage a constructive atmosphere for discussion.

The size five group is the one that our participants seem to like. Among other questions at the end of each of our experimental meetings, we ask them to indicate whether they think the group was too large or too small for its purpose. Below size five, participants say it is too small; and when they get to six, a few say it is beginning to get too large. But nobody says five is too large, and nobody says it is too small.

I surely do not think there is anything magical about the number five for a conference group, although it is a size which gets away from the peculiar difficulties connected with two-man, three-man, and even-size groups, and begins to allow a leader a little room to operate. And it seems to me that the fact that an optimum size does appear under our particular conditions indicates that there may be an optimum size for other conference conditions also.

DESCRIBING WHAT GOES ON

In order to study problems like the effects of size, and many others, we need to be able to obtain precise observation and description of the behavior of group members. What really does go on?

In our studies so far we have not attempted to evaluate the content of the discussion or the actual decision that our people make. That will differ, of course, in every type of group, according to technical requirements of a good decision in a particular context. We are, however, interested in how groups go about reaching their conclusion.

Thus, we concern ourselves with the ways the members react to each other, how they appraise and evaluate each other, who likes whom and why, who dislikes whom and why, whom they regard as their leader, and how much active participation goes on. We want to know who talks when, and how people talk: whether they agree or disagree, what the rate of giving suggestions is compared to the rate of giving information and opinion, how often the participants ask for opinion, and so on. At the end of the meeting we request our participants to appraise each other's performance along these general lines. We also ask their opinions about the decision they came to and about the conduct of the meeting as a whole.

In order to obtain a description of the behavior in the meeting, we make a classification of every act that takes place. Every time a person makes a remark or a meaningful gesture it is classified. We worked quite a while to develop a classification system, and I am happy to say that it is now outstandingly simple.

To give you a crude, fourfold breakdown first, we say that social interaction and decision making consist of (1) questions, (2) problem-solving attempts, (3) positive reactions, and (4) negative reactions. In formal terms, that about takes care of what happens when people get together.

Actually, our research classification breaks the process down finer than that. We have divided the "problem-solving attempts" into three types: (a) those giving information, (b) those giving opinion, and (c) those offering suggestions. The "questions" are cognate with these: (a) asking for information, (b) asking for opinions, and (c) asking for suggestions. Similarly, we have marked out three types of "positive reactions": (a) simple agreement more or less on the intellectual level, (b) a demonstration of tension release which is generally smiling or laughing, and (c) an instance of solidarity or friendliness, usually taking the form of pleasant remarks meant to clear the atmosphere, i.e., jokes and attempts to make the other person feel better in some way. The "negative reactions" are parallel to the positive ones: (a) simple disagreement or difference of opinion, (b) disagreement accompanied by tension or anxiety, and (c) outright antagonism and mutual frustration.

This gives us 12 categories of activity, and is actually a very simple kind of breakdown. However, it has proved effective. We can fit every act that occurs in our experiments into one category or another, and we have obtained many useful results with it, such as those mentioned above on group size.

By using this system, we can tell at the end of the meeting just how many instances of agreement there were, how much disagreement, and so on, either absolutely or in terms of percentages of the total amount of interaction. We can measure how much each person talked and determine exactly what kind of contribution he made, in relation to the group as a whole and to every other participant. We can then chart the progress of the meeting by indicating how activity varied as time went on. This classification tool can be used in the observation of any conference group and is helpful in evaluating individuals as well as groups.

ROLE OF THE LEADER

The role of the leader is a major question with which we have been concerned. As I indicated above, we appoint no formal leaders for our conference groups, and this gives us a chance to find out the characteristics of natural leadership. We also have been interested in seeing whether or not the people who assume leadership can maintain their positions in subsequent sessions, since they have had no formal grant of authority. What makes a "natural leader" in the conference situation?

In the first place, as the size of a group increases, there is a strong tendency toward the centralization of communications around one or two persons. A disparity soon appears between the amount of talking done by the dominant person or persons and the amount that the other people do. We have never observed a group where there was exact equality of participation—or even anything very closely approximating it. No group, in other words, remains undifferentiated and leaderless.

Occasionally in smaller groups where there is a great deal of conflict we get more equal participation; oddly enough, this equality of involvement seems to be about as often associated with trouble as with cooperation. I am inclined to think that when people talk about equality of participation, they ordinarily mean *not* that each person should spend an equal amount of time talking but rather that there should be an opportunity for everyone to react to every remark or proposal that is made and every opinion that is expressed. Equality, then, means a chance for each proposal to be adequately heard.

Most people are willing to let others talk, and are interested in hearing the reactions and views of others. The usual conference membership consists of one or a few very active participants with the rest participating less along a downward gradient. Sometimes there is a gap between a top participator and the others. This gap between degrees of participation indicates that one of the members is assuming central importance. Of course, this does not necessarily mean that he will be chosen leader, but in our short-term groups there is a very high relationship between the amount of talking people do and the leadership rating they get on that session. Our groups, you must remember, meet for only a very short time, the members are not introduced to each other, and no leader is appointed; hence if a man is to gain a strategic position, he must do so by talking. Once the leader has established himself, there is a tendency for him to relax a little during the following sessions. We notice that he talks less than he did at the beginning, provided he feels sure that he is not losing his position.

As a means toward understanding the leadership phenomenon, we ask our conference participants to rank each other on the basis of several criteria. One of these is what we call "task ability." We ask them, for example, who in their group had the best ideas, who did the most to guide the discussion and keep it moving effectively, and other questions of this sort, all centering about task effectiveness. We also try our best to find out how well each person likes each of the others present. We ask the same questions after each meeting in the series of experimental sessions which we conduct.

At the end of the first meeting in five-man groups, we find that the man who receives the most votes on task ability has about a 50-50 chance of receiving the highest popularity rating as well. By the end of the second session in a series, only 25% of the group think the most active and efficient member was also the most likable. At the end of the third session the figure is down to about 17%, and after the fourth meeting only 14% think their leader was also the most jolly good fellow.

There is a tendency in the first meeting, then, for task ability and popularity ratings to coincide, but thereafter they seem to be paired only by chance. We do not know exactly why this happens. It may be that in the first session people fail to make very fine discriminations regarding their fellow conferees. As they get to know each other better, their judgments become more perceptive. Being somewhat pessimistic, however, I lean a little bit to the theory that there is a danger more or less inherent in the role of the task leader which tends to lose him the affection of his associates.

We do not find many cases in which the task leader is highly disliked—he is liked about as much as the average. But typically the best-liked man is not the one who has assumed task leadership. I am inclined to think that this may be due to the fact that the ordinary would-be leader, in sticking to his job and keeping it his first concern, tends to talk more than he listens, and so loses influence over his fellows. They withdraw some of their admiration from him and center it on someone who is not shouldering the main responsibility for getting the job done and who feels he can afford, therefore, to be more sensitive to personal relationships within the group.

What conclusions can one draw from this? I suppose some people might say that task ability and popularity, although both very vital elements of leadership, are important in different ways. A group needs at least one man with task ability if it is to perform its function of decision making in an effective manner; at the same time, there should be at least one man in the conference room who understands and appreciates the several personalities involved, who can conciliate conflicting opinions and act as mediator between opposing points of view, and who can induce agreement by inspiring his associates' confidence, respect, and esteem. Since task ability and likability are both necessary for different and separate reasons, why shouldn't committees choose two separate men to provide these requisite elements?

On the other hand, there are those who believe that the efficient, duty-minded task leader ought to be as good at winning friends as he is at getting concrete things accomplished. No group can ever have two real leaders, according to this view, and there *are* men, however rare they may be, with both a sensitivity to individual re-actions and a talent for guiding discussion toward constructive con-clusions.

We have found, in the course of our research, that people who do have both task ability and general likability are apt to be nominated to leadership posts in other groups we place them in. Men who com-bine both these qualities of excellence are obviously very valuable in conference situations. I might note here that, in moving certain people from group to group, we have found it easier to predict their task ability ratings than to forecast their likability. Often men who have been given high popularity ratings by one set of conferees will not be as well-liked in other groups, while their task ability grades —based largely on how much they talk—are likely to remain more stable.

SUCCESS OR FAILURE?

Finally, my colleagues and I have been thinking about the general effectiveness of conferences, about the conditions which make them successes or failures. What I shall say on this subject, however, is drawn substantially from the experience of those who have had day-to-day conference responsibilities in business settings, as reported, for example, in a fine study made by researchers at the University of Michigan on actual administrative conferences.

By way of general comment on this and other studies, I might say that a good deal appears to depend on the expectations and values of the people who are at the meeting. It is very difficult to say *this* or *that* is the best way for a committee to operate, because its success is heavily dependent on how its participants expect it to operate. Some research studies in this field seem to show that the direct, auto-cratic type of conference procedure produces very bad results. The lesson seems to be that one should be democratic. In other studies, by contrast, especially those made of business groups, indications were that dissatisfaction arises when the leader tries to share leadership. Where time is limited, when the stage has been set and there are certain definite expectations as to how things should go, differences in procedure are often not enthusiastically received—even though they are well-intended attempts to make operations more democratic. In any organization there are probably a number of committees whose members would object were their meetings to be conducted in any way except according to a well-defined, no-nonsense, more or less autocratic, and rigid procedure.

In organizing a committee meeting, it is important to have a clear-cut idea of the purpose of the group. Some meetings, for example, are designed to facilitate upward communication—to let management know how its organization feels about certain issues. Other committees are largely advisory. Still others may be primarily information-gathering devices. Not all committees are actually charged with the responsibility for making decisions. It is necessary to make a distinction between these various committee purposes and functions, for the operation of the conference may be totally different depending, for instance, on whether or not the participants will be held accountable for their decisions.

There may be many instances in business where a committee is not really necessary at all. If some one person is made responsible for a decision, and this person has adequate channels of information and is wholly capable of carrying out his program by himself, he might do much better on his own.

Before a conference is called, then, management ought to ask itself, "Do we *need* a committee here?" A conference can hardly be successful if it is merely a hindrance to effective, direct action.

However, in situations where there is a lack of clear authority and insufficient information on which to base action, or where the many values and motivations involved prevent one person from making and implementing a decision successfully, a committee conference is in order. Participation and involvement are very important when a new policy has to be crystallized from many opinions and motivations and when one wishes a real change in behavior. Decisions stick much better with those who have helped to make them than they do with people who have had no say in the matter.

OTHER POINTS*

Several other points can be made regarding the operation of business conferences. Some people have observed that the most successful discussions occur among people who themselves have had experience in leading such sessions. These men seem to be more aware of the problems at hand, and are able to seek out the facts more quickly and reach an understanding or a decision with greater dispatch than an ordinary group.

Adequate preparation for the conference is very important. All of us have attended meetings where no chairman had been provided and no agenda prepared—and we would probably agree that these conferences were usually dismal failures. It is helpful to know before the meeting who is to be in attendance, who will be moderator, and precisely what problems are to be covered.

When the executives in one business firm found that their meetings were degenerating into bull sessions and accomplishing little in the way of effective decision making, they set up an informal "conference code" among themselves to remedy the situation. Now before anyone calls a meeting, he must have a definite agenda in mind, must outline the topic in advance, must prepare charts or visual aids of some kind, and, most important of all in this company's experience, he must see that written records of decisions reached, postponed, or rejected are prepared and distributed to the conferees.

The question of time limits on meetings is often raised. At New York University they have done some research in this field, and have found that 90 minutes is about long enough for most conferences. At Harvard three-hour sessions conducted for observation purposes show that long meetings grow less productive with each passing hour. The fatigue element certainly plays an important part in the effective-

* From the discussion.

ness of a conference, along with such physical factors as location of lighting, comfortableness of chairs, distribution of participants around the room, and so forth.

In conclusion, most businessmen will agree on the usefulness of meetings as a tool in planning future strategy. Knowledge about the ways in which small groups operate should be of value to men whose businesses require skillful conference leadership.

NEW TRENDS IN COMMERCIAL BANKING

Charles Cortez Abbott and Morris A. Schapiro

THE WORD *trends,* as used in this chapter, applies to three kinds of development in banking: services, methods, and the structure of the industry. In brief, rapid changes are taking place in all three of these areas. Also, it appears that the changes which have taken place so far are only a beginning; in other words, an era of new developments in banking is barely underway.

These changes stem partly from the economic pressures within banks, and partly from the economic, social, and political developments taking place outside the banking world. Some of these forces have been long in the making; some are of recent origin.

As we look back over the last few years, or even the contemporary

Note: Mr. Abbott, who introduces this chapter, was formerly Converse Professor of Banking and Finance at Harvard Business School and is now Dean of the Graduate School of Business Administration, University of Virginia; Mr. Schapiro is head of M. A. Schapiro & Co., Inc.

scene, it is quite clear that there have been rapid and rather astonishing developments in the area of *banking service.* We note the growth of the "pay as you go" check plan and the "charge account" plan; the latest statistics indicate that about 75 banks have instituted these plans, although some have since discontinued them. In Boston, the First National initiated the "check credit account" operation.

In the late 1930's, we observed the development of term loans and of equipment financing. Significantly, since World War II, more banks have entered the field of "retail banking." There has been a striking expansion in consumer financing, in all of its many forms, as well as in loans on real estate. We also have seen the rise of "common trust funds." Again, banks have been called on, in effect, to finance the deficit, or at least the seasonal needs, of the United States Treasury.

The list of recently developed services can be extended almost indefinitely.

Turning to *banking methods,* we are witnessing a sequence of developments in the area of mechanized accounting and bookkeeping. Banks now have a relatively new device—the posted check bookkeeping arrangements of various banks throughout the country. Electronic accounting is just around the corner. David Rockefeller, Vice President of Chase Manhattan Bank, recently disclosed some of the thinking regarding the impact of atomic energy on banks and banking. Vast changes are ahead as banks make ready to reach for new efficiencies.

As Mr. Breech pointed out in an earlier chapter, Ford Motor Company's operations in 1965 will not be conducted with the methods or the tools of 1955. This is as true of the banking business as it is of the automobile business.

Now, considering banking as an industry, new developments are best viewed in perspective against the economic and business characteristics of the industry—that is, in the light of the *banking structure.* Banking primarily is a service industry; further, it traditionally has combined the services of safekeeping, transfer of funds, provision of means of payment, lending, trust administration, and so on.

However, no stern logic limits banking to this particular combination of services. Already we can see new services being combined with these traditional ones as banks adapt themselves to a changing world.

Aside from the service industry characteristic, there are other aspects of banking which should be noted:

1. Like many service industries, banking has a small capital base and, like most service industries, it must follow its customers when they move, as for example, from city to suburb. New plant expansion in *growth* areas, decentralization, and other powerful factors have caused major population shifts.

2. Banking has a high percentage of fixed costs, primarily due to salary expense.

3. The industry is heavily regulated.

4. Its resources have various origins in varying amounts—capital, time and demand deposits, both stable and volatile money, payroll accounts, banking balances, public funds, and so on. What a bank does with the resources at its disposal is determined largely by the characteristics of these individual types of funds.

Let us look briefly, but more closely, at one of the new developments: consumer financing. Here is a demonstration of health and vitality in the banking industry, and a sign of adapting to a changing environment. Business, like other types of organisms, must adapt or wither. That banks have entered the consumer financing area, which in many cases has been a more profitable endeavor than business financing, we may interpret both as a sign of vitality and as an indication of a new area of competition not only among individual banks but also among commercial banking and other types of lending agencies.

The fact that new trends are discernible in banking services, banking methods, and the commercial banking structure is a sign that banks are alert to the challenge of changing conditions. Were such trends not apparent, there would be reason to be concerned about the vitality of an essential industry.

BANK MERGERS*

Because banking is so closely regulated, it is possible to identify trends and changes by examining pending banking legislation. For example, among the bills recently considered in Washington is a minor one which would repeal that section of the National Banking Act which requires national banks, wherever located, to advertise intended liquidations in a New York City newspaper:

> In a recent issue of the *American Banker* is a page of such notices, one advising the reader that "the First National Bank of Dawson, located at Dawson in the State of Pennsylvania, has closed its accounts. All creditors are notified to present claims to the undersigned at Dawson, Pennsylvania. (Signed) J. Ford Knox, Liquidating Agent." Among the other liquidation notices were those of the First National Bank of Point Marion, Pennsylvania, the Lincoln National Bank of Newark, New Jersey, the First National Bank in Bloomington, Indiana, and a bank in Riverdale, California! There was a total of nine, all in one day.
>
> However, it is no longer essential that these banks advertise notice of liquidation in New York. This requirement goes back to the circulation privileges which national banks enjoyed years ago, and which were terminated in 1935. Prior to that date, advertising in New York City was necessary—it was the quickest means of preventing cashiers and tellers from recirculating the notes and bills which were issued by the national bank in question. Now that the circulation privilege is gone, the advertising requirement is an anachronism. The bill to abolish this requirement indicates a realization of the need to free the banking industry from a regulation outdated by 20 years.

Federal legislative activity in the banking field is currently concentrated on two major fronts—mergers and holding companies. Although the regulation of bank holding companies has been an issue since before World War II, it is only now that enactment of a new federal law appears probable, despite the fact that public interest in the question hardly exists. The situation differs in the case of bank mergers. That trend took hold after the war, and more recently has

* By Mr. Schapiro.

been underlined by a series of large transactions in New York City, beginning with the Chemical Corn merger in the fall of 1954. Bank mergers everywhere have been in the news, and so a larger public is interested in their significance.

A House Judiciary Subcommittee has been inquiring: Are these mergers in the public interest? This is an important question, and its resolution will be by far the most important single influence on the shape and dimension of banking and on the investment status of private capital in the industry. Opinions are taken earnestly; thus, there are those who firmly believe branch banking is an unmitigated evil, while others insist branch banking is absolutely essential to the functioning of banks under the private enterprise system. There are those who see reduced competition and monopoly; others, a trend adding needed vitality and releasing new competitive forces.

In the years 1948 through 1954, there were 742 bank mergers in the country. Many of these were in effect liquidations in which shareholders of the merged bank received cash for their holdings. At the end of 1954, the number of insured commercial banks stood at 13,303. Since then we have witnessed more mergers impressive in both number and size.

Much of the interest in merger developments has been focused on New York City because the largest and most important transactions have taken place there. Since September, 1954, there have been five mergers. The total resources of the absorbed banks exceeded $7 billion or one quarter of the city's banking resources. In less than ten years, the membership in the New York Clearing House Association declined from 25 to 15.

The impact of these mergers reaches far and to all levels: directors, managements, employees, customers, and correspondent banks, at home and around the world. Banks which have not participated in mergers are also affected, since their positions are set against a background of uncertainty. All banks today, everywhere in and out of New York, are probing their futures, trying to identify the reasons for the trend, and seeking to determine what each should do to assure continuance in the competitive race for position.

Why are banks merging, then? Businessmen and others familiar with the consequences of the financial inflation of the last 20 years understand and accept the trend. However, those in charge of the Congressional inquiry say that big banks are anxious to get bigger, and bigness means power. Some people look at big banking with reservations. They have heard again and again that, unless the merger trend is halted, we shall soon be down to a mere handful of giant banking concerns. But do they know the facts?

Let us examine the trend in more detail. The pressures forcing bank mergers arise primarily from the economic, political, and social changes of the last 20 years. We have experienced an enormous increase in bank deposits, although this increase has not been uniform. Concurrently, the great diffusion and shift of deposits throughout the economy has followed the population movement into new areas of industrial expansion. In the Northeast (the First, Second, and Third Federal Reserve Districts), there has been an increase in deposits, but gains in the rest of the country (the other nine districts) occurred at a much more rapid rate.

The migration from city to suburb, a nationwide trend, has further affected the flow of deposits. As the First National Bank of Boston pointed out, the 67% increase in suburban population since 1940 compares with 20% for the total population. To illustrate the impact of these changes on old metropolitan areas: Deposits in the 6,639 member banks of the Federal Reserve System outside New York City have risen from $89 billion in 1945 to $122 billion in 1954, or 37%; while in New York City the total of its member-bank deposits has hardly changed from the $28 billion held in 1945. Lately the deposit increase has taken place entirely outside New York. When we break down the figures by cities and states, we find that the diffusion of deposits has been on a vast scale.

Nevertheless, Congressional critics have charged that already the 100 largest banks in the country hold 46% of all commercial bank deposits. But it is also true—and this should be borne in mind by the House Judiciary Subcommittee—that in 1940 the 100 largest banks held 58% of all such deposits! And this should not be an unexpected figure, since the diffusion has been, and continues to be, away from old financial centers.

EXAMPLE: CHASE AND MANHATTAN

When Chase National Bank and the Bank of Manhattan merged, the Honorable George A. Mooney, New York State Superintendent of Banks, was asked by the Subcommittee's Chairman, the Honorable Emanuel Celler, if the Bank of Manhattan had not been eliminated from business. The Congressman apparently feared that removal of the Bank of Manhattan would mean a reduction in competition or at least a tendency toward such reduction. He challenged the Superintendent's earlier statement that the Chase-Manhattan consolidation intensified competition in New York City and did not tend toward monopoly. The Superintendent's answer is well worth repeating. He said (to paraphrase):

> Of course, there was some reduction in competition which existed prior to the merger, but it was not too great, since the banks had been engaged in complementary activities and had not been directly competitive.
>
> However, fresh competitive forces were introduced into New York City by the merger. The Chase National, a banker's bank, had operated primarily in Wall Street, making large loans at low rates; it had not operated throughout the city. As a result of the merger, Chase Manhattan, with its city-wide branch system, now competes effectively with the First National City Bank, Chemical Corn, Manufacturers Trust Company, and others. Thus, the release of this new competitive force throughout New York City far outweighs whatever lost competition resulted from the merger.

The Superintendent also pointed out that, in weighing the competitive scene before and after the merger, the presence of competition from nonbank sources should not be overlooked. The functions of commercial banking are not exclusive. Others engage in the business, others who are not themselves commercial banks. There are savings banks, savings and loan associations, pension funds, insurance companies, and a host of other lenders. Also, the investment markets are always available for fresh funds and large borrowings.

Commercial banking, then, finds itself, as an industry, in open competition with a vast complex of nonbank sources. In addition, New York City banks are in competition with banks throughout the rest of the country. Metropolitan banks have been forced to consider mergers in order to maintain their competitive position not only with such concerns as large insurance companies but with banks in other centers where deposits and capital have shown such striking gains.

There has been discussion about the suitability of the premium that a large bank pays to acquire a small bank. Have premiums been too high, too low? Have premiums been paid at all? There is really no rule to be observed in this type of situation; actually there are many variations.

Although newspaper accounts always label such acquisitions "mergers," the fact is that basically different methods have been used. The recent transaction between the First National Bank of New York and the National City Bank, for instance, was effected in cash, $165 million. First National shareholders redeemed their holdings at $550 a share. National City assumed all liabilities and purchased all assets. The excess of appraised value of those assets over liabilities was about $157 million; so National City received $157 million and paid out $165 million. The premium which the latter bank paid was, therefore, about $8 million. Banking capital of $165 million was released from the system and added to the deposit structure.

National City had capital funds of $550 million, which was reduced to $542 million by the $8 million premium. How is this $8 million figure to be judged—was it too much or not enough? Here we are dealing with a cash transaction, in effect no different from the liquidations we have noted. Hence, as a liquidation resulting in severance of ownership, this is a taxable transaction for the stockholders of First National.

The $8 million premium must be considered in relation to the earning power of the net assets—about $550 million—which National City acquired, and to other expected benefits. First National earned over

$7 million in 1954, and theoretically, therefore, National City would get back its investment—the premium—in a little more than one year, since it had acquired all the First National's business. Actually, however, the added earning power will be less, due in part to the release of former capital and in part to customer duplications, usual in many mergers. A more conservative estimate of added earnings would probably be about $4 million, and therefore the $8 million premium would be recovered in two years.

Where merger is accomplished through exchange of shares, there is a continuity of ownership and the transaction becomes nontaxable to the shareholders of the merged bank. Here again, the premium varies, often widely, depending on the ratio of size of the larger bank to the smaller: generally, the higher this ratio, the higher the premium. Where the shares of the larger bank already command a premium over book value in the market place, the financial advantages to the stockholders of the smaller bank can be great, sometimes astonishing, in terms of the market value of their holdings.

In mergers based on exchange of stock, as compared with liquidations, the calculations are somewhat more involved because of the partnership nature of the deal. The merger formula affects the future division of equity, earnings, and dividends between the shareholders of the participating banks.

We may generally say that when a large bank acquires a small bank for cash, there is a premium which can be measured in terms of the length of time required for anticipated earnings to cover the cost of acquisition.

RELATED QUESTIONS

Another important phase concerns the effect of mergers on officers and employees of the selling banks. We might well refer readers to the report on this subject made by the Federal Reserve Bank of Philadelphia, dated January 1955. This detailed study indicates that bank employees in 85% of recent mergers have benefited through higher salaries and better job protection. With the premium paid by shareholders of the purchasing banks there came substantial improvements in the lot of the bank personnel—both the officers and the staff members.

Some people wonder if the country shouldn't have an antimerger law of some sort. It has been suggested to the House Subcommittee that authority be given to the Justice Department to pass on all mergers to judge whether they are in the public interest. But many are convinced that antimerger legislation is neither necessary nor wise. With all the laws and public agencies which now regulate and supervise banking procedures, if the Justice Department entered the picture too, the interests of private banking could suffer. The forces behind the merger trend are basic and powerful; they will continue to operate regardless of any unnecessary and perhaps injudicious restrictions on formal combinations.

There is increasingly more reason to ask the country's lawmakers and banking authorities to bring their thinking into line with current merger and branch banking trends. For example, when will a bank like the First National of Boston be able to move out of Suffolk County? Like many others, it is confined to the metropolitan area, while a lot of good business is free to move out.

In the New York area, the industry and population move to the suburbs has been on a spectacular scale; the new Thruway and other construction accelerate this trend. In New York City's immediate neighbors, Westchester and Nassau Counties, commercial bank deposits have risen from $350 million in 1941 to $1,600 million today. New York City, as a financial star, has spun off the equivalent of the total deposits in Houston, Texas, or in Portland, Oregon, cities which rank tenth and eleventh in the country.

The question now being discussed is how soon will banks in New York City be permitted to cross the city limits and follow industrial and population movements. Much has happened since 1914 when the State Banking Law was last revised. Recently, in March, 1955, the State Legislature authorized a Joint Legislative Committee to Revise the Banking Law. Undoubtedly, it will review and consider the statutes which confine branch banking within the city limits.

Of course, there will be opposition by those who believe that any change will adversely affect the public interest.

Of greatest importance to banking developments in New York State are the consequences of pending federal legislation which would define bank holding companies, empower the Federal Reserve Board to control their creation and expansion, and force such companies to divest themselves of assets unrelated to banking. It is claimed that statewide banking in New York actually *does* exist by virtue of the bank holding companies. Enactment of proposed legislation would allow existing bank holding companies to function but would make difficult, perhaps impossible, the formation of new ones. Will the state of New York, merely by inaction, protect the exclusive position of existing holding companies, or will it make adjustments and authorize branch banking on a wider scale?

The question of whether, when, and how restrictions on branch banking in New York State will be relaxed is difficult to answer. The pressures for change, however, are great in New York, much greater than in Boston, for example. Even before the merger trend hit Wall Street, interest in the New York banking scene was already spreading to outlying areas.

Undoubtedly, in re-examining the situation, the lawmakers will hold the public interest paramount. Fortunately, basic questions are now being widely discussed and more facts are available for public analysis.

Part Four

PLANNING FOR YOUR OWN FUTURE

CRITICAL PERIODS IN
PERSONAL HISTORY

Case Discussion

WHAT CAN HAPPEN if you fail to plan your personal strategy with the same care that you calculate the future of your business? What kinds of problems may arise to plague you because of faulty planning for your own future? When you find yourself in an unfortunate situation, how can you shake yourself loose and start again? James Short and John Redmond, whose case histories will be discussed below, found themselves forced to consider these vital questions.

Mr. Short, an able and successful person in his early fifties, was the

Note: This chapter is a combined summary of two sessions on *Critical Periods in Personal History*. Joseph C. Bailey, Professor of Human Relations, Harvard Business School, led the discussion on the James Short case, under the heading of "Personal Strategy—Around Twenty Years Out." Kenneth R. Andrews, Associate Professor of Business Administration, Harvard Business School, acted as discussion leader for the John Redmond case, bearing on "Personal Strategy—Ten Years Out." The analysis of each case represents a synthesis of the views expressed by the participants in the discussion of that case.

No. 2 man in the Hudson Corporation, a large and vigorous concern headed by a 70-year-old president who refused to retire and let the younger man take over. Frustrated by what he considered the increasing incapacity of his chief, and torn between his equity in the concern and his ambition to be the Man-in-the-Front-Office, Short was tempted by several outside offers which had been made to him. Should he go or stay? If he stayed with the Hudson Corporation, what could he do about his deteriorating relationship with the "old man"?

John Redmond, the second of our two protagonists, faced a different but equally tough problem. Redmond seemed to be on the threshold of a most fruitful career. After working with the Summers Engineering Corporation for seven years, he had been made factory superintendent in a southern plant and was earning $12,500 a year. Although he himself was fully satisfied with his job and with the progress he had made, his wife Nancy had grown to dislike the small town in which they lived. Thus, to cite one of Redmond's own observations, "Nancy is fed to the teeth with this town. . . . I'm sympathetic, but I have a career at stake."

Before discussing these two situations, let us look at the detailed case histories.

THE CASE OF JAMES SHORT *

Early in 1953, David C. Davis, a management consultant, received a phone call from his friend, James A. Short, executive vice president of the Hudson Corporation, requesting a personal conference at the close of business that day. Although Mr. Davis had some social engagements for the evening that would need adjustment, he was glad to meet Mr. Short's request because he had been on the point of arranging a meeting for himself with Mr. Short.

* Copyright, 1955, by the President and Fellows of Harvard College. Case material of the Harvard Graduate School of Business Administration is prepared as a basis for class discussion. Cases are not designed to present illustrations of either correct or incorrect handling of administrative problems.

Mr. Davis felt that he could guess what Mr. Short had on his mind. About seven years earlier, when his close acquaintance with Mr. Short began, Mr. Davis had assisted Mr. Short in locating a new job, after he had resigned abruptly from the Hudson Corporation.

Mr. Short had been persuaded to return to the Hudson Corporation two years later. The new job in his old company was a marked improvement for him in terms of remuneration, explicit definition of responsibilities and authority, and a title designation that clearly indicated his post as No. 2 man in the company hierarchy. Mr. Davis knew that matters had gone much more satisfactorily, from Mr. Short's point of view, during the years since his return, although Mr. Davis recently had heard indirectly that some of the earlier difficulties between Mr. Short and the president of Hudson Corporation had arisen once more.

The meeting between the two men began in Mr. Davis' club not long after five o'clock and continued through dinner and into the evening. The information that follows, together with the gist of the conversations reproduced, were written out by Mr. Davis, at the request of a case writer from the Harvard Business School, soon after the conference occurred. The case was cleared for accuracy and disguise with Mr. Short by Mr. Davis.

Mr. Short opened the conversation immediately upon his appearance with the remark, "I expect you know what's up—J. G. can't keep his hands off any longer; and this time, if I quit, it'll be for good, and I want to plan ahead for it a bit more than I did last time."

Mr. Davis smiled. "How long can you hold onto yourself? You act teed off."

"I am," Short replied, "but I managed to finish the day and get up here without calling for a showdown. And tonight is Friday night, so there's the week end ahead of me. Furthermore, I've had two good offers recently which still stand open waiting for my answer."

"That ought to help," Davis said. "Added to which, I have a third offer that was specifically drawn up to appeal to you and about which

I was planning to see you next week. Shall we move over to the dining room and get into all this over dinner?"

Settled at their table Mr. Davis urged Mr. Short to bring him up-to-date on what had been happening in Hudson Corporation since their last meeting about six months earlier. "I thought you had your troubles pretty well cleared up. At least you made no complaints at that time."

Short: That's the devil of it. They were cleared up until somewhere around 12 or 15 months ago. Beginning then J. G. [Connell, the president of Hudson Corporation] has made my job increasingly difficult by postponing decisions I put up to him—ones that require his approval and quickly too, to be worth acting on; by questioning a lot of my smaller decisions—ones I've been making for years without his objection, and really aren't important by themselves but only as a symptom of his intentional meddling; by making more and more suggestions about how I ought to handle my personnel—suggestions he knows damn well I won't accept. They concern the ways he treats people, and are the ways I never have and never will use.

Well, that's the way it's been going for more than a year. This morning when I went in to go over the next budget for my divisions, he said he'd been studying it and thought I ought to cut the figure for promotion and advertising one million dollars. I said, "Not unless I cut the figure for projected sales several times more." He didn't like that, but he wouldn't argue with me about it. We've gone to the mat on that one too often. So he went back to the million dollars he said I could save. I wouldn't take it without a proportionate cut-back in sales. Finally he said, "You aren't the president around here yet." I wanted to say, "Damn lucky for you I'm not." But I held onto it and merely said, "That's right." He said, "I think you ought to cut one million out of that one figure. Think it over." I said, "I will," and walked out. And here I am.

Davis: What's he want?

Short [slowly, after a long pause]: I hate to say this because it ought not to be true, but I think he's afraid of me. He ought not to be. He's the biggest figure in the industry, one of the old-timers too, out of the rough-and-tumble era. He owns a lot of the stock; he controls a solid majority of the company directors; he's a very wealthy man and has been for years. It's taken a long time for me to admit this to myself, but it's the only explanation that fits the pattern of his recent behavior.

The figures for my divisions are coming out the way I predicted them to him almost two years ago. I have lifted two of our perennial money losers out of the red. They're in the black now, and next year they'll both be solid money makers. I think he's afraid to allow the company stockholders and directors, the bankers and the employees to see the transformation from perpetual red to dependable black as a result of the work I have been doing for the last four years. He fears they might figure he wasn't needed, and he's becoming more touchy every day about that since he passed the 70-year mark some time ago.

Davis: He can't last forever, and you're the only possible successor he's got in the whole organization. Everyone in the company knows that, from top to bottom, and a good many are praying for the day. You've put in 25 years all over the company, abroad and at home, getting ready for a take-over when the old man retires—the last ten years as the heir apparent, chosen and trained by himself. You think you can't take the punishment any longer?

Short: It isn't that simple, Dave. I've never taken any "punishment" from him, except lots of hard work and tough assignments —and I asked for those. It's most of the other executives in the company who have taken the punishment, that is, the ones who stayed on for the sake of the high salaries he pays. The ones who wouldn't left. I guess I'm the only one who wouldn't put up with his galley-slave tactics who stayed with him.

Davis: Maybe that's the reason you're the only one he has groomed as his successor.

Short: He groomed me as his successor because I always studied my problems until I was certain what the trouble was. Once that was

done, a promising solution or two were never hard to find. When I
went in to him, I always took along my recommendations and then
fought for them. Usually I won, because I double-checked and triple-
checked on everything. I never minded those combats, and I don't
think he did either. The other guys generally took only the problems to him and then asked him what to do about them. That's
where they got in trouble. He'd tell them, and at the same time call
them stupid or dumb or incompetent—right in front of their own
people, too. It used to make me sick at times, but I'd tell them after-
wards, when they came to see me, that they'd asked for it by going
in that way. I'd try to get them to see that the only way to avoid a
public horsewhipping was to go in with their own plan and battle
for it.

You know he lives for nothing but his business. He lives in a hotel
in the center of town so as to be close to the office. He and his wife
don't own a home anywhere. They have no children. She's been
a confirmed neurasthenic for decades, going from doctor to doctor.
She shifted some time ago to cults and fads and healers.

Any time of night, or on week ends, or on vacations, he'll phone
any officer in the company he wants to and either order him in for
an afternoon or evening of work while the office is closed, or else
keep him on the telephone as long as he wants to bat a problem
around.

He tried it on me not long after I got back from that foreign
assignment. I was expecting it, because some of the other men had
complained about it to me—or, rather, their wives had to my wife.
I told our maid to tell him I was busy entertaining our guests and
that I would be in to see him first thing in the morning. He never
mentioned it and never tried it again.

No, I'm not the one who has had to take that sort of punishment;
it's the other men, the whole executive structure in fact.

Davis: We've gone over some of this before, but I'm still a little
puzzled. Between bonus and salary you went well over the $100,000
bracket two years ago. You don't put up with the bully-ragging old
Connell has been notorious for; on the contrary, you're almost in-

dispensable to him. You've worked hard a long time for what you've almost got in your hand. It can't be so far off now. Why can't you go along until the ship is yours?

Short [after another long pause]: Age is one angle—his and mine. I've just touched 50, and if I'm going to accomplish anything particularly noteworthy in an organization as big as ours, I've got to get a really free hand soon. Ten years is hardly enough. Fifteen may do it.

At least I'm still ready to try hard. I may not feel that same way when the time gets shorter.

He is over 70, but all his close relatives—uncles, cousins, parents —were long-lived, many into their nineties. I believe he's going to hold on as long as he can. I may be wrong on this. He often talked with me about his retirement and I think he meant it. But not during the past two or three years has he mentioned it again. I don't know whether it was his 70th birthday or my breaking into the black with the losers he could never rescue that made him clam up.

He still works like a horse, though he is slowing down and won't admit it. He may keel over one of these days—but I just don't know. It's a question mark, Dave: his retirement. I've speculated over that ever since he got over 65 and stayed on to 70. Now I'm 50, and I've concluded that I'm the fellow who's got to make the decision.

Davis: Jim, what if a taxi ran him down this evening? What would you like to try for most with Hudson Corporation? Why should you stay there rather than go to any of the three openings we are going to look over later on? What's Hudson got that I can't top on behalf of Casper?

Short [startled]: Have you got an offer from Casper?

Davis: I've got the executive vice presidency for you. Not at once, but explicitly inside one year, to give Gene Darnell a decent interval in which to move back to the chairmanship. With it goes a salary, bonus, deferred payments, and pension, tentatively proposed to meet your wishes, and with full authorization to me to meet any offer you get from any firm in the industry on each of the points I mentioned—salary, bonus, and so on.

Short sat silent. He was not prepared for such an offer from the chief rival in his field. His thoughts had been so much preoccupied with the tangled difficulties of his own situation at Hudson that he found it hard to grasp Davis' statements. Finally he asked, "Is that true?"

Davis gestured toward his brief case, "I have the papers in there when you're ready to look them over. Now how about my question: 'What's Hudson got for you that I can't top for Casper?'"

Short: Well, for one thing I know Hudson like the inside of my own house. I know every move I want to make, who I want to make the moves, and when, and how. I know what our weaknesses are and many remedies I am sure will help correct them. I know also where we have unrealized sources of strength which I am confident could be developed to such a degree that, well, before I am through, we could attain a commanding lead in the industry. And that means [with a glance at Davis] that we could overtake Casper's present 10% lead in sales and go 20% to 25% ahead of them.

That's one thing Hudson's got for me.

Another is—and I should have put it first—I think I could release the energies and capabilities of a lot of good men that J. G. has used as chore boys. I think I could attract and hold a lot of good men who would never enter our doors so long as Connell's practices are followed. And this is something I've wanted to do in Hudson longer than anything else. I sort of feel I owe it to a lot of men who never got a decent chance to show what they could do in an encouraging atmosphere. I owe it to some friends of mine whose spirits or health were broken, and to some whose lives were shortened because they worked in Hudson.

That is a serious thing to say, but I mean it. And the funny thing is that I owe more to J. G. than I owe to any man alive. He gave me my chance in sales when I asked to transfer out of the accounting department 20 years ago. He sent me abroad in charge of sales when our subsidiary in Austria looked weak. He put me in full charge in less than one year when they had to replace their general manager there. He gave me a free hand over the whole outfit for nearly a decade before the war ended that operation. He asked for results, sure, but I would do exactly the same thing. During his two visits per year we took our operations apart down to the last penny, and I learned as much about running my own show during his inspections as I did during the rest of the year.

He's a rough and often ruthless man, but you've got to remember the period when he was growing up. He was at work selling at the time of the Spanish-American War! I've told him a good many times that he is a holdover from the old robber barons who built our railroads and steel mills.

Davis: Quite a compliment to pay your boss. How did he take it?

Short: Sometimes he'd frown, sometimes he'd grin. Don't forget he is perhaps the greatest promoter and one of the greatest salesmen our industry has produced. Nobody could touch him ten years ago. Remember he merged the first truly national organization in our field, just as he was the first to move aggressively into the foreign field in a really big way—at least from an American base. And he carried competition to every market that could be made to pay. In our field there's no personality like him left on the scene.

Davis: Sounds like hero worship to me.

Short: Why, yes, I guess it does. I guess I've felt that way about him for years. But I don't any longer. At least not much. Not since I've been continually at headquarters where I've seen him in action every day with the personnel of the organization. I was in Europe nearly ten years, you know, and after I came back he sent me out again to put the southern subsidiary on its feet. I didn't really get to know him, or the situation in the home office, until the war was over, scarcely eight years ago.

I think maybe he's changed too. I'm pretty sure he has in the last two or three years. He lies to me now. He goes behind my back and then denies it. He never used to do that. I've lost my respect for him.

Davis: Well are you ready to look over the material I've got on Casper?

Short: Not yet, Dave. I can't swing around that fast. Nor that far.

What I mean is I never expected that kind of an offer from that source. Except for two years I've worked all my life for Hudson. I can't get up out of the trenches and walk straight across to the principal enemy I've spent most of my business years fighting all over the globe. It sort of makes me feel like a deserter.

It would be a whale of a kick in the pants to the old man, though. Maybe it would jar some perspective back into him. Still he treated me awfully white that first time I resigned. I just walked out. You remember?

Well, he said I had to keep my title and my office until I made a connection. He wanted to pay my salary too, but I wouldn't take that. Furthermore, he met my terms when I was willing to go back, and he kept them, until these past months.

No, Dave. I've got to think out a lot more of the angles on Casper first. Casper does need rebuilding though, doesn't it? I think it's got into much worse shape since the war than anyone seems to realize. Still it's a back-breaking chore to get such a scattered and loose-jointed giant trained into fighting shape, isn't it?

Davis: Well, what about the two offers you mentioned earlier. What have they got?

Short: You'll laugh when I tell you about the first one. Annual sales are barely over $10 million a year. Isn't that something, when both Hudson's and Casper's sales run over $300 million a year?

Still they made it awfully attractive for me personally—and for my family, too. It's the M. B. Madison Co. You know the wonderful country club location they have built for themselves well out in one of the nicest, unspoiled suburbs in the whole metropolitan area? I could live a country life—and you know I like the country—and not have more than a pleasant 20-minute drive to and from the office. I could live with my family once more, which I haven't been doing these past four or five years while I've put in about twelve hours a day trying to pull those divisions out of the red. My boy and girl are in college now, but if my wife and I don't take every opportunity to see as much of them as possible while we can, it will soon be too late.

I owe something to my wife in all this. We were close together in Europe and nearly as much so when we went south. But since this last deal got under way, she must think I'm beginning to resemble J. G. She hasn't said much, but I know how she looks at the way those two have lived their lives. Our years in Europe gave us a lot of interests that I've had to neglect recently. There really isn't much point in working yourself like J. G. does, especially since they tax it away nearly as fast as you can make it.

I'll never get her to make the choice, and I wouldn't want her to, but the M. B. Madison setup is closer to what we both feel makes all-around sense than anything I've got in sight. Let me tell you a bit more about it.

The presidency is opening soon, and that is what they're offering me. The salary is $40,000 with a profit-sharing arrangement which I figure could make me an additional $30,000 after the two or three years we would need in which to substantially increase their sales. There is a capital gains opportunity through an option on 5% of their total stock which is attractive. The stock is low currently but has a growth potential that I believe could triple its price before I needed to sell—all in all, I see almost a quarter million dollar gain between the buying and selling price. My pension possibility is limited, and I'll have to build my own estate along the other lines.

The salary drop is severe, especially over the next five years, so money-wise I have to balance the near-term versus the long-run considerations in this offer against the immediate gains in the other openings.

Probably I'd have a freer hand in that organization because of its size, for one thing. In a year I'd know its people as well—maybe better—than I do my own now. It's officers are decent people; the company has an excellent reputation for its business standards. It's one of the oldest in our line, and I'm confident there is a fine base for doubling its share of the market. Most of all, right now, I'd be on my own again, and the directors who have talked with me are ready to accept any reasonable conditions I want to set in regard to running my own show.

It's a temptation all right: the country, my wife and family once more, a sure chance to make a good record and a dependable nest egg—all without killing myself as I have been doing.

Davis: What about the other offer?

Short: It's another presidency, after a year. I'll go in as executive vice president at $60,000, which will go up somewhere around $80,000 when I take over the president's office. There is a bonus which runs around 10% of the salary each year. The pension would enable me to retire with $30,000 annually from that source alone. The stock option proposal is a complicated formula, but it works out so that I can buy stock on a basis which virtually assures me of doubling my money, and if the stock increases further in value I would secure that additional increment.

From a financial angle it would be hard to beat from my point of view. The salary and bonus are a reduction from what I'm getting now, but about three years ago I found that the huge bonus I got that year melted down to just a few thousand dollars after the Treasury took its bite. As a matter of fact, I bought tax-anticipation warrants with what was left simply to remind myself that a big bonus often doesn't mean a thing.

It's the Martin Brachall Company. A fine old reputable concern with a name for honesty and integrity—a factor that appeals to me more and more as time passes. All the officers are gentlemen. I've known many of them for years, and I've admired the atmosphere of goodwill and cooperation they work in. They know what team-work means, and it is an asset I am definitely counting on when I estimate what I can do for the company.

They have a line of staple products, some of them virtual monopolies, not only because of world-wide consumer preference and brand prestige, but also because of entrenched marketing arrangements. As an old marketeer, I have a deep hunch that there is a tremendous potential, both in the company's position as well as in its products, that is ready for a long-pull expansion. The stock is closely held and hasn't missed a dividend in over two generations. The financial standing is gilt-edge. Actually all that is needed is a period of concentration on promotion and sales—the very kind of assignments I've handled successfully three times straight at Hudson. Sales are running close to $30 million annually, and I can see a dozen ways to begin lifting that figure nearly 10% a year.

Davis: I can't tell whether the Madison company or the Brachall company excites you the most. Aren't there any catches in the last proposition?

Short: That's the question, Dave, I asked myself after my confidential talk with Mr. McKee [President of Brachall company]. I'm sure there is, but I haven't found it yet, and I've gone over it a dozen times. All I've found, in fact, are some more pluses. Their offices occupy part of their own building, which leaves room for a convenient expansion. It is in the part of town I like best. It's very handy for me to reach from where we live now—and where we're really taking roots in the community at last. Even the president's office has exactly the view I like best in all the city, and it combines with an executive office layout that creates a mood in which I feel good and do good work. Maybe I'm oversensitive to such things just now, and perhaps it's silly to mention it, but I'll bet there are a lot of similar hidden considerations that lie deep in these kinds of decisions. I'm only trying to look at mine, and to me the building location and the offices I'll occupy are a clear plus.

Davis: Is it any use to look over the draft proposals I've got from Casper for you?

Short: I don't see why. At least not this evening, Dave. It's getting late, and I've got a lot of thinking and deciding to do this week end. I know the gist of the proposition: they will write me a better ticket financially than I can get anywhere else.

Davis: They'll go further than that. They're ready to . . .

Short [interrupting]: I know, a big organization, Dave. I know what it can and can't deliver. Money it can—the rest is only a chance to try to turn a whale around. Perhaps I'll want to; it's the kind of animal I'm most familiar with. Maybe these smaller organizations are simply "greener pastures" to me right now. I'm grateful to Casper —perhaps I ought to say, to you, because you're probably the prime mover here—but it's good for my morale, coming from my friends the enemy.

Short arose. "Thanks for the evening, Dave. I did all the talking, but I've found that helps clear up my thinking a lot if I find someone who is able to listen—somebody besides my wife, that is. I didn't want to pour all this out to her without a preliminary run-through on you, you see, because this time she's more thoroughly involved than in any other single decision in my whole business career. This time her opinion isn't what I need. I want her to say frankly what kind of life she would like a part of for the next 15 years; from there on it's up to me to make the choice that meets her wishes, and mine too. Doesn't that make sense to you?"

Davis smiled, "It makes sense to me all right, but I'm not the one you have to make sense to from here on.

"Good luck, and call me up any time I can be of use again."

James A. Short was born in Minnesota in 1903; worked part of his expenses off in going through college and graduated from the University of Iowa in 1924 with Phi Beta Kappa honors. He majored in business administration and specialized in accounting. He married in 1925. In 1933, after it was clear that they would not have children of their own, he and his wife adopted twin babies.

Mr. Short began work in 1924 as a cost accountant for a firm in Chicago that was merged with several others in 1927 to create the Hudson Corporation. His work with company figures soon disclosed to him that progress upward in the ranks of management was slow in his department and was most rapid then in foreign sales. He requested a transfer to that department which was effected in 1931. The years 1926–1931 were spent in domestic sales to prepare for entrance into foreign sales.

From 1931 into 1939 he was briefly sales manager for, and then general manager of, the Austrian subsidiary of Hudson Corporation. During his managership sales increased from approximately $100,000 a year to more than $5,000,000. The outbreak of war terminated operations in Austria, and Mr. Short returned to the American headquarters of Hudson Corporation, now substantially larger, and located in the New York metropolitan area. Shortly thereafter he was sent south to liquidate an old-line subsidiary of Hudson that had defied years of effort to make profitable. Close attention to its accounts suggested ways in which money could be saved. These were instituted by Mr. Short, and together with increased sales produced results that led the president of Hudson to encourage Mr. Short to continue his efforts. Between 1940 and 1943 sales rose from $5,000,000 to $7,500,000, though net profits rose much more steeply.

Mr. Short was called back to headquarters in 1943 and made assistant to the president with the title of vice president. He was given trouble-shooting assignments throughout the whole corporation—a position he quickly grew to dislike. He requested, on several occasions, some definite responsibilities on which he could make his own record, pointing out that if he found trouble when dispatched on such missions, it made other vice presidents look bad; whereas if he did not, it made him look bad. Once or twice he was dissuaded from pushing his request; thereafter it was agreed to, but fulfillment was frequently postponed. Mr. Short, at this point, resigned abruptly and worked for the two years, 1945-1946, with a smaller concern in the same industry which was only obliquely a competitor of Hudson.

Upon his return to Hudson in 1946, which was negotiated with Mr. J. G. Connell, Mr. Short was made vice president of the whole company and soon thereafter executive vice president and, in addition, was given direct responsibility, in 1948, for the two most difficult divisions in the corporation. Mr. Short began his conversation with Mr. Davis over events that derived from that assignment.

THE CASE OF JOHN REDMOND *

When John Redmond left the Harvard Business School in 1948, he went to work in Providence, Rhode Island, as a product analyst

* Copyright, 1955, by the President and Fellows of Harvard College. Like the material on James Short, this case was prepared for use at the Harvard Graduate School of Business Administration.

for the Summers Engineering Corporation. He believed that where he lived would ultimately be important to him but not early in his career. "What I wanted then," he recalled seven years later, "was an opportunity to get the broadest kind of experience in the shortest possible time to get qualified for a responsible line position."

In May 1955 Redmond was factory superintendent in a southern plant built by Summers in 1949 for the manufacture of a product formerly made in central Massachusetts. He was fully satisfied with his progress and his job. His wife disliked the midsouthern community in which the Redmonds lived with their three children. She expressed the view more and more urgently that the family return to New England. The factory manager told John Redmond that to raise the question of transfer to old established New England plants would jeopardize his promising career in the company, and to seek employment in other companies in New England would mean a sacrifice in position or income.

The Summers Engineering Corporation was a large organization manufacturing and distributing nationally a wide line of industrial and consumer products. Its older plants were largely located in the industrial Northeast, but the newer plants made necessary by rapid growth since 1946 were being located in favorable labor markets in other sections of the country, particularly in the South and Southwest. Under a stated policy of decentralization, the company attempted to subdivide its operations by product classes. The subdivisions were assigned responsibility for profit and considerable independence of action.

John Redmond was born (1919), brought up, and graduated from college (B.S. in B.A., 1940) in Rhode Island. He spent five years in the Air Force (1941–1946), serving in the European Theater. In 1945 he married an Army nurse in France, and a year later brought her to Boston where he attended the Harvard Business School. Nancy Redmond had grown up on the West Coast and had studied nursing at the University of California. She took private cases as a registered nurse until their first child was born in 1947. The family financed itself with the aid of the G.I. Bill and the school loan fund.

In the spring of 1948, John Redmond decided to go to work for the Summers Engineering Corporation. His starting salary was $4,800. The new products department in the company's home office in Providence maintained a group of 20 "product analysts." These men were mostly young engineering and business graduates whose task it was to make staff studies of the potential of selected existing and all new products and to make proposals to the management committee for the elimination, modification, or initial manufacture of the product studied. During two years of roving assignments, John Redmond made a comprehensive distribution study of a new power tool for the Do-It-Yourself market. This study attracted favorable notice.

In 1950 Redmond was offered a temporary assignment in a new southern plant. The division manager wanted to insure that the old procedures previously used for the manufacture of his products were not perpetuated without analysis in the new plant. He believed that problems of getting the new plant into operation should be scrutinized by other eyes than those that had supervised production in Massachusetts. No hourly workers were transferred to the South.

Seeing this opportunity as another broad assignment with a unique opportunity for experience, Redmond moved his family to the southern location. His wife was reluctant to leave Rhode Island but concurred in the wisdom of the move.

In 1955 Redmond was still at the same southern plant. He had been factory superintendent for two years and was responsible now for the work of 400 employees. Initially assigned to study wage rates for six months (salary $5,400), he was made general foreman in charge of all manufacturing operations after only six weeks. Within the next few weeks, he added a full second shift, attempted to strengthen the supervisory organization, and made plans for reduced operations after making up three months' production lost during the move. He chose 7 foremen from 12 for his permanent organization and reduced the work force from 632 to 400. The consequent impact of this move upon a community of 15,000 people made him determined to stabilize production and eliminate layoffs. His attempts to increase productivity, reduce turnover, and lower production costs became known in the home office of the company. In 1954 turnover in a work force 85% women was 17.5%, the lowest of any plant in the Summers corporation. Excluding pregnancies, turnover was 10%, and for the first quarter of 1955 was down to 9.2%. In 1953 he was made factory superintendent, reporting to the division manager, the senior officer of the company present at this location. His salary in May 1955 was $12,500.

Redmond spent most of his time in direct contact with either his foremen or his work force. His procedure with foremen was to supervise them very closely and to "pay out rope" as they developed. His procedure with hourly workers was to get to know each person as well as possible. Except in three departments, he personally announced all changes, and he attempted to provide regular opportunities for both foremen and workers to say what was on their minds. The division manager, to whom the factory superintendent, chief engineer, inspector, purchasing agent, and industrial relations manager reported, had turned all production operations over to Redmond from the first. He asked Redmond to explain each month the manufacturing variances, unapplied labor costs, spoilage, overtime, and other departures from budgeted performance.

Redmond believed that his work had proved effective, that it was being recognized. He found it thoroughly satisfying. After a year of working 18 hours a day, he was able now to live what he considered a normal life. With his work force and production stabilized, he found he knew his people well and with the help of a roving personnel counselor thought he knew what they were thinking. He took pride in the fact that repeated attempts to organize his plant had failed and was sure that he had solved the problems of communication which appeared to perplex many plant managements in other divisions of the Summers corporation. The excitement of the early crises and his own ignorance of plant operations had passed. But the challenge of continually modernizing production and finding new jobs for those displaced either in the manufacture of components previously purchased or in the manufacture of new modifications of the basic product kept him fully occupied. He felt himself still learning how to manage and to build a continuously improving organization. The opportunity to learn how to plan was now his, and he had time and interest left over for community affairs.

Mrs. Redmond's activities centered upon her home and a social circle of six couples. The Redmonds' second child was born in 1951, their third in March 1955. For several years the Redmonds' social life consisted almost entirely of semimonthly bridge sessions with their closest friends and activity on other week ends with three of the couples of the group. In late 1954, two of the couples moved from the town and illness in two other families sharply curtailed social activities. The social life of the community as a whole took place in private homes, with the exception of church activity in which the Redmonds did not take part. Four larger towns (cultural centers of the region) were an hour's drive away. The Redmonds visited one of these three or four times a year.

Mrs. Redmond wanted to live in New England. She liked the climate, the people, the atmosphere, and the way of life there. She believed her children were being deprived of its cultural advantages. "Nancy would like to see a legitimate show now and then," Redmond said, "and she likes to be able to eat in a good restaurant without making a four-star production out of it. I feel the same way, but a man can overlook many things if his job gives him the kind of satisfaction he requires. But no man can forget that happiness begins at home—after all, we spend 65% of our time there."

When Redmond took his concern to the factory manager, the latter advised him emphatically not to let his wife control his career. He felt he had himself stayed much too long in New England because his wife had opposed moving and that his own progress in the company had consequently been delayed. He added also that Redmond had come and would continue to go a long way in the company. He suggested that he would be a factory manager and a division head within two or three years and that before he was 40 he would be making $20,000 a year in addition to incentive compensation which could substantially increase this figure. He did not believe that Redmond should sacrifice his potential by "agitating within the company" for a change. Moving to another plant for personal reasons rather than being called there to fill an important job damaged relationships with immediate superiors and colleagues, he said, and created the impression that the company came second. He added, however, that if Redmond ignored this advice, he would do whatever he could to help with an in-company transfer. "I owe you everything I can do to help you get what you want," he said.

Redmond himself was troubled about the effect of asking for a transfer to the New England operations of the Summers corporation. To find there the opportunity he now had for building a permanent manufacturing organization high in productivity and morale and for extending his experience would, he believed, be very difficult. The alternative was to seek a similar opportunity outside the Summers corporation. To do this he felt involved the possibility of reduced salary.

The education and upbringing of his family put limits on the price he could pay for a New England job. "As I see it," Redmond said, "this is to a large degree a matter of economic necessity. I came here to get experience. If there is a great deal more to gain by riding with Summers for a couple more years, I would favor that. But Nancy is fed up to the teeth with the town and wants to get on the road back. I'm sympathetic but have a career at stake."

A CLOSER LOOK AT THE PROBLEMS

How do men get themselves into spots like this?

Note that James Short had been with Hudson Corporation for almost 30 years—his entire business life. During that time he had had extensive contacts with the president of the firm. He certainly should have recognized the kind of a personality he was working with. When the boss passed the age of 65 and showed no signs of retiring, Short should have analyzed his own situation.

There were several choices open to him at that time; he could have reconciled himself to being No. 2 man until nature removed the president from the scene; he could have left the company forthwith, at an age when his flexibility would have been greater; he might have faced the old man with the issue then and there; or he could have begun to plan ways in which he could entice or encourage the president to move out. A carefully calculated campaign—part pressure, part selling, and part adjustment of the organizational structure of the company—might have resulted in the desired vacancy in the "front office."

An important part of this picture, of course, is the defining of objectives. Did Short *really* want to be the top executive of this company, or of any other company? He was obviously tempted by the attractions of country living, a 9:00-to-5:00 job in a small business, a chance to exercise responsibility, albeit in a slower-moving operation than the Hudson firm. After all, he had worked hard all his life; 20 or 25 years of harvesting his well-sown crop looked pretty appealing to James Short. He should have decided earlier what his real personal and business goals were; now he was being forced to make these basic decisions under pressure and in an emotional turmoil.

John Redmond, on the other hand, had marked out his objectives pretty clearly—at least his *career* objectives. "What I wanted," he said, "was an opportunity to get the broadest kind of experience in the shortest possible time in order to become qualified for a responsible line position." But Redmond had not taken all considerations into account, and his failure to think broadly enough finally caught up with him: he had forgotten the part that Nancy must play in his life. He neglected to consider the impact of his career plans on his wife —and inevitably, of course, Nancy's attitude would affect him too. "No man can forget," he had come to realize, "that happiness begins at home—after all, we spend 65% of our time there."

Redmond's factory manager advised him, "Don't let your wife control your career." But this advice ignores the fact that if a man has a family, his career must be a *joint* operation. He and his wife must both agree on objectives; both parties must enjoy a feeling of participation.

Redmond had been working 18 hours a day, and was completely

absorbed in his job as factory superintendent. In the process of stabilizing his work force and the plant's production, he had had little time for interests outside the company. Indeed, he had given scant attention to the reactions of his wife and family. His failure to provide for what was a foreseeable contingency—Nancy's social isolation and discontent—resulted in a crisis which forced him to make a choice between a series of bad alternatives.

Short and Redmond were both tied up in log-jams which might well have been avoided through planning and foresight. But *what might have been* is of little help in determining *what is* and *what is going to be*. What could they do?

More likely than not, these two men did not yet understand what was *really* going on, what their *real* problems were. Both had allowed the issues to become clouded by their own emotionalism and irrationalism; their responses were based on faulty estimates of their own self-interest. So their first step had to be to buckle down and study every aspect of their troublesome situations. Let us see how they might go about doing this.

ANALYSIS OF JAMES SHORT

James Short assumed that his boss, in refusing to relinquish the presidency, was just being self-willed and obstinate. Perhaps this *was* the case. To J. G. Connell, the president, the Hudson Corporation was everything. Short himself admitted that his boss was the greatest promoter and one of the greatest salesmen the industry had produced —that nobody could touch him ten years ago. The old man still worked like a horse. His wife was a difficult person, they had no children, and he had no outside interests at all. Short believed that his boss was afraid of him; the younger man had by himself lifted two of Hudson's perennial money-losing divisions out of the red, and Connell, according to Short, hesitated to inform the directors and stockholders of this accomplishment for fear they might figure the old man was no longer needed.

J. G. had always been exacting and demanding with his subordinates. He was a perfectionist, and had never been an easy person to get along with. Now, at least in Short's opinion, he had become impossible, and was hanging on to his post out of jealousy and intransigence. Connell had a comfortable majority of supporters on the board of directors, and there was therefore no pressure on him to move over and out of the No. 1 spot.

On the other hand, Short's view of the situation could have been completely wrong. It was undoubtedly distorted to some degree. Connell had been grooming Short for many years for the position of president. Everyone in the company knew that Short was J.G.'s only possible successor. The old man obviously intended to step aside sometime, but he did *not* want to be pushed. Connell had given Short all the best breaks, and had taught the younger man all he knew. But it seems he was not yet satisfied that Short was ready to take over the Hudson Corporation—he probably wished to continue testing his future successor.

There is evidence that James Short was something of a prima donna. Supremely confident of his own ability, he tended to take business differences as personal insults. He had not fully developed those qualities of patience, understanding, generosity, and appreciation of the efforts of others which are essential to the top executive. His attitude was immature in several respects: for instance, although he admitted he owed much of his success to Connell, the offer made him by the Hudson Corporation's chief competitor would, he thought, "be a whale of a kick in the pants to the old man."

Short's alternatives at this time were to accept one of the three offers he had had from other companies—all of which appealed to him for various reasons—or to stick it out with Hudson. It would seem that he could do best by remaining with his old firm. He knew Hudson, he told a friend, "like the inside of my own house. I know every move I want to make. . . . I know what our weaknesses are and many remedies I am sure will help correct them. I also know where we have unrealized sources of strength which I am confident could be developed to such a degree that, before I am through, we could attain a commanding lead in the industry. . . . I think I could release the energies and capabilities of a lot of good men that J.G. has used as chore boys. . . . And this is something I've wanted to do in Hudson longer than anything else."

Short had been attracted by bids from rival firms because of the temptations of living in the country, of more time to spend with his family, of being able to run his own show, of idealized office layout. At the same time that he itched with desire to put the Hudson Corporation far out in front of all its competitors, he wondered whether he shouldn't begin to take life easier and cultivate some of his old and sadly neglected outside interests. But Short had not given enough thought to the difficulties he was likely to encounter in changing his business affiliation. At the age of 50 a man finds it no easy task to go out and start all over again. The risks are much greater for him than they would be for a man of 35 or 40. It is not improbable that Short would have been bored working for a smaller outfit—and he had a tremendous sense of loyalty and obligation to Hudson which would, in actuality, have been hard to overcome.

In analysis, James Short's strongest desires and ambitions dictated his continuing with Hudson; switching jobs did not seem wise at this stage in his life and career. Only if he could not manage to ameliorate the unpleasant situation within Hudson's executive branch should he strike out in a new direction.

Examination has shown that Short's problem with his aged superior was not insoluble. Part of the difficulty lay in his own stubbornness and unreasonableness. Since the president was not going to step aside until he was satisfied that Short could carry on successfully, the younger man had a fairly well-defined course of action laid out for him. He faced the biggest job of salesmanship he had ever had—he needed to sell himself. His greatest desire was for freedom of operation without interference from a person whom he considered out-of-touch with the needs of the firm. He therefore had to convince the boss that he should be given control of the everyday management of the plant. J.G. might agree to this were it understood that he would retain general supervisory powers.

Were Short to imagine himself in J.G.'s personal situation, it might be easier for the No. 2 man to get along with his boss. In his advanced years, Connell was probably experiencing feelings of insecurity—inevitably a part of every man's personality whether he admits it or not. Short "owed more to J.G. than . . . to any man alive"; he might express his gratitude by being considerate, appreciative, patient, and generous toward his benefactor. He might show the old man increasing deference; he should overlook the little things about Connell which had annoyed him in the past, and chalk J.G.'s crankiness and obstinacy up to old age. He should consciously try to build up his boss's sense of being needed; if J.G. was given a place to go other than the pasture—if he could retain his titular position as president while resigning most of the real authority in the company to Short—he might well prove willing to move over. Up to this time, Short had forgotten an important point in his own climb up the ladder—the finding of an acceptable place for Connell.

In other words, Short was going to have to plan his relationship with the boss as carefully as he always planned his business moves. He would have to change his tactics, basing them on an appeal to the old man's pride, his natural concern for the continued success and growth of the firm he had founded, and his desire to protect his investment. It might be an excellent idea for Short to take a three weeks' fishing trip, during which time the atmosphere of tension at Hudson would clear. The junior executive would return to his desk refreshed and calm, determined to make the best of the situation. He would have gone to the roots of his problem; he would have clarified his objectives and formulated an effective method of achieving them.

ANALYSIS OF JOHN REDMOND

What was the *real* problem—the real underlying difficulty—in John Redmond's case, and how had it developed? These questions must be answered before Redmond could act intelligently to improve his situation.

Redmond was happy with his job; his wife was unhappy with the town in which they were located. What was the matter? Looking at the situation one way, perhaps Nancy just had not grown up to adult responsibilities. Instead of doing something about her lack of friends and social life, she was sitting down and brooding, wishing herself back in New England. Most activities in the community centered around the church, but Nancy had made no effort to participate in its program. She might have arranged her domestic duties to give herself time to engage in neighborhood and community affairs, but she had made no aggressive attempt to build a life for herself in the town. Instead of taking pleasure in her husband's business success, and enduring the sacrifices of today for the rewards of tomorrow, she had become resentful and misanthropic. Perhaps she needed some professional help to assist her in seeing that the drabness was not all outside, but inside.

On the other hand, maybe Nancy had good reason for not liking the community and the people in it. It *was* a small town; perhaps it was ingrown and resentful of strangers from the North. Its social pattern was set, and related closely to the homes and private lives of the citizens rather than to the common life of the town. Nancy might not have appreciated or understood the traditions and customs of the South; she might have found the climate incompatible; she certainly missed the cultural advantages which she had enjoyed elsewhere. Redmond himself told his factory manager: "Nancy would like to see a legitimate show now and then, and she likes to be able to eat in a good restaurant without making a four-star production out of it." And in order for the Redmonds to enjoy diversions like this, they had to drive to one of the larger towns in the area, all of which were over 30 miles away.

There is a distinct possibility, too, that the Redmonds' problem was not as closely connected with the small southern town as both Nancy and John believed. Nancy had been an Army nurse, with a career and interests of her own which she continued until her first child was born. Suddenly—in the space of eight years—she had found herself completely separated from her former life, and burdened with three small children. She was not even given the opportunity to share in her husband's career decisions—John spent most of his time at the factory and was often preoccupied with office problems even when he was at home. Nancy's husband, to all intents and purposes, considered her a backdrop to his life, and she simply was not the backdrop type.

In this sense, it was not the town she really disliked; it was her loss of individuality, of her sense of participation and accomplishment. She just was not a "Kinder, Kirche, Kuche" kind of a girl. And if this was the real heart of Redmond's problem, his situation would not improve with a transfer to New England—John needed an "agonizing reappraisal" of the relationship between his family and his career.

There is one more angle to this situation which Redmond might have missed altogether in his preoccupation with Nancy's discontent. Perhaps he was not, in truth, getting the "broadest kind of experience" he so desired by staying with the Summers Engineering Corporation in the South. He had been in one job in an experimental plant for six years. Was he just being used by Summers for its own purposes, rather than being trained for increased responsibility? Wasn't it perhaps time, now that he had worked himself to the top of this particular job area, to start getting some know-how in sales, finance, or control? He had done an outstanding piece of work, true; perhaps it was *so* outstanding that the company had come to rely on him in his present post, and Summers might be extremely reluctant to move him and disrupt a smooth operation.

Obviously the Summers people thought Redmond was good; his promotions and salary record to that date showed that much. But were they evaluating him in the same terms by which he evaluated himself? They said, "You're doing a fine job," but they might have meant as a permanent general foreman; *he* thought, "I am doing a fine job in equipping myself to be president of the Summers Engineering Corporation." Redmond certainly did not want to be a factory superintendent all his life. Maybe this was a good time to find out what plans the company had for him and to re-examine his entire business career, Nancy's current unhappiness being, in this case, only a side issue.

John Redmond therefore had a considerable amount of information to gather before he could tackle his problem. He needed to know, first of all, exactly what his company had in mind for him. This was a tough question to put, and a hard one to answer, but the facts which John needed could be available: Did Summers plan to keep moving him around from plant to plant and from division to division? Was he to be a trouble shooter for all the company's nationwide subdivisions? Or was he scheduled to get all his training in his present location?

Secondly, what opportunities were available in New England, since this was where Nancy wanted to go? Could Redmond find a favorable spot in one of Summers' northern outfits? Or could he make a propitious move into another New England firm? Possibly the only spots in his line would be in small towns fundamentally similar to the community in which the Redmonds were living.

Once Redmond had carefully investigated the situation in regard to his career opportunities, he definitely ought to take time to sit down with his wife and talk seriously with her about his business objectives and—even more important—about what they both wanted together out of life. A mutual soul-searching had probably been put off much too long in the Redmond family; discussion of John's career aims, of how much money he wanted to make, how much time he wanted to give to his job, and what kind of work he wanted to do would be bound to help immeasurably in solving the family's difficulty.

Nancy, it would seem, had been neglected for too long; if she were included in the planning of her husband's career, she would be more willing to adjust to distasteful environments.

John Redmond had certainly given far too little thought to his wife's personal desires. Busy as he was with his office problems, he had probably been totally taken aback when Nancy announced that she was fed up with the South—he had quite conceivably been taking his wife for granted for several years. Now he was forced to move quickly and aggressively in order to salvage Nancy's peace of soul.

If Nancy and John together decided that his best bet *career-wise* was to remain with the Summers corporation in the South, then Nancy, newly aware of the reasons for her husband's decision, might agree to staying on.

In this event, one would think, it was up to John to help his wife become integrated into the community, to find some enjoyable interests for her outside the home, to make her feel a sense of participation in his life. Perhaps the family could move to one of the larger towns—an hour would not be too long for John to spend commuting if such a move would make Nancy happier. Or the Redmonds might make a sincere effort to become acquainted with and understand the community in which they had been living. John himself had given no time to civic affairs, and it was time that he began to do so, if only because the top executives in a big manufacturing concern located in a small town *must* cultivate—for business reasons—the goodwill and amity of the townsfolk. And John presumably wanted to become president of this branch of the Summers corporation.

Together the Redmonds could work at extending themselves both culturally and socially. Nancy had been a nurse before her marriage; if she could interest a group of teen-agers in a home-nursing course, she might again obtain some feelings of individual accomplishment. Or she might get interested in the Red Cross, the Y.W.C.A., or even the church. John could certainly help his wife in her attempts to come to terms with her surroundings. And a good baby-sitter might do wonders for Nancy's morale—husband and wife could take more time off together. The Redmonds might even promise themselves a regular trip to New York, and perhaps an occasional visit to New England.

Equipped with a new recognition of the importance of his family and his wife—both in themselves and in regard to his career—John Redmond could come to consider time spent with them as a real investment in his future happiness and success. Certainly Nancy's participation in the establishment of objectives and the reaching of decisions is one of the most necessary considerations in solving John's problem. He would have to include such participation in all his future planning.

CONCLUSION

James Short and John Redmond found themselves in the dilemmas we have described above because both men neglected to replan their course after unexpected developments arose. As businessmen they were successful strategists, but they neglected to utilize skills developed in business that might have been helpful in their personal lives.

These two men were not *hopelessly* entangled, as we have demonstrated. By examining their situations carefully themselves, and by seeking detachment and an impersonal perspective through discussions with a skillful listener neutral to the problem, they could locate most of the causes for trouble and therefrom draw up some reasonably promising alternatives for action. Their case histories prove that it is never too late to plan your personal strategy in a comprehensive way, although such planning is much harder when it must be done under the pressure of an uncomfortable situation.